1/08

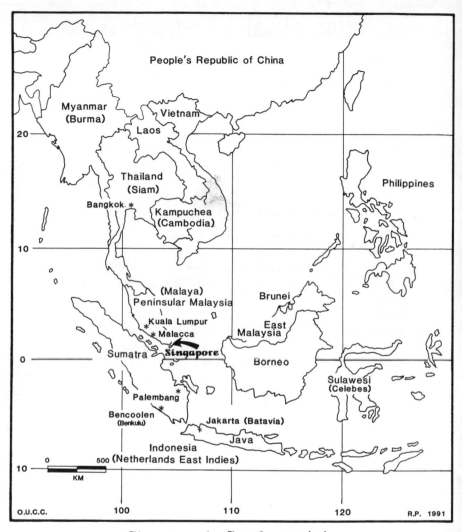

Singapore in Southeast Asia

Historical Dictionary

of

SINGAPORE

by
K. MULLINER
and
LIAN THE-MULLINER

Asian Historical Dictionaries, No. 7

The Scarecrow Press, Inc.
Metuchen, N.J., & London
1991

British Library Cataloguing-in-Publication data available

Library of Congress Cataloging-in-Publication Data

Mulliner, K.

  Historical dictionary of Singapore / by K. Mulliner and
Lian The-Mulliner.
        p.   cm. -- (Asian historical dictionaries ; no. 7)
    Includes bibliographical references.
    ISBN 0-8108-2504-X (Alk. paper)
    1. Singapore--History--Dictionaries.   I. The-Mulliner,
Lian. II. Title. III. Series.
DS610.4.M85   1991
959.57'003--dc20   91-35697

Copyright © 1991 by K. Mulliner and Lian The-Mulliner
Manufactured in the United States of America

Printed on acid-free paper

For our parents:
Our mothers, Harriet and Ina,
and our late fathers, Joe and The Sien Bie

CONTENTS

v

EDITOR'S FOREWORD

Although one of Asia's smallest entities, Singapore is nonetheless one of the most significant. Despite its size, it plays an uncommonly important role in political events and, even more so, the economic development of the region. With one of the world's fastest growing economies, it is not only a model for other countries but contributes mightily to the integration of Southeast Asia. This has made it a popular destination for foreign businessmen and a place not to be missed for foreign tourists who savor the comfortable mixture of past and present, East and West.

Yet, while it has been visited by many outsiders and is frequently covered in the media, it is not as well known as might be hoped. There are still many aspects that deserve to be further explored and some which are misunderstood. Moreover, if it is to be a model, economic or other, it is necessary to fathom the workings of the economy and society. Any effort at understanding Singapore better could well start with this dictionary, with its extensive chronology, useful introduction and broad array of specific entries. The process can then be carried much further, thanks to a comprehensive and well-organized bibliography.

This Singapore volume was written by the capable team of K. Mulliner and Lian The-Mulliner. The former is Assistant to the Director of Libraries at Ohio University and has studied, taught and written on Southeast Asia for over thirty years, including co-editing *Malaysia Studies* and *Southeast Asia, an Emerging Center of World Influence?* Lian The-Mulliner, Head of the Southeast Asia Collection, Ohio University, was born and educated in East Java and co-compiled the pioneering *Treasures and Trivia: Doctoral Dissertations on Southeast Asia Accepted by Universities in the United States.*

Jon Woronoff
Series Editor

ACKNOWLEDGMENTS

The authors acknowledge deep intellectual debts to the hundreds of scholars, reporters, and participants whose research and information have made this dictionary possible. The Bibliography in this volume is an indication of the magnitude; however, because it focuses on monographic titles, it represents only a fraction of that debt. We also are grateful to the friends and colleagues who neglected to warn us of the immensity of the task of preparing this volume. Had we been forewarned, we might have missed the fun and excitement as well as the endless nights of toil.

We extend our appreciation to the staff of the Ohio University Library, where we are employed, and especially of its Southeast Asia Collection, for repeated assistance. Special gratitude is owed to Ms. Siew-Ben Chin, a Southeast Asia Cataloger with the Ohio University Library, for her assistance with Chinese terms, spelling, and cross-references between dialects and Mandarin. Ms. Swee-Lan Quah, Deputy Head of Cataloging at Ohio University, even provided personalized courier and delivery service in conjunction with a personal trip to Singapore. Mr. Takeshi Kohno, a graduate student in the Southeast Asia Studies Program and graduate assistant with the Collection, provided essential support in researching special problems and particularly in collecting the data which made the statistical and cabinet appendices possible.

For timely responses to last-minute questions, we are indebted to Dr. John Micksic and Dr. Edwin Lee, both in the Department of History of the National University of Singapore (NUS), and to Dr. Leo Suryadinata in the Department of Political Science of the NUS. Randall Baier with the Cornell University Libraries was instrumental in enabling us to identify and rapidly borrow a magnificent biographical volume. Even more, Ms. Ch'ng Kim See and staff of the Institute of Southeast Asian Studies (ISEAS) Library in Singapore responded graciously and promptly to frantic requests for timely statistics and other information. Incorporating 1991 election results was made possible by electronic-mail announcement of detailed results prepared by Chew Hong Gian of the Information Technology Institute of the National Computer Board of Singapore.

While we acknowledge the author and publishers who have allowed us to reproduce or adapt their materials in the appropriate places, we would like to repeat our appreciation for their permissions, including Mr. Saran Singh, the University of Pennsylvania Press, and the University of Singapore Press.

Recognizing the assistance of others in no way relieves us of full responsibility for the ideas and opinions expressed herein or for any shortcomings.

K. Mulliner   Lian The-Mulliner

Ohio University Libraries
Athens, Ohio

NOTE ON SPELLING AND NAMES

Spelling

Other than English, the major languages in Singapore are not based on the Roman alphabet. Malay historically was written with the Arabic alphabet (called *Jawi*) and Chinese in ideographs or characters. The same is true for the Indian languages, of which the Dravidian language Tamil is the most widely spoken and is one of the four national languages of Singapore. Standardization of romanized spelling has been effected only in recent decades; therefore, personal and place names have been spelled different ways at different times and in different places.

Because this dictionary is historical and written in English, preference has been given to the most common historic English rendering of place and personal names for entries in the dictionary. M. C. Turnbull's *A History of Singapore, 1819-1988* (see in "General" section under "History" in the Bibliography) has been used in determining the standard in most cases. Variant spellings are indicated with "See" references in the Index. Recognizing that this approach differs from current academic practice, which usually accepts contemporary official spelling and applies it retrospectively, the following notes on the two main non-Western languages may assist a reader in identifying terms found in older and primary sources.

Indonesian-Malay-Malaysian
Even where standardization has been undertaken, such as Indonesia, the standards have changed over time. When established earlier in this century, Indonesian was based on Dutch

orthography, but, after independence, this gradually gave way: "u" replaced "oe," "ch" replaced "tj," and "j" replaced "dj." In the 1960s and since, Malaysians and Indonesians with representatives from Singapore and Brunei have attempted to develop uniform orthographies and, with less success, standardized spelling and vocabulary. In Malaysia, this effort yielded the "new spelling" (*ejaan baru*) adopted in 1972. This reform changed "ch" to "c" and "sh" ("sj" in Indonesian) to "sy."

For example, the kingdom and present-day state north of Singapore is spelled Johor in contemporary official Malaysian and Djohor in Dutch historical writings while the standard English rendering is Johore. Similarly, the island group located immediately south of Singapore is officially spelled Riau in contemporary Indonesian but was Riouw in Dutch usage and Rhio, among others, in English. "Johore" and "Rhio" are used in the dictionary except in referring to the present-day state and province.

Chinese

Similar problems of accepted standards and changes in those standards exist for Chinese; however, these are compounded by the pervasiveness and predominance of dialects over the official language (Mandarin) for much of Singapore's history. A standard romanization system, Wade-Giles, was used from the nineteenth century but was directed primarily at the national official language, Mandarin. Historically, approaches akin to Wade-Giles have been used in romanizing words in the dialects and remain the standard usage for place names--despite some government attempts to replace the dialect word with the Mandarin form.

In 1957, the People's Republic of China adopted a new romanization system, pinyin (*hanyu pinyin* = Chinese spelling), but it also was intended for the national language. Singapore has adopted this system as official--as well as the simplified characters for ideographs promulgated by the PRC.

To address the variations arising from these different approaches, for references to China, the pinyin romanization is added in parentheses. Because Chinese names and places in Singapore and elsewhere in Southeast Asia are best known by the dialect word, that word in traditional spelling has been retained. For general dialect terms (in contrast to place and personal names), the Mandarin term in pinyin romanization is provided in parentheses, e.g., Kwangtung (pinyin: Guangdung).

Personal Names

Indonesian-Malay-Malaysian
Indonesia has largely accepted the Western practice of treating the second or last name as a surname or family name. In Malaysia and Singapore, however, Malays have not accommodated this Western form and do not have family names or surnames. For them, the final part of the name is the father's personal name or the last part of the father's personal name. For example, the first president of Singapore was Yusof Ishak (actually Yusof bin Ishak), with Ishak being the father's name but not a family name.

For Malay names, a name is written and alphabetized in the form used. Thus, using the above example, the first president can be found under "Y" for Yusof. Titles (whether inherited or awarded) are placed following the name (e.g., Yusof bin Ishak, Tun). "Bin" means "son of," and the female counterpart, "binte," "daughter of." Many younger Malays have dropped usage of "bin" and "binte" but retain the father's name as the last part of the name, while others abbreviate them as "b." and "bte."

As with personal names nearly everywhere in the world, there is no standard spelling. To the extent possible, spelling herein follows the spelling used by the individual. In historical cases, such as Temenggong Abdul Rahman, the spelling follows the usual romanization today, rather than the nineteenth century "Abdu'r-Rahman." References are provided in the index from variant spellings to the form used in this volume.

Chinese

For Chinese names, the best known dialect form is retained. Chinese names are written and alphabetized with the family name first, followed by the personal name (usually two syllables, e.g., for Lee Kuan Yew, Lee is the family name and Kuan Yew is the personal name). Occasionally, when an individual has adopted the Western form of placing the family name last, a Western form of entry is used. Commas are used to separate the family name from personal name only in cases where the individual has adopted the Western form. The best guide to variant Chinese names is Russell Jones, *Chinese Names: Notes on the Use of Surnames and Personal Names by the Chinese in Malaysia and Singapore* (see in "Chinese" section under "Society" in the Bibliography).

COMMON ABBREVIATIONS
AND ACRONYMS

For the *reductio ad absurdum* of this section, see the 148 pages in Foo Kok Pheo, ed. *Common Abbreviations and Acronyms in Singapore* (see in "Yearbooks and Handbooks" section under "Reference Works" in Bibliography).

ABL	Anti-British League (also SSABL and SPABL)
ACCORD	Advisory Committee on Community Relations in Defence
ACSU	Army Civil Service Union
ACU	Asian Currency Unit
AEBUS	Anti-Enemy Backing-Up Society
ALS	Area Licensing Scheme (for automobiles)
AMCJA	All-Malaya Council of Joint Action
ASEAN	Association of Southeast Asian Nations
BMA	British Military Administration
BS	*Barisan Sosialis* (Socialist Front)
CBD	Central Business District
CCC	Citizens' Consultative Committee
CEC	Central Executive Committee, of PAP
CPF	Central Provident Fund
CPIB	Corrupt Practices Investigation Bureau
CPM	Communist Party of Malaya, see MCP
CRP	Chinese Revolutionary Party
DBS	Development Bank of Singapore
DP	Democratic Party
EDB	Economic Development Board

FGMSU	Federation of Government and Municipal Servants Unions
FPMS	Federation of Pan-Malayan Students
FUKEMSSO	Federation of United Kingdom and Eire Malaysian and Singapore Students' Organization
GLU	General Labour Union
GRC	Group Representation Constituency
HDB	Housing and Development Board
ICFTU	International Confederation of Free Trade Unions
ISA	Internal Security Act
ISC	Internal Security Council
ISD	Internal Security Division.
ISD	Internal Security Department
JP	Justice of the Peace
KMS	*Kesatuan Melayu Singapura* (Singapore Malay Union)
KMT	Koumintang
LF	Labour Front
MAS	Monetary Authority of Singapore
MCA	Malayan (later Malaysian) Chinese Association
MCP	Malayan Communist Party
MDU	Malayan Democratic Union
MENDAKI	Council of Education for Muslim Children
MIC	Malayan (later Malaysian) Indian Congress
MNDYL	Malayan New Democratic Youth League
MNLL	Malayan National Liberation League
MNP	Malay Nationalist Party
MPAJA	Malayan People's Anti-Japanese Army
MRT	Mass Rapid Transit, Inc.
NBLU	Naval Base Labour Union
NCMP	Nonconstituency Member of Parliament
NCP	Nanyang Communist Party
NEMP	Nonelected Member of Parliament
NMP	Nominated Member of Parliament
NTUC	National Trades Union Congress
NUS	National University of Singapore
NWC	National Wages Council

OCBC	Overseas Chinese Bank Corporation
PA	People's Associations
PAP	People's Action Party
PARF	Preferential Additional Registration Fee
PIEU	Pioneer Industries Employees' Union
PKI	*Partai Komunis Indonesia* (Indonesian Communist Party)
PMFTU	Pan-Malayan Federation of Trade Unions
POSB	Post Office Savings Bank
PP	Progressive Party
PSA	Port of Singapore Authority
PSC	Public Service Commission
PUB	Public Utilities Board
PUTERA	*Pusat Tenaga Ra'ayat* (People's United Front)
PWD	Public Works Department
RELC	Regional English Language Center
RIHED	Regional Institute for Higher Education
RWU	Rubber Workers' Union
RZ	Restricted Zone (for automobiles)
SAF	Singapore Armed Forces
SAP	Singapore Alliance Party
SATU	Singapore Association of Trade Unions
SBC	Singapore Broadcasting Corporation
SBS	Singapore Bus Service, Ltd.
SBWU	Singapore Bus Workers' Union
SCC	Singapore City Committee
SCDF	Singapore Civil Defence Force
SCMSSU	Singapore Chinese Middle School Students' Union
SDF	Skills Development Fund
SDP	Singapore Democratic Party
SDU	Social Development Unit
SEAC	South-East Asia Command
SFPPB	Singapore Family Planning and Population Board
SFSWU	Singapore Factory and Shop Workers' Union
SFTU	Singapore Federation of Trade Unions
SHBLU	Singapore Harbour Board Labour Union

SHBSA	Singapore Harbour Board Staff Association
SIA	Singapore Airlines
SLP	Singapore Labour Party
SMU	Singapore Malay Union
SOE	State Owned Enterprises
SPA	Singapore People's Alliance
SPABL	Singapore People's Anti-British League
SS	Straits Settlements
SSABL	Singapore Students' Anti-British League
SSCF	Straits Settlements Volunteer Force
SSP	Singapore Socialist Party
SSVC	Straits Settlements Volunteer Corps
STC	Singapore Traction Company
STCEU	Singapore Traction Company Employees' Union
STU	Singapore Teachers' Union
STUC	Singapore Trade Union Congress
SVAC	Singapore Volunteer Artillery Corps
SVC	Singapore Volunteer Corps
SVIC	Singapore Volunteer Infantry Corps
TMH	*T'ung Meng Hui* (Revolutionary League)
UMNO	United Malays National Organisation
UPP	United People's Party
USSU	University of Singapore Students' Union
URA	Urban Redevelopment Authority
VOC	*Vereenigde Oost-Indische Compagnie* (Dutch East India Company)
WP	Workers' Party

CHRONOLOGY OF IMPORTANT EVENTS

100s   Sabara, trading emporium, identified in Ptolemy's *Geographike Huphegesis*, at the southern tip of the Golden Chersonese, possibly Singapore.

1200s   Settlement called Temasek reported on Singapore Island.

1300s   Settlement, called Singapura, formed by Tan Sri Buana.

1390s   Malacca Sultanate established by Sultan Iskandar Shah (or Paramesavara).

1511   Malacca fell to Portuguese.

1587   Malacca Sultanate base at Johore Lama destroyed by Portuguese.

1613   Malay outpost on Singapore Island burned by Portuguese.

1641   Netherlands seized Malacca from Portugal.

1699   Sultan Mahmud II, last heir to Malacca Sultanate, assassinated.

1784   Netherlands successfully attacked Rhio.

1819   Thomas Stamford Raffles and party landed in Singapore, January 28/29. Preliminary agreement with Temenggong Abdul Rahman to establish factory on January 30, approved by Sultan Hussein of Johore, February 5. Treaty signed with the Sultan and Temenggong (as de jure and de facto rulers of Singapore island), February 6. Raffles departed, leaving Farquhar as resident under him as Lieutenant Governor of Bencoolen, February 7. Raffles returned with supplies and immigrants from Penang, May. Raffles signed a further treaty with the Sultan and the Temenggong defining settlement in June and then departed.

1820   Opium and spirits farms proposed in March and, despite objections from Raffles, implemented a few months later.

1822   Raffles arrived from Bencoolen, October; declared principle of free trade, November.

1823   Farquhar attacked by an Arab running amok, March 11. Raffles called first meeting for founding of Raffles Institution, April 1. Raffles ousted Colonel Farquhar and named John Crawfurd to succeed him in May. Raffles issued regulations outlawing gambling and slavery, May. Raffles left Singapore, June 9.

1824   *Singapore Chronicle* established as first newspaper in January. Anglo-Dutch Treaty recognized British suzerainty over Singapore in March. Treaty with Sultan Hussein and Temenggong Abdul Rahman ceded island outright in August.

1826   Singapore incorporated into Straits Settlements (with Malacca and Penang [including Province Wellesley on peninsula]) with Robert Fullerton as the Governor, August 14.

1827   Treaty with Sultan and Temenggong ceded entire island of Singapore and islands within ten miles of it to East India Company, October 4.

1830   Fire in China town destroyed several blocks in February. All of Straits Settlements placed under Presidency of Bengal, May 25.

1832   Singapore became center of Straits Settlements in December.

1836   Armenian church consecrated, March 26. Singapore Institution (later better known as Raffles Institution) opened as a school in December.

1837   Chamber of Commerce established.

1839   First ship built in Singapore launched.

1843   Girls' school opened in Raffles Institution.

1844   Foundation of Tan Tock Seng Pauper Hospital laid, July 25.

1845   First Masonic lodge opened.

1846   Chinese Funeral riots, first major secret society trouble in Singapore, began March 3.

1851   Anti-Catholic riots. Chinese Catholics in rural areas attacked by secret society members, beginning February 15. Straits Settlements placed directly under Governor-General of India, September 1.

1854   Riot between Hokkiens and Teochews (either over commercial argument or unwillingness of former to aid rebels driven out of Amoy by Chinese imperial troops), May 5-17.

1857   General strike by Chinese residents, protesting interpretations of Police and Conservancy Acts, January 2. Police and Indians clash at Telok Ayer mosque, February 5.

1858   Queen dissolves East India Company and assumes direct control of Indian territories including Straits Settlements, September 1. Queen's proclamation read in Singapore, November 19.

1859   Fort Canning (on Canning Hill) built in May.

1860   Chong-san Seng-chai Company leaves Chamber of Commerce and Chinese subsequently excluded.

1863   Widespread factional and secret society clashes in October. First recorded importation of Chinese women prostitutes in latter part of year.

1864   Gas street lights introduced, May 24.

1867   Straits Settlements became Crown Colony, April 1.

1869   Opening of Suez Canal caused shipping booms as distance to Europe cut by two-thirds.

1871   Riots among Chinese, primarily Hokkien and Teochew lower classes, October 21-26.

1872   Riot between Teochews and Hokkiens, 1872.

1873   Chinese Immigration Ordinance passed, aimed at improving conditions of coolies.

1875   Mutiny by prisoners killed superintendent D. H. Dent, February 13. Nine prison mutineers executed, June 19.

1876   Chinese Post Office riot in December, over handling of remittances to China.

1877   Chinese Protectorate established with William Pickering as first Protector. Straits Branch of Royal Asiatic Society formed, November 4.

1881   First Chinese-language newspaper, *Lat Pau*, launched.

1882   Volcanic eruption of Krakatoa (*Krakatao*) in the Netherlands East Indies, August 26-27.

1885   Riots at Trafalgar (tapioca) Estate, February 16.

1887   Statue of Sir Stamford Raffles unveiled, June 27. Murder attempt on William Pickering, July 1887, allegedly at instigation of Ghee Hok Society.

1888   Verandah riots, February 20, arising from efforts to clear walkways of merchants and customers, with more than one hundred arrested and several killed.

1889   Riot between Teochews and Hakkas.

1890   Societies Ordinance came into effect, outlawing secret societies, January 1. First tin smelter built on Pulau Brani by Straits Trading Company.

1896   Governor of the Straits Settlements also became High Commissioner of the Federated Malay States, from July 1.

1906   Riot among Hokkiens and Teochews, sparked by a dispute between two ships over berthing on November 13; it continued for five days, resulting in considerable damage to shops and more than three hundred arrests.

1910   Monopolies Department established to take over revenue farms, January 1.

1915   Indian Mutiny, February 15-20.

1930   Immigration Restriction Ordinance implemented.

1941   Japan invades Malaya, landing at Kota Bahru (Kelantan), and Singapore bombed, December 8. Prince of Wales and Repulse Bay sunk by Japanese off East Coast of Malaya, December 10.

1942   Britain surrendered to Japan at Ford Motors Factory in Bukit Timah, February 15. Singapore named Syonan (Light of the South). Top officers of the Malayan Communist Party and the Malayan People's Anti-Japanese Army killed in a Japanese ambush at Batu Caves, near Kuala Lumpur, September 1.

1945   Japan surrendered August 14. Surrender announced in Singapore, August 21. British forces land, September 5. Malayan Democratic Union (MDU) launched as first local, multi-racial political party, December 23.

1946   White Paper on Malayan Union, January 22. Colony of Singapore formed, March 31, with dependencies of Christmas Island and the Cocos Islands included. Pan-Malayan Council of Joint Action (PMCJA) formed in December.

1947   Chin Peng made Secretary General of Malayan Communist Party (MCP) in March. Progressive Party formed in August. PMCJA changed name to All Malaya Council of Joint Action (AMCJA), August.

1948   Six elected members included in twenty-two-member Legislative Council. Progressive Party won March Legislative Council election, March 20. Bill proscribing the Pan-Malaya Federation of Trade Unions introduced in Malaya, May 31. Emergency declared June 25. Malayan Democratic Union dissolved.

1949   Municipal Commission implemented with eighteen seats elected out of twenty-seven. Progressive Party won thirteen seats.

1950   Lee Kuan Yew addressed Malayan Forum in London in January. Lee Kuan Yew and Goh Keng Swee returned to Singapore in August. Maria Hertogh riots in December.

1951   Legislative Council Election. Singapore formally proclaimed a city, September 23, with royal charter.

1953   Nanyang University launched in February. Rendel Commission appointed in July to examine constitution and relationship between municipality and government.

1954   Rendel Commission Report released in February. Chinese Middle School Riots, first clash with police, May 13. *Fajar* trial in August, Lee Kuan Yew defended students charged with publishing subversive editorial. People's Action Party (PAP) formed, October 23, and formally inaugurated, November 21.

1955   Labour Front won Legislative Assembly election, April 2, and David Marshall became Chief Minister, April 6. Chancellor Lin Yutang and staff of Nanyang University resigned, April 6. First meeting of Legislative Assembly, April 22. Hock Lee Bus Company riots, May 12. General strike, June 12-17. Talks with Malayan Communist Party leader Chin Peng in town of Baling in Kedah failed, Dec. 28.

1956   PAP regained control of Malayan Forum in London in February. First Constitutional Conference in London, April 17. PAP Central Executive Committee election in which Communists decline to run, July 8. Chinese student riots, leftist PAP leaders arrested, October 25.

1957   Second Constitutional Conference in London, March 7. By-elections challenge made by David Marshall, won by PAP in Tanjong Pagar constituency and Liberal Socialists in Cairnhill constituency (Marshall did not contest), June 29. Communists gained control of PAP Central Executive Council, August 5. Communist trade unionists detained, August 22. T. T. Rajah resigned as Secretary General of PAP, August 25. Ong Eng Guan became mayor, December 21.

1958   Third Consitutional Conference in London, May 12. PAP won Kallang city council by-election, July 26. State of Singapore Act passed United Kingdom Parliament, providing for the State of Singapore and Singapore citizenship.

1959   PAP won general election with forty-three of fifty-one seats, May 30. Lee Kuan Yew became Prime Minister and Singapore declared a state, June 3. Detainees released, June 4.

1960   Ong Eng Guan's sixteen resolutions, June 19.

1961   Hong Lim constituency by-election, PAP defeated by Ong Eng Guan running as an independent, April 29. Lee Kuan Yew told "Plen" that merger unlikely, May 10. Tunku Abdul Rahman announced possibility of merger, May 27. PAP defeated; David Marshall representing the Workers' Party elected in Anson constituency by-election, July 15. Eden Hall Tea Party, July 18. *Barisan Sosialis* formed by PAP defectors, July 26. Lee

Kuan Yew's radio broadcasts on merger began September 13. White Paper issued on merger, November 17.

1962   Anti-merger Malaysian Socialist Conference in Kuala Lumpur, January. *Barisan Sosialis* no-confidence motion defeated, July 13. U.N. Commission on Colonialism rejected criticism of referendum, July 27. Referendum yielded 73 percent acceptance of merger, September 1. Brunei uprising, Dec. 8.

1963   Barisan leaders detained in "Operation Cold Store," February 3. Malaysia Agreement signed in London, July 9. Riot at rehabilitation camp on Pulau Senang for secret society members resulted in death of superintendent, July 12. Malaysia Agreement, August 1. Declaration of Singapore's independence, August 31. Malaysia formed with Singapore as a component, September 16. PAP won Singapore general election, September 21, with 33 seats (47 percent of popular vote), 17 to Barisan (32 percent of popular vote), and 1 to Ong Eng Guan, September 21.

1964   PAP won only one seat in Malaysian general election, April 25. Communal riots (Indonesian instigation blamed), July 21. More communal rioting, September 2.

1965   Hong Lim constituency by-election won by PAP over *Barisan Sosialis*, July 15. Singapore expelled from Malaysia, declared independence as republic, August 9. Republic of Singapore admitted as 117th member of the United Nations, September 21. Eighteen of the Pulau Senang rioters in 1963 were hung, October 29. *Barisan Sosialis* party boycotted December Parliament session. Singapore Independence Bill passed, December 22.

1966   Bukit Merah constituency by-election won by PAP against an independent, January 18. Chua Chu Kang, Crawford, and Paya Lebar constituencies by-elections won by PAP uncontested, March 1. Ngee Ann College sit-in in October and November. Bukit Timah, Joo Chiat, and Jurong constituencies by-elections won by PAP uncontested.

1967   Bukit Panjang, Havelock, Jalan Kayu, and Tampines constituencies by-elections won by PAP uncontested, February 24. Thomson constituency by-election won by PAP against two independents, March 7. Compulsory National Service introduced in March, opposed by *Barisan Sosialis*-led street demonstrations. Singapore issued own currency, June 12. Britain announced withdrawal of forces, July 18. Association of Southeast Asian Nations (ASEAN) formed, August 7.

1968   PAP swept first Parliamentary general election, April 13, boycotted by *Barisan Sosialis* party. Jurong Town Corporation established in June. Singapore Development Bank established. Employment Act and Industrial Relations (Amendment) Act passed by Parliament in July.

1970   PAP won uncontested by-elections in Delta, Havelock, and Whampoa constituencies, April 8. PAP won contested by-elections in Kampong Kapor and Ulu Pandan constituencies, April 18.

1971   British Far East Command ceases, October 31.

1972   PAP won all seats in general election, September 2.

1974   Combined Japanese Red Army and Popular Front for the Liberation of Palestine terrorists attacked Shell Oil refinery at Pulau Bukom and took hostages in escape attempt, January 31. Terrorists released hostages and allowed to fly to Kuwait and then South Yemen, February 7.

1976   PAP won all seats in general election, December 23.

1977   PAP won Radin Mas constituency contested by-election, May 14. PAP won Bukit Merah constituency contested by-election, July 23.

1979   PAP won Geylang West and Nee Soon constituencies uncontested by-elections, January 31. Anson, Mountbatten, Potong Pasir, Sembawang, and Telok Blangah constituencies contested by-elections won by PAP, February 10.

1980   PAP won all seats in general election, December 23.

1981   Anson constituency by-election won by J. B. Jeyaretnam of Workers' Party, October 31.

1984   PAP lost two (of seventy-nine) seats in general election, its first general election loss of a seat since 1964, December 22.

1987   Sixteen people detained in raid by Internal Security Department for alleged involvement in Marxist conspiracy, May 21. Four detainees released, six others arrested, June 20. Three of June 20 detainees released, July. Nine detainees released, September. Remaining detainees except Vincent Cheng released, December.

1988   Nine of those detained and later released in 1987 issued statement denying involvement in conspiracy and accusing government of mistreatment, April 18. Eight signatories of statement rearrested, April 19. Francis Seow, former Solicitor General and ex-president of Law Society detained, May

6. PAP won eighty of eighty-one seats in general election for expanded Parliament with Group Representation Constituencies, September 3. Court of Appeal asserted right to review detention orders, December 8.

1989   Internal Security Act amended to exclude judicial review, January 26.

1990   Lee Kuan Yew stepped aside as Prime Minister, replaced by Goh Chok Tong, November 28.

1991   Singapore commandos killed four Pakistanis involved in hijacking attempt of Singapore Airlines plane from Kuala Lumpur, March 26. PAP won seventy-seven of eighty-one seats in general election, August 31, 1991.

OVERVIEW

Singapore, from the Sanskrit *Singapura*, means "lion city." The name is explained in the half-history, half-mythology *Malay Annals* as arising from a sighting of a strange animal by the founder of Singapore. It is described as having been larger than a billy goat with a red body, white breast, and black head. When the founder asked what it could have been, his trusted associate and father-in-law said that there were legends of a lion (*singa*) having such an appearance. The founder, Sri Tri Buana, named his new settlement in its honor. Now adopted as the national symbol (as below but red), it is said to symbolize courage, strength, and excellence. Five divisions in its mane represent the national ideals of democracy, peace, progress, justice, and equality. The lion's tenacious nature symbolizes "the nation's single-minded resolve to face any foes and overcome any obstacles."

The island nation lies at the junction of mainland and insular Southeast Asia and of the South China Sea and the Indian Ocean, at the southern terminus of the Straits of Malacca. Although sometimes described as a third China (after the People's Republic of China on the mainland and the Republic of China on Taiwan) because of its population, it is even more, as proclaimed in past government campaigns, a global city.

Southeast Asia has been viewed as the crossroads of the Indian and Chinese worlds--vividly reflected in the term Indochina. Both cultures have been pervasive historically in the Malay Archipelago and continue until the present in Singapore, as does the Islamicized Indonesian/Malaysian. During the colonial era (in which, excluding Thailand, it was divided among the Dutch, French, British, and Americans), there was little inclination to it as a distinct or coherent region. The term Southeast Asia (South-East Asia in British usage) gained wide usage only after World War II, during which it was designated a theater of operations. Today Southeast Asia includes the ten nations of Burma (officially identified as Myanmar), Thailand, Laos, Cambodia (also called Kampuchea), Vietnam, the Philippines, Indonesia, Malaysia, Singapore and Brunei. The first five are classed in Mainland Southeast Asia and the latter five as Insular (or Island) Southeast Asia--although most of Malaysia is joined to the mainland.

Singapore lies between Malaysia and Indonesia. Under a common British colonial administration, it was administered jointly with the peninsular (and, later, the Borneo) territories comprising present-day Malaysia and generally is included in the geo-political identification of Malaya. Earlier, however, it also had close ties with Indonesia, especially with the Rhio Islands immediately south and kingdoms on the island of Sumatra to the West--whence legend says that it was founded. Because of centuries of contact, some attention must be given to people and events in the territories now identified as Indonesia and Malaysia. With these two, the recently independent sultanate of Brunei Darussalam, Thailand, and the Philippines, it shares membership in the notable regional organization, the

Association of Southeast Asian Nations--usually referred to as ASEAN.

Geography

Located at the tip of the Malay Peninsula, separated only by the narrow Strait of Johor from the mainland, it is a nation of more than fifty islands; however, nearly all of its population and 92 percent of its territory are on the largest island, also called Singapore. The main island is roughly oval shaped, 26 miles (41.8 km) east-west and 30.4 miles (22.9 km) north-south. Despite its high population density, less than half the land has been developed for residence, industry, or commercial use, and 8 percent is used for agriculture. The total land area of all islands is 241.7 square miles (626 sq. km). About half the islands are small and uninhabited. It is separated from the Indonesian islands to the south, comprising the Province of Riau, by the Straits of Singapore.

Sitting just eighty-five miles (137 km) north of the equator (between 1°9'N and 1°29'N latitudes), it has an equatorial climate--hot, humid, and rainy with little seasonal change. Annual average temperatures range from a high of 87° Fahrenheit (30.7° Celsius) to a low of 73°F (23°C). Temperatures are moderated by sea breezes and profuse greenery, the latter resulting from a government initiative to make Singapore a "Garden City." Humidity ranges from 60 to 70 percent on dry afternoons to 95 percent in the early morning. Its only seasons are the result of the northeast monsoon and the southwest monsoon. The former, from November to January, brings increased rainfall and somewhat cooler temperatures. It has an annual average rainfall of seventy-nine inches (2 000 cm) and receives two inches (50 cm) several days each year. Rain tends to fall in brief intense showers. Between monsoons, April-May and October-November, it occasionally is subjected to violent morning thunderstorms, called Sumatras, which were much dreaded by sailors in the Straits of Malacca.

The main island is largely flat and less than fifty feet (fifteen meters) above sea level. Of its hills, the highest, Bukit Timah (Tin Hill) Peak, reaches 541 feet (165 meters). The center of the island features granite hills and valleys. The modest heights do give birth to several streams, such as the Jurong, Seletar, Serangoon, and Kallang, which have carved broad shallow valleys over the centuries. Many small hills have been flattened to permit urban expansion.

Settlement in the nineteenth century was concentrated close to the Singapore River, which is the present main business district, and the remainder of the island was covered by tropical rain forest and swamps. The forest region was used for small gambier and pepper plantations (often called *bangsal*, referring to the makeshift processing shed). These relied on a specialized form of slash-and-burn agriculture to clear new planting areas and are blamed for denuding much of the landscape after the middle of the nineteenth century. In the twentieth century, swamps have given way to reservoirs and nature preserves in the center of the country, and the rivers flow through concrete canals rather than a natural course. Agriculture has greatly diminished, but about 14 percent of the main island is used for commercial vegetable gardens and livestock farms, mostly along the less-populated Johor Strait.

Today, nearly the entire landscape has been marshalled to the service of man but it includes an ample number of parks and designated natural areas. With limited space, most people live in large apartment buildings, called flats, and not single-family residences, called bungalows. Housing has been one of the government's proudest accomplishments, as it first built sufficient buildings to accommodate the masses displaced by the burgeoning commercial areas and then arranged for the renters to gain ownership by borrowing against mandatory retirement savings (the Central Provident Fund [CPF], similar to--but at a substantially higher rate than--Social Security in America). Home ownership exceeded 90 percent in 1990.

An increasing population after World War II brought heavy demands for new housing and jobs, which the government met

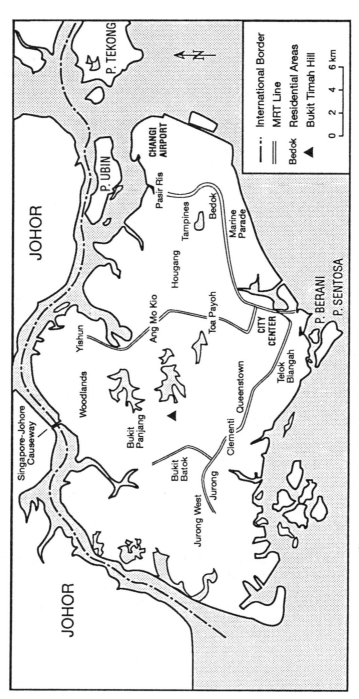

Singapore in 1990 -- Rapid Transit Rail System and Housing Estates

by dispersing the population, commerce, and industries across the island into "New Towns." These pioneering settlements in the 1960s are now linked by an efficient mass-transit rail and bus system and have grown to make the island nearly as much one city as one nation. To meet space needs, 12.5 acres (50 square kilometers) have been reclaimed from the sea. Despite these efforts, a part of the population and industry is increasingly settling in neighboring Johor and Batam Island in Riau--a fact recognized in the government's recent emphasis of the "growth-triangle" that seeks closer ties with its immediate neighbors.

The People

Its 302 million inhabitants are divided among four general ethnic categories--Chinese, Malays, Indians and others--but each has many important divisions. Chinese comprise the predominant majority, 77.7 percent of the population. Historically, they have tended to live and work according to their dialect group (*bang*). Dialect groups are largely determined by the territory of origin of forebears in China, indicated on the following map. Historic populations of the major dialect groups are presented in the Appendix, "Percentage Distribution of Chinese by Dialect Group." Into the twentieth century, dialect group lines often were the source of intra-communal conflicts and riots, most often pitting the Hokkiens against the Teochews and possibly other groups from Kwangtung (Cantonese and Hakkas). In addition to the dialect groups, a further division is represented by the *Babas* or *Peranakans*, who were born in Southeast Asia and whose families may have lived there several generations. While these came largely from Hokkien ancestry (historically from Malacca), over the years and generations, they lost command of Chinese and used English and/or Malay to communicate. In the post-war era, immigration has been a minor factor for the Chinese population and the traditional basis for distinguishing between *Babas* and *Singkehs* (new arrivals or sojourners) is disappearing although the cultural distinction is more resilient.

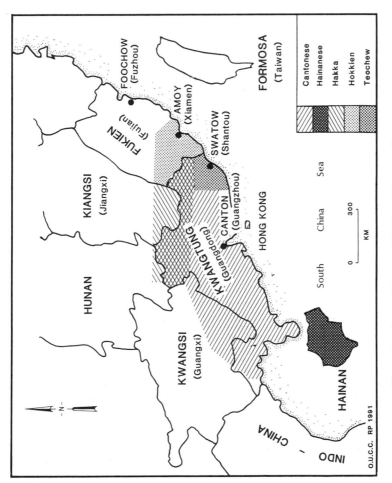

Homelands in China of Major Dialect Groups

Initially encouraged by the Beijing government early in this century, the use of Mandarin (the dialect which emerged as the national language of China)--especially as the medium of education--is one means of eroding dialect-group separation. The present government has re-emphasized this policy, making a second language mandatory for all students and encouraging those of Chinese ancestry to learn Mandarin. Dialects continue to be used in many Chinese homes; however, the pervasiveness of English in commerce and daily life has further eroded the dialects' importance.

Malays are the second largest ethnic group, accounting for 14.1 percent of the population. Although Malays were resident on Singapore in 1819, most of the present population traces its parentage to elsewhere in the Malaysian/Indonesian Archipelago, especially Peninsular Malaysia, Riau, Sumatra, and Java--with the tiny island of Bawean north of Java contributing an identifiable Boyanese element. Not included in the total is a substantial number of Malaysians who come as temporary foreign workers. Unlike the other ethnic groups, most of the Malays are united by a common religion, Islam.

Indians account for 7.1 percent of the population, but this designation includes all the diversity and antagonisms of the Indian sub-continent. Tamils are the largest group among the Indians (explaining why Tamil is one of the official languages) but also included are Malayalams, Punjabis, Telegus, Bengalis, and Sikhs as well as about twenty-eight thousand Indian Muslims.

The fourth ethnic category, "other," accounts for 1.1 percent of population. In the 1980 census, this was about 45 percent white (from Britain, Europe, North America, Australia, and New Zealand), 15 percent Japanese, 20 percent Eurasian, and 5 percent Arab.

Population growth is low, estimated at 1.3 percent in 1989 compared to 2.4 percent in 1960 and over 3 percent in the 1950s. This was cut to 1.5 percent by 1970 and dropped to 1.2

percent in 1980, prompting the government to reverse its family planning policies and encourage the educated and those better off to have more children, which has yielded limited success. Projections for the 1990s are for a .6 percent growth rate in the second half of the decade. The low rate of increase is striking considering advances in health care (an infant mortality rate of only 7.3 per thousand live births in 1987) and longevity (a life expectancy of 71.2 years in 1980, ten more years than in 1957). One result has been an aging population with the 30-59 age group accounting for 46.5 percent of the population compared to 31.1 percent in 1980.

The Economy

Prosperity has enabled the nation's transformation from an ideological battleground and an economy dependent on entrepôt trade or processing resources from Malaya and Indonesia into one of the most vibrant growth economies in the world. Looking at its first twenty years after independence, its real gross national product grew an average of 7.8 percent, considerably better than South Korea, Taiwan and Hong Kong, other Pacific Rim "smaller tigers" with which it is often compared. By the mid-1980s, its per capita income of US$7,260 greatly exceeded many European countries, including Italy, and in 1989, its per capita gross domestic product was US$19,415. Excluding the recession and recovery years of 1985 and 1986, its growth was near 10 percent for much of the 1980s.

Contrary to contemporary conservative economic theory, that transformation can be largely attributed to active government involvement in the economy. Transforming an economy requires capital, part of which the government was able to generate by mandating savings through high contributions (35 to 50 percent of wages, at various times) to the Central Provident Fund (CPF) as well as foreign investment. The high savings not only fueled the economy but, through an enlightened borrowing policy, financed the transformation of the society from renters to home-owners (actually apartment-owners) and cut domestic consumption almost in half between 1960 and the mid-1980s. Simultaneously, the government mobilized the savings to undertake the massive building projects of the Housing Development Board and the Jurong and other new Town Corporations. Other government agencies, such as the Economic Development Board, actively solicited foreign investors, offering financing and concessions to attract them.

As one front of its political struggle against communists and leftists in the 1960s, the government tamed the labor movement and ended the recurrent strikes and work stoppages of the 1950s. Labor leaders amenable to the government were elevated and the membership benefitted from the prosperity. Unifying business, labor, and government in the National Wages Council (NWC) afforded a responsive mechanism for linking rewards and productivity, an approach that has yielded dramatic success in both areas.

The major drag on the economy is its labor supply. By the late 1980s, unemployment was under 3 percent, and future growth is likely to come from foreign workers (who numbered 312,700 in the 1990 census). This reality prompted the NWC policies (including sharply increasing CPF contributions) in the early 1980s aimed at discouraging labor-intensive businesses. Labor demand also contributed to rising wages and greater job opportunities for much of the population. The government has courted Hong Kong residents dreading the takeover by China in 1997 following the Tiananmin massacre in June 1989. It is recognized that an adequate labor shortage will require further foreign workers and even greater emphasis on capital-intensive industries. One other response is evident in the "growth triangle" concept in which Singapore will headquarter companies whose actual facilities are based in Riau and southern Johor. The limited labor supply also poses a dilemma for the government, which would prefer that the country produce its own labor supply but finds that women comprise more than half of the potential (and over 40 percent of the actual) labor force. In the 1984 elections, present Prime Minister Goh Chok Tong stirred a controversy when he suggested that women should concentrate on child-bearing and -rearing. That the labor scarcity is no greater is evidence that few heeded his advice.

History

As proven in the last century, Singapore is ideally situated to serve and control sail-powered shipping between Europe or the Middle East and China, but there is little evidence that it served this function other than for brief periods before the founding of modern Singapore in 1819.

As early as the first century A.D., Western sources describe a land called Chryse in Asia which scholars have equated with the Malay Peninsula. In the second century, Claudius Ptolemy reported the collected wisdom on the world in *Geographike Huphegesis* (*Guide to Geography*), including more detail on Chryse, which is described as a peninsula called the "Golden Khersonese." He mentions a city, Emporion Sabara (sometimes reported as Sabana), at the tip of the peninsula. Emporion suggests a center where foreign trade was permitted. With the scientific decline in Europe, nothing further is recorded until the thirteenth century. Archaeology is of little additional help. A stone said to contain undecipherable inscriptions was once prominent at the mouth of the Singapore River, but it was destroyed by the government engineer in the 1830s and only fragments were preserved. Excavations have yielded limited cultural material, mostly identifiable with the thirteenth and fourteenth centuries.

Temasek and Singapura

The story of Temasek must be culled from folklore, myth, and occasional reports of foreign visitors, many of which contradict each other. In the thirteenth century, Chinese records reported a settlement called variations of the name Temasek, a name corroborated in a 1365 Javanese chronicle describing it as a dependency of the Majapahit Empire. The Chinese descriptions placed it at or near Singapore Island and described it as a haven for pirates. Another further described a battle between Temasek and Siam.

The *Malay Annals* (*Sejarah Melayu*) describe the legendary resettlement of Temasek after the attack by Siam. Two widows living near Palembang in Sumatra observed that their rice fields and a nearby hill had turned to gold. On investigation, they met three handsome young princes who claimed to be descendants of Alexander the Great (*Raja Iskandar Dzu'l-Karnain*) and, further back, King Solomon (*Raja Sulaiman*). Learning of this encounter, the king of Palembang invited them to the city. Two of the princes were invited to be rulers of other parts of Sumatra, and the youngest, who was given the title *Sri Tri Buana*, remained as ruler and married the daughter of the former king. Deciding that he needed a coastal city for his capital, he sailed to Rhio where he was welcomed by the female ruler. While preparing to depart, he stopped at nearby island and went hunting. Chasing a wounded deer, he climbed a rock and sighted a white sand beach. Advised that was the land of Temasek, he and his party sailed over. On landing he spotted the strange animal. Advised that in ancient times a lion was said to appear similar, he decided that was the site which he had been seeking and called it *Singapura*. It grew into a great city, which he ruled for 48 years, until ca. 1347.

His son, *Paduka Pikrama Wira*, succeeded him and reigned for fifteen years (until ca. 1362), during which the ruler (*Batara*) of Majapahit became angry because *Singapura* did not acknowledge his suzerainty. A battle ensued but the Javanese eventually were beaten back. His son, *Raja Muda* (crown prince), was married to an Indian princess and acceded to the throne with the title *Sri Rana Wikerma*. He ruled thirteen years (until ca. 1375) and was succeeded by his son, under the title *Paduka Sri Maharaja*, who ruled twelve and one-half years (until ca. 1378). During his rule, *Singapura* was attacked by flying swordfish. The fish would soar onto shore, impaling anyone in their way. To repel them, *Paduka Sri Maharaja* had his men form a human wall, resulting in deaths beyond number. A boy observing the slaughter asked if it wouldn't be better to make the wall of banana trees rather than human legs. When the fish stabbed the banana trees, they became stuck and could be easily killed. Fearing that the youth was too clever, on advice of courtiers, he had the youth executed, bringing a curse on Singapore.

Paduka Sri Maharaja was succeeded by his son, Sultan Iskandar Shah. During a subsequent attack by Majapahit, an offended courtier opened the gates for the troops from Java. During the ensuing slaughter, Sultan Iskandar Shah fled to Muar (in present-day Johor) and eventually Malacca, where he became the founder of the Malacca Sultanate in 1395.

Portuguese versions of the history claim that the city was sacked by Majapahit about 1375 and that Sultan Iskandar Shah (whom they called Parameswara) was a Javanese, possibly a Majapahit prince, living in Palembang who fled to *Singapura*, where he murdered the ruler or senior officer (*Paduka Sri Maharaja*) and assumed the throne. Several Portuguese sources credit the destruction of the city to an attack by Siam (probably Ayudhya or Patani; others blame Pahang) rather than Majapahit. One modern scholar, O. W. Wolters (see in "Pre-colonial History" section under "History" in the Bibliography), argues that the recounting in the *Malay Annals* is really the story of the founding of Malacca but has been moved back in time to disguise a period when Palembang was subservient to Jambi.

Under Malacca and Johore

No matter which realm conquered *Singapura*, the foundation of the Malacca Sultanate eclipsed the island as Malacca succeeded Srivijaya in dominating trade through the Straits. After the conquest of Malacca by Portugal in 1511, the court moved to Johore and maintained a trading official on the Singapore Island. Skirmishing continued between Malay rulers and the Portuguese, resulting in attacks on Johore and Singapore. In 1613, the Portuguese destroyed a Malay outpost at the mouth of the Singapore River, having earlier destroyed the

Sultanate's headquarters at Johor Lama (Old Johore). During the Portuguese era, Malacca remained a major trading port, linking Portuguese settlements in India (Goa), China (Macau), the East Indies (Timor), and Japan (Nagasaki). The conquest of Malacca by the Dutch in 1641 marked Malacca's end as a trade emporium. The Dutch were far more interested in developing their empire on Java, although sporadic attempts were made to force ships passing through the Straits to stop at Malacca and pay duty.

Despite the *Malay Annals*, some scholars believe that *Singapura* and Temasek were little more than a pirate's den. In the seventeenth and eighteenth century, Singapore was left largely to the Sea Gypsies (*Orang Selat* = straits people or *Orang Laut* = sea people), who were not above attacking lightly armed craft or those weakened by the seas. Late in the seventeenth century, a new empire, the Johore Kingdom, was emerging--based in Johore and Rhio--following the assassination of the last heir of the Malacca throne. A dynastic struggle in the early eighteenth century divided that realm between the Malays and the Bugis, who were invited to assist one of the factions. This struggle continued, but, by 1762, Rhio under a de facto Bugis ruler emerged as a major trading center, based at Tanjung Pinang on the island of Banten, attracting British country traders and others. Its success annoyed the Dutch, prompting an unsuccessful invasion in 1784 and a retaliatory siege of Malacca by Rhio and Selangor. A fleet from Batavia broke the siege and then attacked Rhio, killing the sultan. The Dutch victory eliminated the only effective power in the area and dispersed the Rhio forces throughout the region, with little recourse but piracy.

Two parallel royal lines reflected the division between the Malays and the Bugis. The Sultanate remained Malay but power was exercised by a Bugis with the title of Yamtuan (shortened from Yang Dipertuan Muda--crown prince), evident in the installation of the infant Sultan Mahmud III in 1762. When he died, although he had designated his son Sultan Hussein as heir, the younger and more pliant son, Abdul Rahman, was installed on the throne while Sultan Hussein was away in Pahang being married. This official usurpation provided the basis for British East India Company claims to Singapore.

Raffles and the Founding of Modern Singapore

Although he lived in Singapore for less than a year in total, Sir Thomas Stamford Raffles is rightly honored as the spiritual and, at least partially, material father of the modern city-state and nation. Coming to Penang after service in the East India Company Offices in London, he rose quickly to garner the designation as lieutenant governor of Java, which the British seized in 1811 from the Napoleon-dominated Netherlands. During the brief British occupation, he introduced many reforms, such as land laws, indigenous education, and emancipation of slaves, that had enduring impact. When Java was returned to the Dutch in 1816 to contribute to the Netherlands' recovery from the French occupation, he was given a similar title at the Sumatran settlement and penal colony of Bencoolen. He chafed at the demotion and, given the task to advance Company interests in the Straits, he sailed for Singapore against the wishes of the Governor of Penang, Colonel James Bannerman, who wished no rival trading port.

With Colonel William Farquhar, who had negotiated a treaty with Rhio the previous year that was later abnegated, he landed in Singapore at the end of January 1819. There he negotiated with the chief charged with administering the territory, Temenggong Abdul Rahman, rights for the company to establish a settlement. Both Raffles and the Temenggong lacked authority to independently authorize the settlement. Farquhar was sent to Rhio and to Lingga to obtain approval of the agreement. The Yamtuan was reluctant to provoke Dutch ire and the Bugis-designated sultan, Abdul Rahman, declined to ratify the agreement. The passed-over heir-designate, Sultan Hussein, agreed to return with Farquhar, where he approved the Temenggong's agreement and on February 6 signed a separate agreement, claiming to be the legal sultan. Under the terms, Sultan Hussein received S$5,000 per year and Temenggong Abdul Rahman received S$3,000 per year. Raffles returned to Penang the following day, designating Farquhar as resident.

Anticipating Dutch anger at the treaties, Sultan Hussein wrote to Sultan Abdul Rahman and the Yamtuan claiming that he had been coerced into signing. The Dutch reacted as the Sultan anticipated but, believing that pressure from Penang and London would force abandonment of the new settlement, did not attack. Reaction in India was supportive of the new enclave, and the Governor-General of India, the Marquis of Hastings, ordered it reinforced--preempting any armed attempt to displace it. In treaties with the Dutch (the Anglo-Dutch Treaty), the Temenggong, and Sultan Hussein in 1824, the Company's right was affirmed, and title was given to the Company for Singapore and any islands within ten miles.

Raffles returned for about a month at the end of May 1819, but the settlement in fact was Farquhar's responsibility (given the delays with communications with either Bencoolen or India). As the Dutch suppression of Rhio was to divert trade to Batavia (present-day Jakarta), Singapore was ideally situated to attract Chinese and native traders who previously had lived or done business in Rhio. With a commitment to free trade and a wish to develop the settlement, Farquhar lured settlers from Rhio and Malacca (which he had helped wrest from the Dutch in 1795 and administered from 1798 to 1818) and within two years had a settlement of five thousand, about 60 percent Malay and 20 percent Chinese. With no tariff revenue, he introduced a revenue farm system for opium, spirits, and gambling to support the administration. Raffles had prohibited the latter and, when he returned in 1822, was disappointed at the practical measures Farquhar had introduced to cope with building and administering the settlement. In April 1823, he removed Farquhar from office. While Raffles was responsible for the actual creation of modern Singapore and for delineating its development path, Farquhar was the midwife and wet-nurse who assisted with the birth of the colony and nurtured it through its infancy.

A month before Raffles departed for the final time in July 1823, he defined the constitution for the settlement in a proclamation. Presciently, he observed that "nine-tenths of the population probably will be natives of China and the Malay Archipelago" and cautioned that British laws would be unenforceable. He appealed to "universal and natural justice" and identified principles such as the rights of personal security, personal liberty, and property as well as the equality of all before the law. He rejected the English principle of allowing a guilty person to plead innocent, contending that such was an "aggravation of the crime."

Company, Colony, and Independence

Because most of the dictionary entries provide detail on Singapore after Raffles and the Appendix, "Chronology of Important Events," highlights developments, it is possible to sketch the remaining history to the present with broad strokes. In 1824, Britain's and the East India Company's claims to Singapore were confirmed in treaties with the Dutch, recognizing British authority, and with Temenggong Abdul Rahman and Sultan Hussein, permanently transferring the territory to the Company and to Britain. Having won the territory, the East India Company was more concerned with its growing possessions in India and lumped Singapore with Malacca (which it also received in 1824 from the Dutch) and Penang as the Straits Settlements.

If neglected by the Company, it did attract some pioneer British traders and Chinese in great numbers. To these were added Indians, many of who were initially sent there as prisoners. Major attractions were the settlement's commitment to free trade and its location near major East-West shipping lanes. As the East India Company's fortunes waned, it repeatedly asked Singapore to introduce fees to cover its costs; however, these requests were rejected by the citizenry.

In the wake of the Sepoy Mutiny in India in 1857, it was learned that the Company planned to ship dangerous prisoners to Singapore to clear Indian jails for the mutineers. This prompted a Singapore demand to Parliament to sever the Straits Settlements and bring them directly under British rule. The Company objected but in 1858 found itself dissolved; however, the Straits Settlements remained under the Government of India. In 1867, the Straits Settlements were declared a crown colony, under the direct authority of London.

Simultaneously, the opening of the Suez Canal and increasing use of steam power greatly facilitated trade between Asia and Europe as the transit time between China and London was cut in half. Singapore also found a new birth as a coaling station and a British naval post. Domestically, it faced the turmoil of competing secret societies. With the growth of mining and agriculture in the Malay States, as they increasingly came under British influence, Singapore became a center for the coolie trade and, from the masses of migrant workers arriving at the port, there was money to be made. The secret societies were also deeply involved in the opium market, and these opportunities for wealth led to battles over the spoils-- which sometimes were fought along dialect group, as well as organizational, lines. Despite outlawing the societies in 1890, they remained an important element in Singapore business and life until the 1960s. One problem was blurred distinctions between the various types of Chinese organizations, be they *huays*, *huay guans*, *kongsis*, secret societies, or businesses.

The distinctions were further complicated in the twentieth century as China-oriented political parties were added to the mix. The *Kuomintang* (KMT; Chinese Nationalist Party) began as a quasi-secret society under Sun Yat-sen and, at various times in its history, worked closely with the secret societies--as did the Malayan Communist Party (MCP).

The great depression in the late 1920s struck Singapore hard, and thousands of Chinese laborers found themselves out of work as international commodity markets collapsed. Large numbers were repatriated to China, where conditions were no better. In the 1930s, immigration resumed, but with a marked difference: wives and other women came in great numbers, laying the basis for a greatly enlarged and settled Chinese community.

With the Japanese attacks on China in the 1930s, differences between political organizations and other concerns gave way to a pervasive support movement to help China. Too soon, it was Singaporeans who needed help but none could reach them. Simultaneously with bombing Pearl Harbor in 1941, the Japanese bombed Singapore and then invaded the Malay State of Kelantan. In less than fifty days, they had captured the peninsula, and two and one-half weeks later accepted the surrender of Singapore. Through spies, the Japanese knew not only of the island's defenses but also of the support extended to China. In a bloody frenzy, thousands of Chinese men (and some family members) were arrested and killed. A number, including the MCP leadership, sought refuge in the jungle in the Malay States, from which they waged sporadic guerrilla war as the Malayan People's Anti-Japanese Army.

After the initial massacres, the policy toward the Chinese moderated, and blatant brutality abated but was never completely eliminated. In 1945, Britain had planned a staged campaign from India to recapture Singapore and Malaya but the surrender of Japan after two atomic bombs took them by surprise. It took three weeks for British forces to arrive to accept the surrender of Japanese forces in Singapore and Malaya. British records attribute the delay to a demand by American General MacArthur that local surrenders be delayed until he received the formal national surrender in Tokyo Bay on September 2.

The British returned with grand plans but found a populace no longer accepting that Europeans somehow were uniquely qualified to govern. Because of its campaign against the Japanese, the MCP found a role as a legal political party--a status that lasted less than two years as the Malayan Emergency began in June 1948. The party had ample opportunity, however, to build an infrastructure for recruitment of sympathizers--giving birth to the worker and Chinese student strikes of the 1950s.

The British severed Singapore from its plans for the Malay States, which in 1948 were incorporated with Malacca and Penang as the Federation of Malaya. Few felt that the largely Chinese island of Singapore could exist separately from the Malayan hinterlands, and communists, conservatives, and radicals accepted the aim of unification. As Britain worked toward granting independence for the Federation, Singaporeans were ill-content to remain a colony. In 1959, Lee Kuan Yew was elected Chief Minister of internally self-governing Singapore, beginning a tenure which would last until November 1990.

Lee's vehicle was the People's Action Party, formed in 1955--one of the only times in history that a national party collaborated with the communists and emerged victorious. In the early 1960s, the leftist and communist elements objected to Lee's plan for merger with Malaysia--precipitating a series of crises which left Lee and his friends in control of the party and their opponents mostly in jail.

Merger lasted less than two years, from September 16, 1963 to August 9, 1965. If nothing else, the experience won independence for Singapore and vividly demonstrated the clash of cultures between the Chinese majority in Singapore and the Malay majority in Peninsular Malaysia. Although the break was mutually agreed upon, it was less than cordial. Fortunately, it was followed shortly after by the ouster of Sukarno in Indonesia, bringing an end to Confrontation and producing concentrated efforts aimed at reconciliation.

In the aftermath, Singapore emerged as a dynamic, if not always diplomatic, partner with its neighbors in the Association of Southeast Asian Nations (ASEAN). It also emphasized diversifying its economy and reducing dependency on processing Indonesian and Malaysian commodities and, after a brief fling at import substitution, returned to its historical commitment to free trade. This, coupled with the foresight of its leadership and the quality of its citizenry, produced a wealthy city-nation.

Along the way, it has voiced commitment to democracy but has not always shown great concern for individual liberties and democratic values. Like Malaysia, it continues the colonial policy of interning without trial persons believed to be threats to the political or social order. It also exercises control over domestic media and has claimed the right to respond to articles in foreign media (under the threat of suspending distribution). Individually, Singaporeans are among the best-educated citizenry in the world (with over 90 percent literacy), but many remain convinced, based on their experiences in mid-century or on what they have been told by the government, that such restraints are necessary. On the verge of the twenty-first century, the government has embraced the idea of Singapore as a world information hub; however, it is unclear how such a role can be reconciled with government policies aimed at controlling the flow of information to its citizenry.

DICTIONARY

-A-

ABDUL RAHMAN, TEMENGGONG (-1825). Signatory with Raffles (q.v.) of the 1819 agreement for the settlement of Singapore. As a member of a minor branch of the Johore Kingdom (q.v.), he had settled in Singapore (and claimed the territory in the southern Malay peninsula) after the restoration of Dutch rule in Rhio in 1818. Raffles recognized that the Temenggong was a secondary chief and had Farquhar (q.v.) go to the court at Lingga to have the agreement approved. Farquhar returned with Hussein, who claimed the title of Sultan, and approved the agreement in that capacity. The Temenggong was given land and a pension in exchange for the 1819 and subsequent 1824 agreements. Later in the nineteenth century, his heirs assumed the title of Sultan of Johore and founded the present royal family of the Malaysian state of Johor.

ABDUL RAHMAN PUTRA AL-HAJ IBNI AL-MARHUM SULTAN ABDUL HAMID HALIM SHAH, TUNKU (1903-1990). Prime Minister of Malaya, 1957-1963, and of Malaysia, 1963-1970. Known as the Father of Malaya and of Malaysia, he announced the concept of Malaysia in 1961 when he feared that an independent Singapore likely would be communist controlled. Once it was included within Malaysia, he found the candid and confrontational style of the PAP exacerbated existing tensions. Confronted by rising racial antagonisms in Peninsular Malaysia (q.v.) and in Singapore, aggravated by PAP attempts to extend its influence, senior Malaysian cabinet members

23

convinced him in July 1965 that Singapore should be separated from Malaysia for the good of both. The separation was announced August 9, 1965.

ABDUL SAMAD ISMAIL (1924-). Prominent journalist, Malay intellectual, award-winning author, and admitted early clandestine communist. Born in Singapore, he became a reporter for *Utusan Melayu* and worked for *Berita Malai* under the Japanese which brought him into association with Malay nationalists, such as Ibrahim Yaacob and Ishak Haji Mohammad. When the British returned, he was arrested for articles which he had written during the period. After his release, he rejoined *Utusan Melayu* and was closely associated with left-wing activities and friends with Devan Nair (q.v.)--with whom he was detained from 1951 to 1953. He was a co-founder of the PAP but later broke with the party. In 1958 he joined the *Berita Harian*, part of the influential *Straits Times* Group and shortly after moved to Malaya. In 1972, he convinced the Malaysian Government to force the Singapore-based *Straits Times* to sell its Malaysian operations to Malaysian interests, giving birth to *The New Straits Times*. In June 1976, three weeks after receiving an award as a literary pioneer from the Malaysian Prime Minister, he was detained--reportedly on evidence provided by the Singapore Government. In September, he confessed on Malaysian television to having been a dedicated communist for much of his life. In 1981, he was released and resumed his journalism career, eventually rejoining *The New Straits Times*.

ABDULLAH BIN ABDUL KADIR, MUNSHI (ca. 1795/97-1854). Foremost Malay-language author and teacher. A *Peranakan Keling* from Malacca, Munshi Abdullah taught Malay to leading European missionaries there and moved to Singapore shortly after its founding. His *Hikayat Abdullah* describes Raffles, the founding, and life in the early years of the colony. He continued teaching Malay to Westerners and also served as a translator, as on a voyage to Kelantan which provided material for his *Kesah Pelay-*

aran Abdullah, and transcriber, reflected in a number of Malay manuscripts in the Library of Congress, procured during the stopover by the U. S. Exploring Expedition led by Charles Wilkes in 1842.

ABU BAKAR, SULTAN (1833-1895). Ruler of Johore, 1862-1895, and its first Sultan. Son of Temenggong Ibrahim (1810-1862), he grew up in Singapore where he received an English education under the independent missionary B. P. Keasberry (q.v.). The treaties of 1819 and 1824 gave his family extensive land holdings in Singapore which provided substantial income; however, the 1824 treaty included a clause forfeiting his property if he moved out of Singapore. He negotiated relinquishing some prime land in exchange for canceling the residency requirement, allowing him and his successors to occupy the capital of Johore Bahru without losing residences and other land in Singapore. He ascended the throne with the title Temenggong, continuing from the division of responsibilities in the Johore Kingdom, but received recognition by the British as Maharaja in 1868, relieving him of possible rival claims, and as Sultan in 1885. In the 1860s, he visited Europe and was received by Queen Victoria. During his reign, he extended the realm to include Muar and surrounding territory--comprising the present Malaysian state of Johor. Shortly before his death, he issued a constitution to regularize the government and even to limit the power of the sultanate.

AGENCY HOUSE. Initially, a company engaged in the country trade enjoying a sub-monopoly from the East India Company (q.v.) and later a vertically integrated trading organization. With the growth of plantations, especially for rubber, the agency houses operated plantations, processing facilities, and export agencies for products, especially rubber, and also served as importers for a variety of products for their operations and wider markets. The earliest and most successful continuing agency house is Guthries, now Malaysian owned.

ALL-MALAYA COUNCIL OF JOINT ACTION (AMCJA). Non-Malay front opposed to the federation proposed to replace the Malayan Union. Organized in December 1946 as the Pan-Malayan Council of Joint Action and renamed in August 1947, it was chaired by the respected Straits Chinese, Sir Tan Cheng Lock (q.v.), and included the Malayan Democratic Union (q.v.), the Straits Chinese British Association, the Pan-Malayan Federation of Trade Unions (q.v.), and a variety of other organizations including the communist Malayan People's Anti-Japanese Ex-Service Comrades' Association. Largely ignored by the British, it allied itself with the Malay front *PUTERA* (*Pusat Tenaga Ra'ayat*; Center of the People's Power) comprised of the Malay Nationalist Party and allied organizations to form the AMCJA-PUTERA. The AMCJA, with the support of the Singapore Chinese Chamber of Commerce (q.v.), staged a successful *hartal* (q.v.) throughout Singapore and Malaya in October 1947. Opposition to restrictive citizenship proposals and increasing communist influence prompted the withdrawal of the Chinese Chamber of Commerce support, which doomed a second *hartal* in January 1948. In March 1948, the Malayan Communist Party (q.v.) also abandoned the organization, taking its grassroots support and leading to its collapse.

ALL-PARTY CONSTITUTIONAL MISSIONS (1956-1958). Talks held with Britain regarding transition to self-government in April - May 1956. Led by David Marshall (q.v.) as Chief Minister and including the parties represented in the Legislative Assembly (q.v.) (Marshall's Labour Front [q.v.], the PAP, and the Progressive Party [q.v.]), the mission won numerous concessions from the British including citizenship for China-born residents, but the British refused to relinquish control over internal security. Marshall had demanded full self-government by April 1957. With these irreconcilable positions, the mission was a failure and Marshall resigned on his return in June. A subsequent mission in March 1957, led by Lim Yew Hock (q.v.) as Chief Minister, yielded substantial agreements and a third conference in April and May 1958 provided for internal self-rule in 1959.

ALLIANCE. Ruling political coalition in Malaya (q.v.) and early Malaysia (q.v.). Coming to power in 1955, the Alliance was formed by communal parties representing Malaya's three major ethnic groups: the United Malays National Organisation (UMNO), the Malayan Chinese Association (MCA) and the Malayan Indian Congress (MIC). After the May 13, 1969, racial riots and an interim National Operations Council, the Alliance was replaced by a much broader coalition, the *Barisan Nasional* (National Front).

ALLIANCE PARTY SINGAPURA. Opposition coalition comprised of Singapore branches of Malaysian political parties. Following the defeat of the Singapore Alliance in the 1963 election, the component parties reformed under this label, and the Singapore People's Alliance was dissolved. The party did not field candidates in the 1968 election.

ANDERSON, SIR JOHN (1858-1918). Governor of Straits Settlements (q.v.) and High Commissioner of the Federated Malay States, 1904-1911. After twenty-five years of service in the Colonial Office, he was an outsider to leaders in Singapore who felt that London did not understand their situation. He became popular as he tried to more closely link Singapore with the Malay States (q.v.). Under his administration, the opium farm was taken over by the government. He also sought to reform the municipal administration. He simultaneously served as High Commissioner for Brunei (1906-1911). After leaving, he was made permanent under-secretary of state for the colonies, 1911-1916.

ANGLO-DUTCH TREATY OF 1824. Agreement demarcating British and Dutch spheres of influence in the archipelago. The British gave Bencoolen (q.v.) (Fort Marlborough) and the surrounding area to the Dutch in return for Malacca. The Dutch abandoned any claims in India while the British relinquished claims in the Netherlands East Indies (q.v.), including Rhio (q.v.).

ANTI-BRITISH LEAGUE (ABL). Also referred to as Singapore People's Anti-British League and People's Anti-British League. Front organization and recruiting tool for Malayan Communist Party (q.v.). It mirrored the communist party with cellular organization and clandestine activities; however, it afforded a nationalist, anti-colonial venue for people unwilling to join the party as well as a testing ground for recruits to the party. It gained greatest importance after the 1948 demise of the Malayan Democratic Union (q.v.). It had a variety of wings including English-speaking intellectuals such as Devan Nair (q.v.) and John Eber (q.v.), Chinese wings with close ties (and often overlapping memberships) with secret societies and school organizations to identify and socialize potential young recruits. Eber edited its outlawed newspaper, *Freedom News*. Others closely associated with it included Abdul Samad Ismail, Lim Kean Chye (q.v.), P. V. Sharma (q.v.), and Eu Chooi Yip (q.v.). Detentions in 1951 removed most of its best known English-speaking membership, but others escaped and increasingly focused on student organizations.

ANTI-CATHOLIC RIOTS. Also called Anti-Christian Riots. Chinese, who had converted to Catholicism and had established agricultural settlements in rural areas, were attacked by non-Christian Chinese probably associated with secret societies beginning February 15, 1851. During five days of attacks and counter-attacks, five hundred people were killed and twenty-eight plantations burned.

ASSOCIATION OF BRITISH MALAYA. Organization formed in 1920 in London to better represent commercial, mining, and planting interests. Succeeding the Straits Settlements Association (q.v.), this organization reflected the increasing importance of British economic activities in the Malay States (q.v.) outside the Straits Settlements (q.v.).

ASSOCIATION OF SOUTHEAST ASIAN NATIONS (ASEAN). Organization for regional cooperation among non-communist nations in Southeast Asia. In the aftermath of Sukarno's removal from power in Indonesia and the end of Confrontation (q.v.), Indonesia, Malaysia, the Philippines, Singapore, and Thailand launched it as a regional cooperative organization on August 8, 1967. Initially, it provided a forum for renewing relations between Malaysia and Indonesia and for formalizing relationships between Malaysia and Singapore following separation. With the end of British protection, Brunei joined in 1984. Beyond intergovernmental cooperation, it also served as a focus for private sector and organizational cooperation (e.g., the ASEAN Tours and Travel Association and the Confederation of ASEAN Journalists). Its successes have come largely in international politics as the members have formed a united front in discussions with major powers (such as the U.S. and the European Community) and in responding to Vietnam's military dominance in Indochina following the American withdrawal and the fall of the Republic of Vietnam (South Vietnam). Its efforts to stimulate regional economic development have been less successful because of conflicting national interests in seeking foreign investment. Despite its limited economic accomplishments, it is one of the most active and durable international regional organizations.

AW BOON HAW (1893-1957). Pharmaceutical and publishing magnate. Born in Rangoon, Burma, he was one of the few Hakka to become a prominent business person. With his brother, Aw Boon Par, he developed a line of patent medicines. In 1926, he opened the Singapore branch of the Eng Aun Tong Medical Hall and these were later found in most major cities in Asia. He was known throughout Southeast and East Asia as the "Tiger Balm King," after the popular ointment which made his fortune. Before World War II, he owned the *Sin Chew Jit Poh*, the largest circulation Chinese newspaper in Singapore and Malaya and Chinese papers in other large cities. After World War II, he also launched English papers, the *Tiger Standard*, in Singapore and Hong Kong. In both of these cities, he built "Tiger Balm Gardens"--known as Haw Par Villa in the latter--which combined plants with statuary from Chinese mythology.

-B-

BABA. Originally applied (in Singapore) to descendants of Chinese (q.v.) who had settled in Malacca (q.v.), often marrying Malay women. Later, it was used for second-generation and later Chinese born and settled in the Straits Settlements (q.v.). The *Baba* community tended to adopt a style of Malay dress and speak at least market Malay. The distinction between them and the *Singkeh* (q.v.) was that they considered the Straits Settlements home whereas the latter were new arrivals or sojourners. With the incorporation of Singapore, Malacca, and Penang as the Straits Settlements, English became the preferred language, although in the twentieth century, some emphasized regaining mastery of Chinese. See also STRAITS CHINESE and *PERANAKAN*.

BANG. From Chinese, a gang or group. In Singapore, it usually referred to a dialect group, e.g., Hakka or Hokkien (q.v.). The Singapore Chinese Chamber of Commerce and Industry (SCCCI) was organized in a *bang* structure, separate organizations for the different dialect groups under a general umbrella.

BARISAN. Literally, front. Often used as a short form of *Barisan Sosialis* (q.v.).

BARISAN SOSIALIS (Socialist Front). Foremost leftist opposition party in the 1960s. Announced on August 13, 1961, by dissidents expelled from the People's Action Party (PAP) (q.v.) for failing to support the party leadership on issues of internal security and merger with Malaysia, the *Barisan* began with thirteen seats (of fifty-one) in the

Legislative Assembly. Three PAP political secretaries, Lim Chin Siong (q.v.), Fong Swee Suan (q.v.), and S. Woodhull (q.v.), and a party Parliamentary secretary, Dr. Lee Siew Choh (q.v.), formed the leadership of the new party. The party also attracted much of the lower-level and grassroots organization of the PAP. The split leading to the formation of the party was reflected in the labor movement as the Trade Union Conference (TUC) split into the PAP-supported National Trades Union Congress (NTUC) (q.v.) and *Barisan*-led Singapore Association of Trade Unions (SATU) (q.v.). The split threatened the PAP's continuance as only one-fifth of the previous members paid dues in 1962 and two-thirds of the labor supported *Barisan*. In 1962, the *Barisan* joined with socialist parties in Malaysia and Brunei in opposing merger with Malaysia. The December 1962 uprising against the British by the *Parti Rakyat Brunei* (Brunei People's Party) prompted the Internal Security Council to detain more than one hundred opposition, labor and student leaders who had favored the rebellion in February 1963--a sweep known as Operation Cold Store (q.v.). Included were Lim Chin Siong and half of the Central Committee of *Barisan*. Protests which turned into riots led to arrest of many middle-level party leaders. In the September 1963 general election, detained persons were not allowed to contest for office, and the *Barisan* captured only thirteen of fifty-one seats. In October 1963, *Barisan*'s labor base, SATU, was dissolved. *Barisan*'s defeat in the 1965 Hong Lim (q.v.) by-election was its final bow in electoral politics. When Parliament met again in December 1965, the five *Barisan* Assemblymen who had avoided arrest boycotted the session and resigned their seats ten months later. In 1968, it continued its boycott of Parliament by refusing to contest elections. Lacking a public forum and with many members detained, the party dwindled.

BENCOOLEN. British Colony on West Coast of Sumatra, centered on the present-day city of Bengkulu (then called Fort Marlborough) and used originally as a prison colony. Raffles (q.v.) was appointed as its Lieutenant Governor in

1818 after Java was returned to The Netherlands. In this capacity, he founded Singapore (q.v.), and it remained under Bencoolen until 1823 when it came under the East India Company's (q.v.) Supreme Government of India. Bencoolen was given to the Dutch in the 1824 Anglo-Dutch Treaty (q.v.) in exchange for Malacca and recognition of Singapore.

BRADDELL, SIR ROLAND ST. JOHN (1880-1966). Leading lawyer in and author on Malaya and Singapore. In 1948, he served as a private legal adviser to the Council of Rulers of the Federation of Malaya (q.v.) and, in 1946-1948, to the United Malays National Organisation (q.v.). He helped draft the 1948 State and Federation Agreements and a model state constitution for the Federation. He was the first Chair of Council of the University of Malaya from its establishment in Singapore in 1949 and received its first honorary degree in 1950.

BRADDELL, THOMAS (1823-1891). Colonial Secretary of the Straits Settlements (q.v.) (1874-1876) and leading citizen. Initially coming to Penang to manage a sugar estate in 1844, he joined the East India Company (q.v.) as deputy superintendent of police in 1849 in Penang. When the 1854 Chinese riots in Singapore spread to Malacca where he was stationed, he attacked the rioters and ended the disorder. In 1859, he entered the bar in London and in 1862 resigned from the East India Company to practice law in Singapore as a partner with Abraham Logan, who had edited and then owned the *Singapore Free Press* in the 1840s. He was named crown counsel in 1864 and, when the Straits Settlements were transferred to the colonial office, he served as attorney general through 1882. He avidly collected stories of Singapore for a history which was never written but his collection provided the basis for Buckley's *An Anecdotal History of Old Times in Singapore: 1819-1867*. In 1875 he was named colonial secretary to Sir Andrew Clarke (q.v.). A coach accident in 1882 compelled him to retire to England. His eldest son,

Sir Thomas de Multon Lee Braddell, was the father of Sir Roland St. John Braddell.

BRITISH MILITARY ADMINISTRATION (BMA). Government following the Japanese surrender until restoration of civilian rule in March 1946. With the landing of British forces in September 1945, Singapore came under the BMA, overseen by Lord Louis Mountbatten as Supreme Allied Commander for South-East Asia. Authority was exercised by Sir Ralph Hone as Chief Civil Affairs Officer for Malaya and Patrick McKerron as Deputy Chief Civil Affairs Officer responsible for Singapore. Its main tasks were restoring public services and infrastructure, but many officials took the opportunity to profiteer, accounting for the counter definition of the BMA as "Black Market Administration." It did reopen the port and re-establish food and water supplies. It also instituted a special War Crimes Commission to investigate Japanese behavior and local collaborators--focusing on treatment of Europeans but largely ignoring the massacres of Chinese.

BROOKE-POPHAM, SIR ROBERT (1878-1953). Air Chief Marshall made commander of all land and air forces in the Far East in November 1940. He conveyed little sense of urgency, assuring the British government that the Japanese had no intention of attacking south, countering Percival's plea for reinforcements. He publicly stated, in October 1941, that Singapore and Malaya needed no help from the American Navy and, as late as December, assured the press that the Japanese were afraid to attack British might in Malaya. As had been planned before the outbreak of war on December 8th (December 7th in the U. S.), on December 23rd his replacement, General Sir Henry Pownall, arrived and replaced him.

BRUNEI. Oil-rich state on the island of Borneo. The ruling sultanate dates from the fifteenth century and once dominated much of northern and western Borneo. The Malaysian states of Sabah and Sarawak occupy territory once controlled by the sultanate, the former being sold to a

commercial company and the latter gradually acquired by
Rajah Brooke in return for suppressing rebellions. The
discovery of oil in the 1920s brought immense wealth to
the country and its rulers. It came under British "protection" in the twentieth century, achieving full independence only in 1984. It was scheduled to join in the formation of Malaysia but refused following an uprising in
December 1962 and a dispute about sharing of oil revenues. Described as a "Shellfare state," the annual per
capita income is well over twenty thousand dollars, and
the ruling sultan has been identified as the richest man in
the world. Despite a citizenry which is overwhelmingly
Malay (a large number of Chinese work there but are
denied citizenship) and Islamic and a royal system of
government, it gets along well with Singapore--the currency of each circulating freely in the other. Brunei has
allowed the Singapore Armed Forces to train in its territory and the royal family invests heavily in Singapore.
Both are members of ASEAN (q.v.).

BUCKLEY, CHARLES BURTON (1844-1912). Leading lawyer
and chronicler of early Singapore. He was invited to
Singapore by W. H. Read to recover his health in 1864
and later became active in law. He served as confidential
adviser to Sultan Abu Bakar (q.v.) of Johore and his successor, Sultan Ibrahim. In 1884, with others, he revived
the *Singapore Free Press*, and his contributions to the
Press, entitled "Anecdotal History of Singapore," provided
the body of his later magnum opus of the same title,
covering Singapore under the East India Company (q.v.).

BUGIS. Malay group and dialect from southern Sulawesi
(known as Celebes under the Dutch) famous for their
sailing prowess. In the eighteenth century, they replaced
the *orang laut* (q.v.) as the predominant naval force for
Johore (q.v.) and successfully joined the royal line of the
Johore Kingdom (q.v.) based in Rhio-Lingga. They also
provided the royal lines for a number of other sultanates
on the Malay Peninsula. They dominated trade between
Singapore and eastern Indonesia through the early years

and remained a major trading force into the twentieth century.

-C-

CABINET. Prime minister and other ministers who are individually responsible for particular government activities (called portfolios) and collectively responsible for government policies. They must be members of Parliament but, in their cabinet posts, are the seniormost officers of the executive branch of government. See "Cabinets of Singapore" in Appendices for membership.

CANTONESE. People and dialect from Kwangtung (*pinyin*: Guangdong) Province in China, in the area around Canton (*pinyin*: Guangzhou) and Hong Kong. They also were referred to historically as Kwangtungs and Macaos. Most were artisans and laborers; others included Hoo Ah Kay (q.v.) (Whampoa) and a wealthy few who made fortunes from tin mining and later in banking and finance. With the encouragement of migration from Hong Kong in the 1980s and 1990s, the numbers are likely to increase.

CAUSEWAY. Bridge connecting the island of Singapore with the Malayan peninsula. Opened in 1923 as the Johore Causeway, it has served as the only land connection between Singapore and neighboring Johore. With the growth of motor transport, it has provided the major route for bringing in rubber for processing and other raw materials and manufactures for export. In January 1942, it was the main route for retreating British forces and then a section was blasted to prevent Japanese troops from following. With warming relations and interdependency between Malaysia (q.v.) and Singapore, a second causeway is planned for the mid-1990s.

CENTRAL PROVIDENT FUND (CPF). "Social Security" system created in 1955 to provide benefits for the old, disabled, and widows. Financed with contributions, which in the mid-1980s slump were reduced to 10 percent of salaries from employers and 25 percent of salaries from employees, it is the national retirement system as well as a form of forced savings which provided development capital after independence. To encourage home ownership, participants have been allowed to remove a portion of their contributions for home purchases. Since 1986, a market-based interest rate is paid on CPF contributions. In July 1991, the employers' share was raised from 16.5 percent to 17.5 percent, with employees' contributions at 23 percent.

CHAN HENG CHEE (1942-). Prominent scholar, past ambassador to the United Nations, and Director of Singapore International Foundation. With advanced degrees from Cornell University and the University of Singapore, she appeared set for a life of teaching and scholarship. Her studies of the PAP were internationally acclaimed and her controlled criticism of the government marked her as an outspoken intellectual among quiescent Singaporeans. In 1974, she appeared on the cover of *Newsweek* as representative of the new Asian woman. In 1988, she was named to head the prestigious government think-tank, the Institute of Policy Studies. In 1989, she became the first woman ambassador in the nation's history when she accepted the appointment to head the mission to the United Nations. In 1991, she returned to Singapore to head a new Singapore International Foundation which the government established to enhance the nation's reputation abroad.

CHANDU. Hindi word for opium (q.v.) processed for smoking, widely used by Europeans and some Chinese as a synonym for opium. This was the preferred form of consumption before the war. A 1908 government study reported that a ball of raw opium would yield 28 tahils (37.35 ounces; 1 *tahil* = 1.34 ounces or 583 grains) of *chandu*, which were then divided into *chee* (1/8th ounce or 58.3 grains) and then *hoon* (5.8 grains). The residue from smoked *chandu* was scraped from pipes and sold at a lower price (without being subject to the revenue farm [q.v.]). When the government assumed responsibility for distribution in 1910, this residue was collected and reprocessed (denying, at least in theory, poorer users access to the cheaper product).

CHANGI. Located on the Eastern end of the island, Changi was best known as the site of Japanese internment camps for European prisoners during World War II and political detainees prior to independence. Today, the nation's modern international airport carries the name.

CHEANG HONG LIM (-1893). Major controller of opium (q.v.) and other revenue farms (q.v.) in second half of the nineteenth century. His father, Cheang Sam Teo, had controlled the opium and other farms between 1847 and 1863 under a Hokkien-Teochew syndicate with Cheang leading Hokkien interests and Lau Joon Tek heading the Teochew. After nearly a decade of competition with Tan Seng Poh (q.v.), brother in law of Seah Eu Chin (q.v.), Cheang Hong Lim (and his Cheang Hong Guan) formed a new syndicate with Tan and Tan Hiok Nee (leader of the Tan-family gang, *Seh*-Tan) which controlled the farms not only in Singapore and Johore but also in Rhio and Malacca in the 1870s. After it lost the farms to bidders from Penang, syndicate leaders (Tan Seng Poh had been replaced by his son Tan Keng Swee) were implicated in the early 1880s of trying to bankrupt the farm through illegal sales. Some minor alleged conspirators were banished but the leaders were Straits-born and not subject to deportation. Cheang Hong Lim, however, was removed from office as justice of the peace. Despite the public disgrace, Cheang Hong Lim built on his great wealth through real estate development but was also widely appreciated for his support of schools and charities. His name endures in modern Singapore in the Hong Lim Constituency and massive Hong Lim housing estates.

CHELATES (*Celates* in contemporary spelling). Sea gypsy people or boat people whose naval activities were dominant in the Straits and the Rhio-Lingga Archipelago during the eras before, during, and after the Malacca Sultanate. The name, used by the Portuguese, is believed derived from the Malay *orang selat* or Straits people, although they are also referred to as Chelate Bajuus (possible references to the Bajau of Borneo or the Bugis (Wajus) of Sulawesi. They provided the naval forces for the Sultanate. See also *ORANG LAUT*.

CHENG KIM CHUAN, VINCENT (1947-). Catholic activist, detained in May 1987. With a master's degree in theology from Trinity Theological College, he was a staff member of the Catholic Centre for Foreign Workers in Geylang, 1982-1984. Subsequently, he worked for the Archdiocesan Justice and Peace Commission as well and was appointed executive secretary of the Commission in 1985. He was among sixteen persons detained May 21, 1987, for alleged connections with a clandestine communist network. He was the only one of these detainees to receive the maximum two-year detention order. In a heavily edited television broadcast, he seemed to accept the accusations that he was associated with Tan Wah Piow (q.v.) and leader of the conspiracy.

CHIA THYE POH (1941-). Former *Barisan Sosialis* (q.v.) member of Parliament and Singapore's longest held detainee. As a student, he was active in the Chinese Schools movement. In July 1966, he was convicted of publishing a seditious article in the *Barisan* newspaper. After resigning from Parliament in 1966 in protest against government restrictions, he was detained on October 30, 1966. In 1989, he was released from formal detention but restricted to the small island of Sentosa and forbidden to engage in political activities. Since September 1990, he has been allowed to visit the main island during the day but must return each evening. No explanation was given for his detention until 1985 when the Minister of Home Affairs, Jayakumar, charged that he had infiltrated

Barisan on instructions from the Malayan Communist Party (q.v.). Chia repeatedly refused to renounce violence, because he claimed that he had never advocated violence, in order to be freed or to accept exile to another country. A government order in November 1990 bars him from making public statements without Internal Security Department (q.v.) approval.

CHIAM SEE TONG (1935-). Secretary General of Singapore Democratic Party (SDP) (q.v.). and member of Parliament since 1984. With a bachelor's degree from New Zealand and a teaching certificate, he taught before studying law in London and winning admission to the bar. After running well but unsuccessfully as an independent in the 1976 general election and a 1979 by-election, he founded the SDP to compete in the 1980 general election. Although this election saw the PAP sweep 77 percent of the vote, the most it has received before or since, Chiam saw his support increase by 8 percent against the same candidate to whom he had lost in 1979. He was elected in the 1984 general election and again in the elections in 1988 and 1991. Between 1986 and 1991, he was the only elected opposition member of Parliament. His critical but non-combative parliamentary behavior are a marked contrast to J. B. Jeyaretnam (q.v.) and the Workers' Party (WP) (q.v.)

CHINA. As the ancestral, if not immediate, home of most of Singapore's population from the 1820s to present, China has had a real and a symbolic influence on Singapore's Chinese population. China's relations with the *Nanyang* (Southeast Asia) have ranged from great involvement to complete avoidance; both were at various times characteristic of the Ming Dynasty (1368-1644). Historically, China exercised hegemony over the region, with the sending of tribute to and recognition by the emperor vital to the legitimacy of a kingdom. The successor Manchu (Ch'ing; *pinyin*: Qing) Dynasty (1644-1911), which was perceived by Chinese as ruled by northern barbarians, spurred greatest contacts as traders and fugitives from southern

China increasingly looked to Southeast Asia as a land of opportunity or refuge. The eighteenth century was characterized by a letter from the emperor to the European powers asking them to identify any Chinese living in their territories so that they could be returned for execution. Only late in the nineteenth century did the Manchus pay much attention to the Chinese populations in the European colonies in Southeast Asia. This awareness can be traced to the sharp increase in emigration, the importance of remittances from Chinese abroad, and--especially near the end of the century--activities of anti-Manchu groups. In the twentieth century, the Chinese in the Nanyang continued to provide important financial support for the governments and for the improvement of China. A fundamental issue for China and the nations in Southeast Asia as they gained independence was the Chinese concept of *jus sanguinus* (by blood) citizenship or nationality--a descendant of Chinese parents remained a citizen of China no matter where they lived. This, coupled with doubts about the loyalties of some Chinese--especially immigrants--was a justification for limiting the rights to citizenship and voting in Singapore and Malaya (q.v.) in the decade after World War II. Compounding the problem was support given local communist parties, such as the Malayan Communist Party (q.v.), by the Chinese Communist Party. As tensions eased after the Vietnam War, Singapore increasingly sought to capitalize on its Chineseness to engage in trade and economic activities with the People's Republic of China (PRC)--without, however, formally recognizing the PRC until after Indonesia had done so.

CHINESE. Predominant ethnic group in Singapore. While all Chinese accept a common ethnic and cultural identity, through history most Chinese immigrants and sojourners have given greater emphasis to family and dialect groups: Hokkien (q.v.), Cantonese (q.v.), Teochew (q.v.), Hakka (q.v.), and others. Those settled in Southeast Asia for a number of generations, *Baba*s (q.v.) or Straits Chinese (q.v.), tended to look more toward the West than China;

however, even these groups were mobilized from time to time to aid China in times of crisis or to learn standard (Mandarin) Chinese in addition to English and possibly their dialect. In contemporary Singapore, children of Chinese parents are required to learn Mandarin in elementary schools, which has the effect of forging a common Chinese identity transcending dialect associations.

CHINESE DIALECTS. Varieties of spoken language. While they share common written symbols (ideographs or characters), great variety is found in pronunciation. For example, the well known Hokkien family name, Tay, is pronounced Chêng (*pinyin*: Zheng) in Mandarin. Dialects tended to be identified with specific regions (with the exception of Hakka [q.v.] which is spread over several provinces). The main dialects in Singapore have been Cantonese (q.v.), Hainanese (q.v.), Hakka, Hokkien (q.v.), and Teochew (q.v.). Because of the divergence (completely different words rather than simply different pronunciations), speakers of a dialect may be unintelligible to speakers of other dialects. This is the case with the main Singapore dialects with the exception of Hokkien and Teochew, which are from neighboring regions in China. To bridge this gap, the northern dialect called Mandarin in English was promulgated as the standard national language (*putonghua* or the common language) in the People's Republic of China and the Republic of China (*guo you* or the national language). In 1898, the first Mandarin school opened in Singapore, and by 1917 it had become the standard medium of instruction in Chinese schools (displacing the individual dialects which continued to be spoken at home). Chinese Singaporeans are urged to learn and use Mandarin (*huayi* or Chinese language) to overcome dialect barriers. Most today at least learn it as all schools encourage multi-lingualism; however, the dialects have endured, as evident in the large audiences for televised Cantonese soap operas imported from Hong Kong.

CHINESE FUNERAL RIOTS. First major secret society clash in Singapore. On March 3, 1846, the funeral procession for a leader of the *Ngee Heng* secret society (q.v.) (with a Teochew membership) opted not to follow the officially approved route, leading to clashes with the police and with a rival secret society (with a Hokkien membership) during the next weeks, culminating in the attack on the home of a magistrate's clerk on March 30 by a *Ngee Heng* gang member.

CHINESE PROTECTORATE. Government body created in 1877 to monitor and regulate Chinese affairs, especially the coolie trade (q.v.) and secret societies (q.v.). William Pickering (q.v.) was named Protector of the Chinese. With the passage of a Chinese Immigrants Ordinance in 1877, the Protectorate licensed recruiters and inspected ships bringing immigrants. It also assumed control for licensing houses of prostitution. In 1877 Pickering also was named as a Registrar of Societies to control secret societies, activities which may have led to the attack on him with an axe by a secret society member in 1887. In 1890, a law aimed at eliminating dangerous secret societies ended the public visibility of the larger organizations. In the 1920s and 1930s, the Protectorate concentrated on suppressing communist organizers and later on mobilizing Chinese to resist the Japanese invasion.

CHINTENGS (Also called revenue peons). Private police hired by revenue farmers. To protect the revenue goods (most prominently opium but also spirits), the farmers would hire individuals and gangs to protect the merchandise and also to guard against rivals selling competing products illegally. Their arbitrary and bullying behavior was cited as a reason for eliminating the revenue farms. See FARMS, REVENUE.

CITIZENS' CONSULTATIVE COMMITTEES (CCC). Coordinating bodies for community projects and two-way communications channels for the government. Initially established in the mid-1960s, the CCCs were an effort to personalize the government to the citizenry. Each CCC was divided into *kampong* (neighborhood) or street committees. At this level, the purpose was to assure that government policies were adequately explained to the people and that the people had an adequate channel to funnel requests and complaints back to the government. Where the PAP represents the constituency, there is an effort to involve the members of Parliament in the process. There is one CCC for each member of Parliament (totalling 81 since 1988, including three in each of the thirteen group representation constituencies). The CCCs coordinate the activities of other community groups such as the Residents' Committee (serving residents in Housing and Development Board [HDB] apartment complexes) and the Community Centre Management Committees (CCMC). These are all voluntary organizations which help mobilize the population to support government activities and to improve their neighborhoods.

CLARKE, SIR ANDREW (1824-1902). Governor and Commander in Chief of Straits Settlements, 1873-1875. Son of the Governor of West Australia, he was named Governor to succeed Ord (q.v.) after a career in Australian politics and serving as director of works for the British navy. While he was popular in Singapore, he was primarily occupied with the Malay States (q.v.), signing the Pangkor agreement, which provided the basis for British intervention into the peninsular Malay States.

CLEMENTI, SIR CECIL (1875-1947). Governor of the Straits Settlements and High Commissioner to Malaya, 1930-1934. Despite or because of a lengthy career in China and Hong Kong (he was a nephew of the nineteenth-century governor, Sir Cecil Clementi Smith), during which he gained proficiency in Mandarin and Cantonese, his greatest problems--beyond the worldwide depression--came from the Chinese (q.v.). He enforced the ban on the *Kuomintang* (q.v.), censorship of the Chinese press, and strict immigration restrictions, cutting Chinese immigration by 90 percent between 1930 and 1933; the worldwide depression which was especially acute in Singapore also contributed to the decrease. In 1932, he canceled government support of Chinese and Tamil schools.

CLIFFORD, SIR HUGH CHARLES (1866-1941). Early British official in Malay States, prominent author, and Governor of the Straits Settlements, 1927-1929. Coming to the Malay States (q.v.) from school in 1883, he served as British Resident in some of the most remote areas of the Peninsula, particularly in Pahang--from which he led a famous expedition against rebels who had fled to neighboring states in 1894. He left the Malay States in 1903 to serve in a variety of high colonial posts in Ceylon, Africa, and the West Indies. He is best known for his brooding writings about the Malays, which provided grist for the better known work of Joseph Conrad. His short tenure as Governor was a lull between the storms of the Guillemard and Clementi regimes. It was cut short by illness and a mental breakdown, which left him with periodic attacks of insanity until his death.

COLEMAN, GEORGE DROMGOLD (1795-1844). Architect who planned, surveyed, and built much of early Singapore. He was born in Ireland and went to Calcutta in 1815, where he built houses for merchants. In 1820, he went to Batavia and in 1822 to Singapore, where he met Raffles (q.v.), who accepted his design for a government building. Returning to Batavia in 1823, he designed sugar plantations and irrigation systems but, with the outbreak of the Java War in 1825, he moved to Singapore--just after the treaty with the Johore rulers (Sultan Hussein [q.v.] and Temenggong Abdul Rahman [q.v.]) making Singapore a permanent settlement, which prompted a building boom. In 1827 he was employed as an official surveyor and in 1833 as the first superintendent of public works. He continued to engage in private construction as well. Among the better known buildings which he designed and built were a merchant's residence which actually served as the court house (and forms the base of the present Parliament House), the Armenian Church, and the original Raffles Institution (q.v.). The latter, with many warehouses and imposing residences, has since been lost to urban renewal.

COMMONWEALTH. International cooperative organization of former British colonies. Although initially comprised of those territories where Europeans clearly predominated-- Australia, Canada, New Zealand, and South Africa--the contemporary Commonwealth reflects the variety of peoples and territory which comprised the British Empire. In the empire at the beginning of the twentieth century, there was a group of self-governing dominions referred to as the British Commonwealth of Nations. After World II, the term "British" tended to be dropped and the short form, Commonwealth, widely used. With formal and informal consultation, a shared affinity for the Queen (although republics such as India and Singapore do not recognize her as the head of the nation), and a tradition of parliamentary democracy, the Commonwealth contin- ues as an important bond among former components of the empire. The principles of membership were made explicit in the Commonwealth Declaration of Principles approved at the Commonwealth Heads of Governments meeting in Singapore in 1971.

COMMUNISM. Leninist organization which continually chal- lenged the legal governments of Singapore and Malaya. In both, it has been linked closely with the Chinese (q.v.) population and the Chinese Communist Party. In the 1920s, the communists had an alliance with the *Kuomin- tang* (q.v.) in both China and Southeast Asia, consistent with the directives of the Comintern (Communist Inter- national), controlled by the Russian Communist Party, which was broken following Sun Yat-sen's death in 1925 and the violent split in 1927. At the same time, the failure of the communist-led uprising in Indonesia prompted Tan Malaka, as the comintern agent for South- east Asia, to look to the cities and the Chinese in reviving the party. In 1928, a Nanyang (South Seas) Communist Party and a Nanyang General Labour Union based in

Singapore were established, drawing heavily on support in the Hainanese population. The party and union were outlawed, and in 1930 both were dissolved at a meeting in Singapore. In their place, the Malayan Communist Party (MCP) was established under the Far Eastern Bureau of the comintern in Shanghai. The MCP and its front organizations challenged the colonial and the elected governments up through the 1980s.

CONFRONTATION (*Konfrontasi*, in Indonesian). Diplomatic and armed resistance supported by the Indonesian Government to the formation and existence of Malaysia (1963-1966). Indonesia, especially its then President Sukarno, believed that because it was the largest nation in the region, Southeast Asia was its sphere of influence. When the British proposed merging of colonies on Borneo with Singapore and Malaya (q.v.) to form Malaysia (q.v.), it was interpreted as a slight of Indonesian preeminence as well as a "neo-colonial" plot to deny self-determination or absorption within Indonesia of the Borneo people. Through front groups, such as the *Tentera Nasional Kalimantan Utara* (TNKU; North Kalimantan [Indonesian term for Borneo] National Army) in Sabah, the Clandestine Communist Organization in Sarawak (CCO), the Malayan National Liberation League (q.v.) with ties to the Malayan Communist Party (q.v.), and its own military, Indonesia attacked Malaysia openly and subversively. The July and September race riots in Singapore were blamed by the Malaysian Prime Minister, Tunku Abdul Rahman (q.v.), on Indonesian agitators. With the military takeover following the September 30th affair in Indonesia and the emergence of Suharto to replace Sukarno, the attacks abated in late 1965, and--in August 1966--diplomatic relations between Indonesia and Malaysia were restored. The Republic of Singapore also opened relations with Indonesia although these were tested in 1968 when Singapore executed two Indonesian marines convicted of a bombing during Confrontation.

CONFUCIANISM. Belief in following the teachings of Confucius (*pinyin*: Kong Fuzi). In the 1980s, the government became concerned that young people in modern Singapore lacked a core set of values and thus were easy prey to Western materialism and decadence. This prompted an emphasis on values education in the schools with religious beliefs being an important source of such values. Although Confucianism is not a formal religion (there is no mention of God, nor is there a priesthood), the government saw it as preferable to having the Chinese (q.v.) left without moral direction or to embrace Christianity as many had been doing. To develop Confucian models for the curriculum, scholars had to be invited from the United States--those from the People's Republic of China (which denounces Confucius) and from Taiwan (which promulgates) were too likely to bring the political content of those nations. As a further step, in 1991, the government introduced a national ideology which is loosely based on Confucian values (q.v.).

COOLIE TRADE. Recruitment and importation of Chinese laborers in the nineteenth century. Ironically, the international outlawing of the slave trade in the 1814 Treaty of Ghent gave rise to the coolie trade to meet the demand for cheap labor, especially from the West Indies sugar plantations and, later, mines and plantations in Asia and the American railways. In addition to being a destination of Chinese laborers (coolies), Singapore served as a transfer point for laborers headed elsewhere in Southeast Asia, especially in Malaya, and as a layover for laborers bound for the West Indies. Poor living conditions in China (q.v.), combined with economic opportunities abroad, encouraged migration, but there were also reports of forced recruitment. Often dialect and clan organizations served as recruiting agencies and provided assistance to new arrivals. To pay for their passage, coolies had to work for an employer for one year. The coolie population was predominantly male.

COUNTRY TRADE. Intra-Asia trade in commodities. While Asians had been engaged in trade with various ports and kingdoms, the term was especially used under the East India Company (EIC) (q.v.) to refer to trade conducted by Europeans within Asia. The EIC enjoyed a royal monopoly on trade between Britain and Asia, with tea the most important cargo, but it licensed private traders to engage in trade within Asia, such as carrying cotton and opium from India and Southeast Asian products to China (q.v.) and purchasing tea which the EIC would export to Britain. The EIC would allot sub-monopolies, often to former EIC employees, for the trade within Asia. Country traders to and from China were most likely to use the Straits of Malacca and stop in Singapore and/or Penang, while direct trade between China and Europe tended to use the Sunda Straits further south.

CRAWFURD, JOHN (1783-1868). Resident of Singapore, 1823-1826. Before being named by Raffles (q.v.) as Resident to succeed Farquhar (q.v.), he was a respected author (*History of the Indian Archipelago*) and had served in Penang, Java, and as envoy to the courts of Cochin China (southern Vietnam) and Siam. He was a rather taciturn Scotsman whose tenure in office paled following the popular Raffles and Farquhar. Despite Raffles's avowed opposition to legalized gambling, Crawfurd made it a revenue farm (q.v.) to cover the costs of government. During his term, the conclusive treaties for the retention of Singapore were signed. After returning to England, he remained actively concerned with the Straits Settlements and the region, authoring books and articles and participating in a mission to Ava (Burma). He was the first president of the Straits Settlements Association (q.v.).

-D-

DALFORCE. Operational name for Singapore Chinese Anti-Japanese Volunteer Battalion, from the name of its commander, Lieutenant Colonel John Dalley. Organized in January 1941 in response to the demands of the Chinese [Chung Kuo] Council for General Mobilization, headed by Tan Kah Kee (q.v.), it drew Chinese of all political persuasions and fought fiercely beside Commonwealth forces in resisting the final Japanese push prior to surrender by the Governor. Some Dalforce survivors, especially communists, crossed into Malaya where they formed the Malayan People's Anti-Japanese Army (q.v.).

D'ALMEIDA, DR. JOSE (d. 1850). Leading businessman, landowner, and agriculturalist. A Portuguese, Dr. d'Almeida was a surgeon on a Portuguese ship which visited Singapore, and he decided to buy land. He later moved to Singapore in 1825 and, in addition to owning a successful commercial firm, was an inveterate innovator in agricultural endeavors, engaging in banana, coconut, sugar, coffee, cotton, cloves, and other cultivation. His family, nineteen or twenty children, continued active in Singapore after his death.

DE CRUZ, GERALD (1920-). Eurasian co-founder of Malayan Democratic Union (MDU) (q.v.) and communist intellectual. He was a journalist for the communist paper *Democrat*, head of the Eurasian Progressive Movement, and, in 1946, was the secretary-general of the Pan-Malayan Council of Joint Action. Disappointed at the dissolution of the MDU and the communist decision to enter armed conflict, he went to London in 1949, where he remained until 1956--obtaining teaching certification and becoming principal of a school for retarded children. In 1955, he worked with Goh Keng Swee (q.v.) to regain control of the Malayan Forum (q.v.) from the communists, which they accomplished in January 1956. In March 1956 he returned to become organizing secretary for the Labour Front. He supported himself with magazine journalism and teaching, serving as a living resource for the nation's turbulent emergence from the Japanese occupation.

DEMOCRATIC PARTY. Short-lived political party. Formed in February 1955 by persons associated with the Singapore Chinese Chamber of Commerce (q.v.) to contest the Legislative Assembly election that year. Its platform supported Chinese language and culture, conservative economic approaches, and liberal citizenship policies. It enjoyed strong financial backing from Tan Lark Sye (q.v.). Despite hopes to win the 1955 election, it captured only two out of twenty-five elected seats.

DETENTION. Arrest for internal security reason without trial. Detention was introduced by the British. Independent Singapore has continued the procedure under its Internal Security Act (ISA) (q.v.).

DOUBLE TENTH TRIAL. War crimes trial. In early October 1943, the Allies sneaked into Singapore Harbor and damaged or sunk seven Japanese ships. On October 10, 1943, the *Kempeitai* (q.v.) attacked the prisoner camp at Chang in the belief that the raid had originated from there. Fifty-seven persons were arrested, of which one was executed and fifteen died under torture. In 1946, twenty-one members of the *Kempeitai*, including its chief, Lieutenant-Colonel Sumida Haruzo, were tried in Singapore and found guilty. The term "double-ten" is well-known among Chinese, referring to the tenth day of the tenth month--the anniversary of the establishment of the republic in China.

-E-

EAST INDIA COMPANY (EIC). Trading company responsible for settling and administering Singapore, sometimes referred to as John Company. Chartered by Queen Elizabeth I in 1600, it was intended to supply pepper and other spices from the East Indies (present-day Indonesia) to England. It early established "factories" (so-called because they were the bases of factors or agents) as its mode of trade, including one at Bentan (today, Bintang), near Singapore. The Dutch succeeded in gaining control of Bentan in 1682, forcing the EIC to relocate to Bencoolen. The strength of the Dutch prompted the company to concentrate its attention on India. While initially intended to engage in commercial activities, especially in the East, and given monopolies to promote that effort, it found itself possessing numerous sovereign and territorial responsibilities in Asia, including Java under Raffles (q.v.) and the Straits Settlements (q.v.). It was dissolved in 1858, by edict of Queen Victoria following the 1857 Sepoy mutiny in India, after which the British Government assumed control of the territories it possessed (although the Straits Settlements remained under the Government of India until 1867).

EBER, JOHN (1916-). Post-war Eurasian leftist leader. With the finest British credentials (Harrow and Cambridge), he was a legal advisor to the Malayan Democratic Union (MDU) (q.v.) but was more active with the AMCJA-PUTERA and frequently wrote and spoke on leftist issues. In 1951, he was detained for membership in the Anti-British League (q.v.) and for supporting communist causes. After release from detention, he moved to London, where he remained active in leftist causes, especially involving Singapore and Malaysia (q.v.), including the Malaya Forum (q.v.). He was later refused re-entry until 1990.

EDEN HALL TEA PARTY. Consultation by PAP dissidents with British prior to planned putsch within the party. In July 1961, Fong Swee Suan (q.v.), Lim Chin Siong (q.v.), James Puthucheary (q.v.), and Sandra Woodhull (q.v.), representing the left and communist wing of the PAP, met Lord Selkirk, British Commissioner General for South-East Asia, at his residence in Singapore, Eden Hall. The conspirators feared British interference and suspension of independence if they ousted Lee Kuan Yew as Prime Minister. Lord Selkirk affirmed Britain's commitment to the constitution. Publicly enraged, Lee Kuan

Yew denounced it as a meeting of "British lions and communist bears," to whip up public support and demand a confidence vote in the Legislative Assembly, which he survived by three votes.

EMERGENCY. Also called Malayan Emergency. Guerrilla war in Malaya, 1948-1960. As part of its psychological warfare ("winning hearts and minds"), the British administration used this term rather than calling it a war. Similarly, it labelled the Malayan Communist Party forces, who called themselves the Malayan Races Liberation Army, as Communist Terrorists--shortened to "CTs."

ENGLAND. Division of Great Britain. Since it is the site of London, which is the seat of government, and the foundation of Great Britain (which also includes Scotland and Wales), it is often used synonymously with Great Britain and the United Kingdom. See UNITED KINGDOM.

ENTREPÔT TRADE. Warehousing or trans-shipping of goods. Singapore's location between the northeast and southwest monsoons, free trade policies, and port facilities made it attractive for sailing vessels from Europe and India en route to China and returning to layover until winds were right. Moreover, its central location made it an ideal trans-shipping port for natural resources from Indonesia and Malaysia and manufactured goods bound for those territories. It remains an important element in the nation's trade but has declined considerably as neighboring nations have emphasized direct trade for imports and exports.

EU CHOOI YIP (1919?-). Journalist and communist leader. As a graduate of Raffle's College in economics, and classmate of Goh Keng Swee (q.v.) and other PAP leaders, he was Assistant Commissioner of Labour after World War II but resigned to become a reporter for the *Straits Times*. As secretary-general of the Malayan Democratic Union (MDU) (q.v.), he was a major public spokesman. He was a reporter on the *Nan Chiau Jit Poh*, owned by Tan Kah

Kee (q.v.), until it was closed by the government in 1950. In 1951, he evaded police attempts to arrest him for producing communist propaganda and fled to Indonesia. He reportedly had contacts with the Indonesian Communist Party and worked with the Malayan National Liberation League (MNLL) (q.v.) office but also remained in touch with the South Malaya Bureau from a base in Riau. Following Sukarno's ouster, MNLL activists were arrested but later allowed to leave the country for Hanoi.   In 1991, although legally not a citizen, he was permitted to return and was appointed to the government's Institute of East Asian Philosophies, chaired by Goh Keng Swee.

EURASIANS. Descendants of mixed ethnic parentage, European and Asian. In Singapore, it applied to Anglo-Indians and others of mixed descent, but most commonly was used to refer to persons tracing ancestry to the Portuguese era in Malacca. These preserved usage of the Portuguese language and have their own clubs within Malaysia and Singapore.

EUROPEANS. "White" visitors, colonizers, immigrants, or the descendants thereof. While the term implies persons from the European continent, it is, and has been, used for any whites--whether from Britain, Australia, North America, New Zealand, or elsewhere. The pervasive racism of colonial times continues, although declining, in the special attitude (which may be resentment as well as respect) toward individuals perceived as "white."

EXECUTIVE COUNCIL (EC). Under the crown colony structure, senior government officers who advised the governor, created in 1967. Although strictly an advisory body for executive policy, in the 1870s Hoo Ah Kay (q.v.) was asked to sit in. In the reforms in the 1920s, two unofficial members of the Legislative Council (q.v.) were invited by the governor to sit in the EC, leading the Straits Settlements (Singapore) Association (q.v.) to ask that representation be equal between official and unofficial members. In 1948, it was further enlarged but with the assurance of an official majority. In 1951, the Legislative Council was allowed to select two of their members for the EC.

-F-

FAMILY PLANNING. Government policies to first restrict and now encourage larger families. In 1949, the first Family Planning Association was established to improve family welfare and the health of mothers. From 1959, with a population growth rate of 4.7 percent, the PAP government actively promoted family planning, with slogans such as "Girl or boy, two is enough"-- often shortened to "Two is enough"--and tax policies penalizing additional children and giving academic placement preferences to children of sterilized parents. From its establishment as a statutory board in 1966, the Singapore Family Planning and Population Board (SFPPB) became responsible for implementing the policies. By the mid-1980s, with economic growth constrained by labor shortages and faced with the success of the policies which had reduced annual population growth to 1.2 percent, the government reversed itself, giving tax breaks, subsidies, and housing and academic preferences for third and fourth children, generating a new slogan in 1987, "Have three, and more if you can afford." The latter phrase reveals the bias to genetic determinism among some government leaders, emphasizing that the better educated and wealthier should have more children or the overall intelligence level of the population will decrease.

FANG CHUANG PI (1924-). Best known as "The Plen," identified as the leading communist in Singapore in 1950s and 1960s. In 1951, a S$2,000 reward was offered for his arrest for distributing communist propaganda. In 1950, he had barely escaped a raid on the communist paper, *Freedom News*, going to Indonesia (q.v.), where he engaged in communist activities. He was made famous by Lee Kuan Yew (q.v.) in a series of radio broadcasts in

1961, in which Lee described meetings with Fang in 1959 and 1961. Lee referred to him as "The Plen," short for Plenipotentiary. According to Lee, Fang sought communist cooperation with the People's Action Party and, to demonstrate his *bona fides*, forced a clandestine communist to resign from the Workers' Party (q.v.) and City Council. This experience convinced Lee of the Malayan Communist Party's (MCP) (q.v.) iron grip on the membership, no matter now harmless the leaders might appear. In 1963 Fang again fled to Indonesia, eventually joining the MCP's continuing armed struggle based in Thailand, where he was living in 1990 and was interviewed by Singapore journalists following the MCP abandonment of armed struggle. His son who had been living in Beijing, Guan Shao Ping, was hired by Singapore Technology Holdings in 1991, reportedly on the recommendation of Eu Chooi Yip (q.v.) to Goh Keng Swee (q.v.).

FARMS, REVENUE. Government-licensed monopolies for certain products and services. License fees, especially in Singapore, were significant revenue sources. During the nineteenth century, farms were let for pork, pawnbroking, *siri* (betel nut), and a variety of vices, including gambling (q.v.) briefly in its early years. Farms generally were sold in public auctions, and purchasers were among the wealthiest Chinese. Opium (q.v.) was the most significant farm, usually contributing more than 40 percent of government revenue. In 1910, the Straits Settlements Government Monopolies Department assumed responsibilities for opium sales to the public, eliminating the most lucrative farm, which it retained until the Japanese occupation.

FARQUHAR, COLONEL WILLIAM (1770?-1839). First Resident of Singapore and responsible for its early growth. Joining the Madras Engineers in 1790 at age twenty, he was in Malacca for twenty-three years after Britain seized Dutch territories and acted as Resident, 1803-1818--leading Malays to refer to him as the King of Malacca. After unsuccessful attempts to gain a British base in the Rhio-

Lingga Islands (q.v.), he accompanied Raffles (q.v.) to establish a factory of Singapore in 1819. When Raffles returned to Penang in February, he designated Farquhar as Resident, reporting to Raffles as Lieutenant Governor of Bencoolen. When Raffles returned in May, Farquhar had a growing community underway. Although the East India Company was pleased with the new possession, it gave Farquhar little financial support. He had planned to retire after the settlement was established and submitted his resignation in 1820 but then declined to relinquish the Resident position when a replacement arrived. After Raffles returned in 1822, he replaced Farquhar and became Resident himself in April 1923. Chinese and European settlers had special celebrations to express their gratitude to Farquhar, when he sailed for Scotland in late 1823.

FIVE-POWER DEFENSE ARRANGEMENT. Agreement for military cooperation among Australia, Great Britain, New Zealand, Malaysia and Singapore. Signed in 1971, the Arrangement provides for mutual defense of the signatories and joint training exercises. It was developed following the decision to withdraw Australian, British, and New Zealand forces which had been stationed at bases in Malaysia and Singapore.

FONG SWEE SUAN (1931-). Labor and *Barisan Sosialis* leader. Educated at Singapore Chinese High School, he was active in student organizing in the 1950s and helped link student and labor unrest, working closely with Lim Chin Siong (q.v.). He served as secretary general of the Bus Workers' Union during the Hock Lee Bus Company Strike (q.v.). He was a founder of the PAP and, with close ties to the communist wing of the party, was detained, 1956-59. Although he was political secretary to Kenneth Byrne as Minister of Labour and of Law, he was instrumental in the 1961 schism within the PAP following the Eden Hall Tea Party (q.v.). He became a leader of *Barisan Sosialis* but was again detained in Operation Cold Store in 1963 and held until 1965. After his release, he abandoned politics and became a businessman in Johore.

FORCE 136. Southeast Asia division of the British Special Operations Executive (SOE) in World War II. To supply and attempt to direct the activities of the Malayan People's Anti-Japanese Army (MPAJA) (q.v.) and other guerrilla groups operating against the Japanese, it would send submarines with officers and, late in the war, parachute drops of supplies. Most of its activities and the guerrillas, including the MPAJA, were centered on the peninsula where jungles afforded escape routes and campsites away from the Japanese.

FOZDAR, SHIRIN. Pioneer advocate for women's causes. Before World War II, she championed women's rights and, in 1934, presented the causes of Asian women to the League of Nations. She helped form and led the Singapore Council of Women. She later carried her campaign to India and to Malaya after 1955; however, her efforts on behalf of women contributed to the promulgation of the Women's Charter (q.v.) in 1961.

FREE PORT. Trading zone without import or export duties. From its founding by Raffles (q.v.), Singapore was developed without customs duties, often despite demands by the East India Company (q.v.), which sought the revenue such duties would yield. Indeed, over the years, leading citizens opposed such measures as an income tax as infringing on the free economy. In effect, it denied the government the usual sources of income and accounted for the major role of opium (q.v.) in supporting the administrative structure. The PAP's 1959 campaign identified free-port status as a major obstacle for its industrialization program. Before 1960, duties had been solely and selectively used for revenue and had been limited to such items as alcohol, petroleum, and tobacco. In 1960, new products were added, such as soaps. No new tariffs were added during the time Singapore was in Malaysia but import quotas were. In 1965 hundreds of products were subject to quotas and by 1969 nearly four hundred products were subject to tariff. Such policies were justified as promoting industrialization by encouraging domestic production over foreign, under an import substitution policy. In 1969, the government reversed the trend, recognizing the importance of trade for the nation. The number of tariffable items was cut in half and by 1973 only three items were subject to quotas.

-G-

GAMBIER AND PEPPER CULTIVATION. Pioneering agricultural undertakings by Chinese in Singapore and surrounding areas. The two crops, gambier (*Uncaria gambir*) and pepper (*piper nigrum*), were generally grown adjacent to each other, as the waste from processing gambier was an excellent fertilizer for pepper. The crops were grown on freshly cleared land, such clearing producing the fuel needed for boiling the gambier leaves as part of the processing. Because the crops tended to deplete the soil, they continually moved into the areas cleared to provide fuel. The abandoned land reverted to coarse grass (*Imperata cylindrica*; in Malay *lalang*). The cultivation practices were blamed for extensive grass wastelands in Singapore (and Johore) in the mid-nineteenth century. Such areas were favorite haunts of tigers, which accounted for numerous deaths. Gambier initially was exported to China where it was an essential ingredient in tanning; however, Europe replaced it as a destination in the mid-nineteenth century. Pepper found markets in both China and Europe. The crop combination afforded growers some supply elasticity if the market price of one or the other were depressed.

GAMBIER AND PEPPER SOCIETIES. Chinese organizations based on agricultural enclaves in Rhio, the interior of Singapore, and Johore (q.v.). The organizations engaged in the cultivation and export of gambier. Comprised predominantly of Teochews, these organizations probably predated Raffles's founding of Singapore and accounted for the Chinese population present on the island in 1819. They initially were extensions of organizations in Rhio. In early form, the societies are claimed by some to have resembled cooperatives, as those participating pooled their resources and shared in the profits; however, they included secret society organizational and ritual practices. Increasingly, the societies came under the influence of the rich merchants in Singapore, on whom they were dependent to purchase and export their crops, especially to Europe. The juncture of economic power and secret society organizations was an important element in the secret society feuds of the nineteenth century, in the coolie trade (on which the societies depended for replacement manpower), and in the competitions for opium farms in both Singapore and Johore.

GAMBLING. Wagering on games of chance. Chinese generally are considered inveterate gamblers. In the early years, the gambling farm exceeded the opium farm as a source of public revenue. Farquhar licensed gambling in 1819 but Raffles banned it in June 1823. Raffles felt that it created ill will leading to disorder, while his successor John Crawfurd observed that gambling continued and that attempts to suppress it contributed to the corruption of the police. Within months, Crawfurd lifted the ban. The ban was restored in 1829 and continued until World War II, when the Japanese again legalized it. Exceptions were made for the Chinese New Year. Legal gambling in modern Singapore is restricted to the public lottery and betting on horse races--making casinos elsewhere, such as Malaysia's Genting Highlands or Las Vegas, popular destinations for Singapore tourists.

GARDEN CITY. Concept of integrating plants into all parts of the island city. As early as 1963, Lee Kuan Yew (q.v.) had launched a tree planting campaign but the full planting and beautification campaign aimed at creating a garden city was not launched until 1967. A Garden City Action

Committee drew on most public and statutory bodies to actively incorporate greenery and parks into projects. The success of the campaign has improved the living and aesthetic environments of the city.

GENERATIONS OF LEADERSHIP. Term identifying age divisions among leaders in post-independence Singapore. It was first used in the 1970s to refer to a "second" or "successor" generation in contrast to the older "first" or "founding" generation. Included in the successor group were Goh Chok Tong (q.v.), Richard Hu, Tony Tan, and Lim Chee Onn. With Lee Kuan Yew's (q.v.) longevity in office, by the late 1980s a third generation (or second successor generation) of leaders emerged, including Lee Hsien Loong (q.v.) and George Yeo (q.v.).

GIMSON, SIR FRANKLIN. Governor of Singapore 1946-1952. Following the debacle of the British Military Administration (q.v.), he restored civilian rule, guided by an advisory council to which he added unofficial members in 1948. In November 1947, he accomplished what predecessors had been unable to effect in 1860, 1910, and 1921, introduction of an income tax. During his administration, political parties were introduced, and elections were held for the Legislative Council (q.v.) in 1948 and 1951. He also added two elected members of the Legislative Council to the Executive Council (q.v.).

GOH CHOK TONG (1941-). Second prime minister of Singapore, from November 28, 1990. He grew up in the quiet coast village of Pasir Panjang and, after secondary education at the Raffles Institution, he received a B.A. in economics from the University of Singapore and an M.A. in development economics from Williams College in the U.S. After a brief civil service career, he joined the national shipping company, Neptune Orient Lines. In 1976 he was recruited into electoral politics as one of the "second generation" of leaders and won a seat in the Marine Parade constituency. He quickly was brought into the cabinet as a minister of state for finance in 1977 and subsequently held portfolios for trade and industry, 1979-1981; education, 1981; and health, 1981-1982. He also held secondary portfolios in defense. In 1985, Lee Kuan Yew (q.v.) named him First Deputy Prime Minister, Minister for Defence, and heir apparent.

GOH KENG SWEE (1918-). Architect of nation's post-independence prosperity. Born in Malacca, he graduated in arts from Raffles College and subsequently won a B. Sc. from the London School of Economics and a Ph.D. from the University of London. In 1949, he became a founder and first chairman of the Malayan Forum. In 1952, with Lee Kuan Yew (q.v.) and Kenneth Byrne, he formed a Council of Joint Action to protest the special allowances paid British civil servants in Singapore. He was back studying in London when the People's Action Party (PAP) (q.v.) was founded, but in 1959 he was elected to the party Central Executive Committee and to the Legislative Assembly for the Kreta Ayer constituency. With Lee Kuan Yew (q.v.), he, S. Rajaratnam (q.v.), and Toh Chin Chye (q.v.) comprised the inner leadership group of the PAP and the nation. He held a number of ministries, including defense, finance, and education, and served as the Chairman of the Monetary Authority of Singapore (MAS). In 1984, he retired from politics and the cabinet but has retained posts as deputy chairman of the MAS and as chairman of the Institute of East Asian Philosophies. In 1985 was named by the People's Republic of China as economic advisor for development of the southern enterprise zones.

GOODE, SIR WILLIAM A[LLMOND]. C[ODRINGTON]. (1907-1986). Last colonial governor and first Head of State (*Yang di-Pertuan Negara*). After an Oxford education, he came to the Federated Malay States as a Malayan Civil Service (MCS) cadet in 1931. He served in Pahang and Selangor prior to being named assistant financial secretary in Singapore in 1939, the same year that he was called to the bar in England. He was interned by the Japanese and in 1948 was named Chief Secretary in Aden.

He returned to the same post in Singapore and in 1957, at age fifty, became one of youngest colonial governors. He served as *Yang di-Pertuan Negara* for six months after Singapore achieved internal self-government in 1959.

GREATER EAST ASIA CO-PROSPERITY SPHERE. Japanese phrase for the Asian territories which it seized during World War II, including China, Manchuria, and Southeast Asia. Although conveying the impression of interdependence and mutual advantage among Asians, in practice it was a thin facade for Japanese domination of other Asian peoples and exploitation of their resources. Nowhere was the facade thinner than in Singapore, with its predominantly Chinese, population which the Japanese saw as extensions of their seemingly endless war in China.

GROUP REPRESENTATION CONSTITUENCY (GRC). Parliamentary constituency in which the electorate cast a single vote for a team of candidates from each party. After the PAP saw two opposition party members elected and its popular vote drop by nearly 13 percent in the 1984 election, it sought alternatives to the voting system. Also, with Malay and Indian minorities increasingly diffused through the population, then Deputy Prime Minister Goh Chok Tong (q.v.) proposed a system which became known as the GRCs, which would enable minorities to be elected as team members rather than relying on non-communal voting by the Chinese majority in most constituencies. The constitutional amendment provided GRCs could be used for between one-fourth and one-half the parliamentary seats, with each team including at least one minority member. At least three fifths of the GRCs must be designated a Malay (q.v.) minority and the rest for Indians (q.v.) and other minorities. In the 1988 election, thirteen GRCs were established to fill thirty-nine out of eighty-one seats. Prior to the 1991 election, fifteen four-member GRCs were created, accounting for sixty of the eighty-one seats. In both the 1988 and 1991 elections, the PAP won all GRC contests--although the Eunos GRC was close on both occasions.

GROWTH TRIANGLE. Concept of mutually beneficial cooperation for development among Indonesia (q.v.), Malaysia (q.v.), and Singapore, focusing on Riau Province in Indonesia and southern Johore in Malaysia. With its limited manpower supply, Singapore in the 1990s seeks to establish itself as a center for corporate, financial, transportation, and information services. Indonesia and Malaysia, with larger land areas and manpower supplies, would provide sites for corporate operations. In addition to enhancing Singapore as a center for corporations doing business in Southeast Asia, Singapore is also seeking to assure accessible water supplies in exchange for assistance with the economic development of neighboring areas.

GUILLEMARD, SIR LAURENCE NUNNS (1862-1951). Governor of Straits Settlements and High Commissioner for Malay States, 1919-1927. After lengthy service with the Treasury in Britain, as Governor, he unsuccessfully attempted to reform the administration through decentralizing authority to the Malay States (q.v.). He introduced the nomination of municipal commissioners by organizations representing the various ethnic groups. His reforms, especially an unsuccessful effort to introduce an income tax, were opposed by the Singapore branch of the Straits Settlements Association (q.v.) and the Association of British Malaya (q.v.).

GUTHRIE AND CO. Oldest major "British" trading company in Singapore. Shortly after the Scot Alexander Guthrie arrived in 1821, he began a company in his own name which continues today. He engaged in various partnerships and remained active in business until 1847. He was succeeded by a nephew, James Guthrie, who came to Singapore in 1837 and retired in 1876. He was succeeded by Thomas Scott, who arrived in 1851 and was a partner in the firm for forty-five years, during which it launched the Tanjong Pagar Dock Company with Tan Kim Ching. It engaged in banking and insurance as well as trade and in 1896 began buying coffee estates in the Malay States, which were converted to rubber plantations. Scott was succeeded by John Anderson, who had grown up in Singapore and joined the company while still a boy in 1876. Before Anderson retired in 1923, he launched Guthrie's into a commercial agricultural venture--oil palm--which would rival rubber as an export earner and exceed it as a corporate income earner. The company has since been bought out by Malaysian ownership.

-H-

HAINANESE. (Also known as Hailam). Chinese dialect group from the southern Chinese island of Hainan, believed to have originated in southern Fukien (*pinyin*: Fujian) Province. They occupied the lowest rung of Chinese society in Singapore. Most were sailors, servants, and laborers. Hainanese women were barred from emigrating until 1918, and the men seldom married outside their community. In the 1920s, Hainanese--especially youth--were receptive to communist agitation. A predominantly Hainanese rally to commemorate Sun Yat-Sen's death triggered the Kreta Ayer Incident in 1927.

HAKKA(S). People and dialect from internal districts of Kwangtung (*pinyin*: Guangdong) and Fukien (*pinyin*: Fujian) Provinces in China. Also called *Keh*s or *Khek*s, meaning guests. Generally looked down on by other dialect groups, the Hakkas were isolated from the larger societies in which they lived--probably because they had moved into the provinces after the other dialect groups were well established and their dialect was unintelligible to their neighbors. In other parts of Southeast Asia (Borneo, Malaya, and Bangka in the Netherlands East Indies), they were active in mining, but they were always a small percentage of the Chinese population in Singapore. They largely engaged in construction crafts, black- and gold-smithing, shoe-making, traditional herbal medicine, and pawnbroking. Despite their low repute among other groups, Hakkas such as Tiger Balm king Aw Boon

Haw (q.v.) and past prime minister Lee Kuan Yew (q.v.) demonstrate the fallacy of the stereotype.

HARTAL. Work stoppage or strike. A term of Indian origin, it was widely used to describe particularly general strikes and public boycotts in Singapore and Malaya during the late 1940s and the 1950s.

HERTOGH, MARIA. See MARIA HERTOGH RIOT.

HOALIM, PHILIP (1895-1980). Co-founder and Chairman of Malayan Democratic Union (MDU) (q.v.). Born of Chinese descent in British Guiana (today, Guyana), where he became active in anti-colonial politics, he studied at the University of London. After receiving his law degree, in 1932 he visited his sister in Penang, who was married to Lim Cheng Ean--a Straits Settlements Legislative Councillor and father of Lim Kean Chye (q.v.). Passing through Singapore, he was convinced by Song Ong Siang (q.v.) to join his law firm. While he was wealthy and opposed to the Malayan Communist Party (q.v.), his commitment to the MDU principles led him to lend his active presence to the organization despite the strong communist influence on its activities.

HOCK LEE BUS COMPANY STRIKE. In the midst of strikes at Chinese middle schools, in May 1955, a strike by students and workers supporting the Singapore Bus Workers Union (SBWU), with Fong Swee Suan (q.v.) as secretary, degenerated into violence as police and demonstrators were killed and injured. Marshall's government refused to call out British troops, and the riot was viewed as a victory for the SBWU, leftist labor leaders, and extraconstitutional tactics. In the aftermath, the Singapore Chinese Middle School Students' Union was also recognized.

HOKKIEN(S) (also called Fukinese or Fukienese). Chinese people from southern Fukien (*pinyin*: Fujian) Province, especially the prefectures of Ch'üan-Chou and Chang-

Chou with Amoy (*pinyin*: Xiamen) as the main seaport. They are the largest dialect group in Singapore (as well as Java, Malaya, and the Philippines), especially when *Peranakan*s (q.v.) are included, as they were among the earliest Chinese to settle in Southeast Asia. Hokkien trade and settlements in Southeast Asia are traceable to the late seventeenth century when the Manchus (Ch'ing; *pinyin*: Qing) extended control over Amoy, prompting the revolt and resettlement to Taiwan of Koxinga (*pinyin*: Cheng Ch'eng-kung) and his followers. *Peranakan*s of Hokkien ancestry living in Malacca were among the early merchants to settle in Singapore. They have tended to dominate the business and social life of the city since its founding.

HOKKIEN - TEOCHEW RIOTS. Violent disturbances between the two leading dialect groups in 1854. While battles between the two largest dialect groups were not uncommon in the latter half of the century, the name is usually used for the battle which began May 5th between the multi-ethnic Ghee Hin (including Hakka [q.v.] and Cantonese [q.v.] as well as Teochew [q.v.]) and the Hokkien Ghee Hok secret societies. The battle was sparked by the return of a number of Singapore Hokkiens who had participated in the ill-fated Short Dagger Rebellion in Amoy (*pinyin*: Xiamen). When a subscription was asked to support the rebels, the non-Hokkiens declined. An argument over a rice purchase was the spark for a battle that spread through Chinese settlements around the island, leaving four hundred people dead and three hundred homes burned.

HONG LIM BY-ELECTIONS. Election constituency which was the scene of two pivotal by-elections in the 1960s. In 1961, when the People's Action Party (PAP) (q.v.) dropped Ong Eng Guan (q.v.) from the cabinet and expelled him from the party, he resigned his seat in the Legislative Assembly (q.v.)--forcing a by-election. Ong contested against a PAP candidate in April 1961 and won, despite communist support for the PAP. In July 1965,

Ong again resigned, and the election battle pitted the PAP against a *Barisan Sosialis* (q.v.) candidate. The PAP won by a large margin. It was alleged that the second by-election was arranged by the Malaysian Government in the hopes of embarrassing the PAP and forcing Lee Kuan Yew (q.v.) to step down as Chief Minister. The PAP victory demonstrated that separation was the only way, short of arrest, that Malaysia could rid itself of Lee.

HOO AH KAY (1814-1880). Leading nineteenth century Cantonese (q.v.) merchant and supplier for the British navy. He was best known among the English-speaking community as Whampoa, the name of his company and city of his birth in Kwangtung. Arriving in Singapore in 1830 to assist his father, he quickly rose to prominence in the Chinese and European communities as a businessman. With a command of English, he often hosted spectacular international parties and important foreign visitors, such as Admiral Keppel. His home and gardens were considered the city's greatest attraction, and he opened the gardens to the public each Chinese New Year. In 1869, he became the first Asian member of the Legislative Council (q.v.) and later was a special member of the Executive Council (q.v.). In 1876, he was decorated by the Queen of England.

HOUSING AND DEVELOPMENT BOARD (HDB). Agency offering public housing and related schemes. Launched February 1, 1960, and absorbing the Housing and Urban Development Company in 1982, it has been among the nation's most dramatic successes. By 1989, 87 percent of the population lived in public or subsidized housing. Through 1989, 653,836 apartments had been built. In 1964, provision was made for sale of the apartments to the residents, and purchasers were allowed to draw on their Central Provident Fund (q.v.) savings for the purchase. By the end of 1989, 79 percent of the occupants owned their apartments. Reflecting the government's propensity for social engineering, in 1989 an Ethnic Integration Policy mandated integration by establishing maximums for any single ethnic group in the neighborhood and in any block of apartments. The policy bars sales which will result in ethnic concentrations beyond the maximums.

HU TSU TAU, DR. RICHARD (1926-). Leading economist and cabinet minister. Although his education at the University of California at Berkeley (B. Sc.) and the University of Birmingham (Ph. D.) was in chemistry and chemical engineering, in the 1980s he emerged as the government's financial expert, serving first as Minister of Trade and Industry and then as Minister of Finance in the 1988 and 1990 cabinets. He joined the Parliament after a career with Shell Oil, rising to Chairman and Chief Executive of Shell Companies in Singapore. He also serves as a director of the Monetary Authority of Singapore.

HUA-CH'IAO (pinyin: HUAQIAO). Overseas Chinese; usual reference by Chinese governments to persons of Chinese ancestry living outside of China (q.v.). The term is predicated on the concept of jus sanguinus: anyone born of Chinese parents anywhere is a citizen of China, with the corollary that China is the sole repository of true Chineseness. Today, it is resented by many Chinese, especially Peranakans (q.v.), who have assumed the citizenship of their land of birth or adoption.

HUAY. Hokkien term meaning association, with implications of brotherhood. It occurs with variant pronunciations and romanized spellings in other dialects. It generally refers to associations based on place of birth, which usually also indicates speakers of a specific dialect. Historically, the term was also used to refer to secret societies.

HUAY KUAN. Hokkien rendering for district and dialect associations. All of the major dialect groups had Huay Kuan, but the Hokkien (q.v.) Huay Kuan, formed in 1860, was the most influential, as its leaders tended to dominate the Singapore Chinese Chamber of Commerce (q.v.), including Tan Kah Kee (q.v.) and Tan Lark Sye (q.v.). In 1953, it donated a beautiful site at Jurong for the nascent Nanyang University. In the twentieth century, the Hokkien population divided into a number of smaller associations based on districts. Important associations of other dialects included the Teochew Ngee Ann Kongsi, led initially by Seah Eu Chin (q.v.), the Nanyang *Khek* Community Guild, the Hainanese *Kiung Chow Hwee Kuan*, and the Cantonese *Ku Seng* Association. The first such association was the *Ning Yeung Wui Kun*, formed in 1822.

HUSSEIN MOHAMED SHAH, SULTAN (also spelled Hussain)(-1835). Proclaimed by the British as the legal Sultan of Johore and signatory to the permission for a British settlement in Singapore. Although his father, Sultan Mahmud, had indicated that he (who was also known as Tengku Long) should inherit the title, the dominant Bugis (q.v.) ruler in the Johore Kingdom (q.v.), centered in Rhio and Lingga, bestowed it on Hussein's more tractable younger brother, Abdul Rahman. After Raffles (q.v.) had signed an agreement for the East India Company to occupy Singapore, Farquhar (q.v.) took it to Lingga to be ratified. Sultan Abdul Rahman declined to ratify it; however, Hussein returned with Farquhar and signed as the Sultan of Johore. In return, he was given a pension and a residence. In 1824, he signed a further treaty permanently ceding the territory of Singapore and surrounding islands to the East India Company. When the Sultan died in 1835, no heir was named and, a half-century later, it was claimed by Temenggong Abdul Rahman's (q.v.) heirs. The grant of property to the Sultan remained in force, and, in 1991, Singapore passed a special Sultan Hussain Ordinance (q.v.) to deal with the property rights.

-I-

INDIA. Country in Asia second only to China in size and population. In the pre-colonial period, Indian traders and kingdoms were active in Southeast Asia, most notably the Tamil Chola dynasty in the eleventh century, whose king--Raja Chulan--was identified as the father of Tan Sri Buana. The East India Company was based in India and governed the Straits Settlements (q.v.) from there, an arrangement continued until the Settlements were declared crown colonies in 1867. Both Singapore and Malaya were identified as offering better opportunities than India and attracted thousands of immigrants from there.

INDIAN MUTINY. Revolt of Indian troops in Singapore in 1915. At the outbreak of World War I, the German Navy was a threat, and a cruiser, *Emden*, attacked Penang in October 1814 but bypassed Singapore. With its destruction the following month, the threat disappeared, but German prisoners--including some from the *Emden*--proved an equal danger. Normally two regiments were stationed in Singapore, one British and one Indian. The British King's Own Yorkshire Light Infantry was moved to the front in Europe at the end of 1914, which left the Indian 5th Light Infantry to guard the prisoners and provide security for the colony. The Germans told their guards that the Germans, with their allies the Turks, were winning the war. On February 16, the 5th Light Infantry was to be moved to Hong Kong, but Punjabi Muslim soldiers of the unit believed that this was a cover story and they were really going to fight fellow Muslims in Turkey. On the eve of departure, the troops seized their barracks and murdered a number of their officers. By seeking help of ships' crews in the port and mobilizing anyone with any military experience, the mutiny was suppressed, although it took somewhat longer to round up mutineers who had fled to Johore to hide. About thirty-five people were killed by the mutineers. Following court-martials, 47 mutineers, including two officers, were sent to firing squads, 137 were sent to penal colonies (64 for life), and 17 were given jail sentences. Eleven troops from the Indian Malay States Guides were sentenced to prison for support of the mutineers.

INDIAN NATIONAL ARMY (INA).   Army formed to oust
   Britain from India during World War II, supported by the
   Japanese (q.v.).   In the invasion of Malaya, the Japanese
   encouraged Indians to desert the colonial British and join
   with the Japanese.   Led by a deserter from the British
   Indian Army, Captain Mohan Singh, more than two
   hundred Indians took part in the assault on Singapore.
   The Japanese were accompanied by Pritam Singh, an
   organizer for the Indian Independence League, who appealed for Indians to support independence for India
   rather than colonialism.   Rash Behari Bose, founder of the
   Indian Independence League, moved to Singapore from
   Japan, and Mohan Singh became the leader of the first
   Indian National Army in Singapore until he was arrested
   by the Japanese in December 1942 and the first INA
   disbanded.   The concept of the INA had considerable
   popular appeal among Indians but they remained disorga-
   nized until the arrival of Subhas Chandra Bose in 1943.
   Bose had resigned as President of the Congress Party of
   India at the beginning of the European war when his
   colleagues refused to capitalize on events to wrest independence from Britain.   In October 1943, he proclaimed
   the *Azad Hind*, or provisional government of Free India.
   Indians from throughout East Asia came to Singapore to
   join, and a special women's section was formed: the Ranee
   Jhansi Regiment, led by Dr. S. Lakshmi.   In 1944, the
   armies went to Burma to carry the battle into India, or at
   least help repel British attempts at reconquest.   At the
   climactic battle of Imphal, the INA was virtually decimated, and scattered survivors straggled back to Singapore.   Subhas Chandra Bose returned to Singapore in
   1945 but was unable to rekindle the same emotions.   In
   August, he was killed in a plane crash in Taiwan, en route
   to Japan.

INDIANS. Migrants from India or their descendants, although
   it often includes Tamils from Sri Lanka (Ceylon) as well.
   Because Singapore began an outpost of the East India
   Company (q.v.), Indians comprised most of the early
   military forces and lower bureaucracy, for their command

of English and absence of family ties and allegiances with contending Chinese factions. With the cessation of Bencoolen (q.v.) to the Netherlands in 1824, Singapore received Bencoolen's convict population and replaced it as the prison colony for India. Until 1859, there was no provision for repatriation after completion of the sentence and the released convicts melted into the society. Singapore sent its convicts to India but found they always returned while Indian convicts chose to remain. Faced with the likely arrival of many convicts arising from the 1857 Sepoy Mutiny, public demand resulted in their being sent to the Andaman Islands. The development of rubber estates in Malaya increased Indian migration to the Straits Settlements (q.v.) in the twentieth century; however, the greatest increase came in the decade following Indian independence. Before and after World War II, Indians were especially active in the labor movement.

INTERNAL SECURITY ACT (ISA). Legal basis for detention without trial. Based on the Emergency Regulation promulgated by the colonial government, it permits detention of individuals believed to threaten national security. An individual may be detained for up to two years initially and indefinitely thereafter, subject to renewal every two years. Special arrest powers are given to any policeman who believes that an individual may be a threat to the public order to take that person into custody for up to thirty days without a warrant for interrogation. When the appeals court in 1988 ordered the release of four detainees, the ISA was amended in 1989 to deny any right of judicial review of detentions or of appeal to the Privy Council.

INTERNAL SECURITY COUNCIL. Joint body vested with maintaining internal security in Singapore after 1959. In the negotiations for limited self-rule in 1959, it was agreed that a seven-person council would be established with Britain and Singapore equally represented and a representative from the Federation of Malaya having the final vote. It was a contentious issue in Singapore and within the PAP as the moderates saw it as a first link with Malaya and the leftists as a continuation of colonial dominance. This joint body played a pivotal role in controlling communist activities and in detaining opponents in the *Barisan Sosialis* (q.v.) in Operation Cold Store (q.v.) in February 1963. The cover of collective responsibility enabled the PAP to deny responsibility for the detentions, blaming Malaya and Britain, yet still enjoy having dangerous rivals removed from contention.

INTERNAL SECURITY DEPARTMENT (ISD). Police agency responsible for internal security. It carries out detentions ordered under the Internal Security Act (q.v.) and conducts interrogations of those detained. The human rights organization Asia Watch has charged that its officers have physically and psychologically abused detainees. The described incidents, slapping or other blows, are not justifiable but are relatively mild compared to the torture so prevalent elsewhere in the world. The government has denied that detainees were mistreated.

-J-

JAPAN. After nearly three centuries of self-imposed isolation, it emerged in this century to discover Southeast Asia as a source of raw materials. Although its occupation of the region in World War II failed to produce the resources imagined--as a result of destruction before occupation and ill-equipped administration--in the post-war period it has become a major economic force. While it has become an important market for goods from the region, its greatest success has been in exporting to the growing consumer markets. In the 1980s, it became the largest supplier to Singapore. While its imports of Singapore products are less than half those of the United States, it has displaced the U.S. as the largest supplier of foreign investment, surpassing US$3 billion in the 1980s. Beyond finances, its economic success has encouraged Singapore to look to it for alternatives to Western models, including activist government involvement in industrial policy and labor relations and adoption of its *Koban* system as a Neighbourhood Police Post System. While resentment remains among older Singaporeans for the World War II atrocities, younger Singaporeans see it as a model of success and supplier of the best and most desirable products.

JAPANESE OCCUPATION. Early on December 8, 1941, Japanese planes bombed Singapore. At the same time, attacks were launched on the American bases at Pearl Harbor and the Philippines and on Hong Kong. Japanese troops landed at Singgora and Patani in Southern Thailand and in Kota Bharu, Kelantan, to begin the capture of the Malay Peninsula. Under the command of Lieutenant General Tomoyuki Yamashita (q.v.), the 25th Japanese Army overran the peninsula on foot and bicycles by February. Japan had air and sea supremacy as the pride of the British fleet in Asia, the *Prince of Wales* and the *Repulse*, were sunk off the east coast of Malaya on December 10th. The invaders captured Johore Bahru on January 31st and Singapore surrendered on February 15th. Despite its preparation for the occupation--it intended to make Singapore a permanent colony--the brutality of its forces, led by the *Kempeitai*(q.v.), in the early weeks provoked continued resentment and resistance by Singaporeans, especially the Chinese majority. Like previous colonial governments, the occupation needed revenue--which it raised by levying a subscription against the Chinese. Faced with an inability to feed and provide for the population, the occupation government established agricultural settlements at Endau in Johore (q.v.) and in Negri Sembilan. It also was called on to supply labor for the Burma-Thailand railroad--which it met by sending prisoners of war and some six hundred civilians--and for industries in Japan. The Japanese surrendered on August 15, 1945, but this was not announced in Singapore until the 21st. Occupation personnel and troops retreated to an internment camp to await the arrival of Commonwealth (q.v.) troops on September 5th.

JAVA. Most populous island in Indonesia. In the fourteenth and fifteenth centuries, the Java-based empire of Majapahit dominated the archipelago and attacked *Singapura* (q.v.), which refused to acknowledge its suzerainty. In the colonial era, it was a major rice supplier to Singapore. In the twentieth century, migration led to an identifiable Javanese segment among the Malay population.

JERVOIS, SIR WILLIAM FRANCIS DRUMMOND (1821-1897). Governor of Straits Settlements, 1875-1877. After military service in the Boer and Kaffir Wars in South Africa, he joined the War Office and undertook a number of missions around the empire, including an inspection of Singapore defenses in 1869 (which he judged inadequate). As governor, he focused on British intervention in the Malay States; however, he also established the Chinese Protectorate (q.v.) in the Straits Settlements (q.v.) and allowed Sultan Abu Bakar (q.v.) of Johore to take control of Muar.

JEYARETNAM, J. B. (1926-). Ousted opposition member of Parliament and Secretary General of the Workers' Party. In 1981, Jeyaretnam became the first opposition member of Parliament since the withdrawal of *Barisan Sosialis* (q.v.) members in 1965. In a number of successful lawsuits, Lee Kuan Yew (q.v.) has charged him and the party with libel, burdening both with a substantial debt. In 1986, he was found guilty of making a false declaration of party accounts. The size of his penalty (a S$2,500 fine) led to his expulsion from Parliament (q.v.) in 1986 and disqualification for five years until November 1991. In January 1987, Parliament also found him guilty of abusing Parliamentary privilege and contempt of Parliament, levying a S$13,000 fine. In the August 1991 election campaign, he charged that the election was held early to prevent him from contesting.

JOHOR. Present official spelling for the southernmost Peninsular Malaysian state. For its history, see English spelling, JOHORE.

JOHORE. Sultanate at the southern tip of the Malayan Peninsula. The Anglo-Dutch Treaty of 1824 (q.v.) effectively severed the kingdom and afforded independence for the Johore family. In 1835, Temenggong Tun Ibrahim Ali succeeded Temenggong Abdul Rahman (q.v.) and assumed leadership in building what became the sultanate of Johore. He invited Chinese settlers to help develop the state. He was succeeded in 1862 by his son, Abu Bakar (q.v.), who in 1885 was recognized as Sultan of Johore. The sultan's son and successor, Ibrahim, held office from 1895 to 1959. He accepted a British advisor in 1910 but kept Johore as an Unfederated Malay State. He was known for his attachment to England, where he owned substantial property and where he died. In 1946, Johore was incorporated into the Malayan Union (q.v.) and then into the Federation of Malaya in 1948.

JOHORE KINGDOM. Successor to Malacca Sultanate (q.v.) and dominant realm in the Malay Peninsula and islands south thereof. After the defeat by the Portuguese in 1512, the Malacca Sultan Mahmud and his followers moved to Johore where they continued the Sultanate's reign over Rhio and Singapore. The kingdom had various capitals, both in Johore and Rhio. In 1699, the last heir to the Malacca (q.v.) throne was assassinated, resulting in a civil war culminating in a new dynasty with the Bugis (q.v.) predominating as result of their naval power. Malay factions received lesser titles and specific territories. The Bugis controlled the most powerful title, Yamtuan Muda (contraction of Yang di-Pertuan Muda; crown prince), while Malay families controlled the titles Sultan, Bendahara, and Temenggong. In the eighteenth century, Rhio (near Tangjong Bentan) was the major trading center of the Johore Empire, attracting traders from the East India Company, coastal Malay states, and China as well as Chinese miners and agriculturalists. The wealth of Rhio (which the Dutch considered a tributary of Java) and the threat posed by a Malay plot to oust the Bugis prompted Dutch conquest in 1784. The center moved further south to the Lingga Islands; however, the Dutch abandoned

Rhio in 1895 when the British seized Malacca and extended their influence in support of the Napoleonic Wars in Europe. In 1812, the death of the Sultan allowed the Yamtuan Muda (Ja'afar) to bypass the heir designate, Hussein (q.v.), and name his younger son, Abdul Rahman, as Sultan. Dutch control offered greater latitude to the Johore branch of the dynasty, carrying the Malay title, Temenggong (responsible for internal affairs). As Singapore was part of the sub-realm of Johore, Raffles made initial agreements with this branch of the Johore dynasty. The original heir, Hussein, moved to Singapore and ratified Raffles's agreement with Temenggong Abdul Rahman (q.v.).

JOSEY, ALEX (1910-1986). Free-lance journalist, socialist, and close associate of Lee Kuan Yew (q.v.). He was brought to Malaya from the Middle East by Sir Henry Gurney, High Commissioner to Malaya, 1948-1952, and made a staff officer responsible for public information operations in the Emergency. He was released following a furor over his remarks on possible nationalization of the rubber industry. He was active in socialist circles, although there were stories of connections with British intelligence. He was closely associated with S. Rajaratnam (q.v.) and worked for the *Singapore Standard* and a number of British and Australian papers. He chronicled Lee Kuan Yew's speeches and life in several books and was considered by Malaysian leaders as Lee Kuan Yew's press officer rather than a legitimate journalist.

JUNK TRADE. Intra-Asian trade conducted by Chinese, primarily from southern provinces. The name refers to the Chinese sailing ships, junks, in which goods were carried. In the early decades of the colony, Singapore received annual arrivals of a fleet of traders from China and a Bugis (q.v.) fleet from around Sulawesi (spelled Celebes by the Dutch), which coincided with the monsoons. It was also responsible for the emergence of Rhio as a major trading center in the eighteenth century.

Later in the nineteenth century, the Chinese junks carried human cargo, the coolie trade (q.v.).

-K-

K'ANG YU-WEI (*pinyin*: Kang Youwei) (1858-1927). Chinese reform leader. China's embarrassing defeat in the Sino-Japanese War (1894-1895) prompted intellectuals to seek reform of the imperial system and eliminate rampant corruption. Their ideas were realized in the brief reign of the Kuang-hsu (*pinyin*: Guangxu) Emperor in 1898. When the Emperor was overthrown in September 1898 by the Empress Dowager, T'zu-hsi (*pinyin*: Cixi), K'ang fled to Japan to avoid execution. In 1900, he came to Singapore, where he established a clandestine chapter of the *Pao Huang Hui* (Emperor Protection Society), the first Chinese political party in the Straits, seeking restoration of the Emperor and his reforms, which attracted many of the prominent Chinese citizens. Blatantly anti-Manchu organizations, such as Sun Yat-sen's *Hsing Chung Hui* (Society for the Revival of China) and *T'ung Meng Hui* (Revolutionary League) with its Singapore branch established in 1906, had greater appeal for the masses and particularly for secret society members. The death of the deposed Emperor in 1908 ended the reformist appeal.

KANGCHU. Chinese headman at a river's mouth, used in reference to up-river Teochew pepper and gambier plantations. He usually had a village, *kangkar*, which could control traffic up and down the river, but *kangkar* was sometimes used to include the plantations. A *kangkar* was identified with the headman, e.g., the *kangkar* of a *kangchu* named Lim would be called Lim *Chukang*. This structure and vocabularly is elaborated in Karl Trocki's *Prince of Pirates: The Temenggongs and the Development of Johor and Singapore, 1784-1985* (see in "Founding and East India Company Rule" section under "History" in Bibliography).

KAPITAN. System for controlling foreign communities, by making one member of the community responsible for assuring compliance with the laws. A similar system was applied under the Malacca Sultanate (q.v.) and continued after European conquest. The most familiar form, *Kapitan China* (Captain of the Chinese), was used in Singapore from its founding until incorporation into the Straits Settlements (q.v.) in 1826.

KEASBERRY, B[enjamin]. P[each]. (1811-1875). Pioneer printer and leader in Malay education. Born in India, he initially entered commerce, opening a store in Singapore and then serving as a clerk to a British firm in Batavia (present-day Jakarta). There he opted to devote his life to religion, learning printing from Dr. Medhurst of the London Missionary Society. He studied in America where he married an American. Together they were sent to Singapore as missionaries to the Malays in 1837 by the American Board of Commissioners of Foreign Missions. In 1839, he joined the London Missionary Society and taught printing. When most missionaries left Singapore for China, he elected to remain, supporting himself in part through printing. His operation, long known as the Mission Press, was a major publishing source in the nineteenth century. He also operated a Malay vocational school in conjunction with the press.

KEMPEITAI. The military police of the Japanese Occupation (q.v.) which took control of Singapore immediately after the British surrendered. With only two hundred regular *Kempei*, hundreds of auxiliaries were recruited from the army. During the first week, the Japanese admitted to killing five thousand Singaporeans, mostly Chinese. Chinese estimates are five times higher. Throughout the occupation, the *Kempeitai*--relying on secret agents and informers--were free to jail and torture anyone they suspected of anti-Japanese sentiments. Following a daring sabotage raid (Operation Jaywick) by a few Allied forces based in Australia on shipping in the harbor, on October 10, 1943 ("double tenth") the *kempei* invaded the intern-

ment camp at Changi and took fifty-seven formerly prominent British officials for interrogation. One was executed
and fifteen died from torture, including the Bishop of
Singapore, H. Fraser. For their brutality, the *Kempeitai*
are remembered as the symbol of the Japanese occupation.

KESATUAN MELAYU SINGAPURA (KMS; Singapore Malay
    Union). First Malay political association. Formed in
    1924, it was intended to support Mohammed Eunos bin
    Abdullah (q.v.), who had just been named to the Legisla-
    tive Council as the first Malay member, and to assert
    Malay independence from Arabs and other Muslims who
    claimed to represent and speak for the entire Muslim
    community. Mohammed Eunos was chosen as its first
    president, an office he held until his death in 1834. He
    was succeeded as president by Embok Suloh--who also
    assumed his Legislative Council seat. KMS was generally
    supportive of the colonial government but also undertook
    to solicit support for Malay self-improvement projects,
    such as the *Kampong Melayu* (Malay Settlement) project
    which provided housing for Malays being displaced from
    Kampong Glam by rising rents. Other projects included
    a ferry service, a cemetery, and the establishment of
    Malay sports clubs. While its platform was modest, its
    accomplishments were concrete, and it marked the first
    efforts of the Malays to assert a leadership role.

KIASU. Hokkien term meaning literally fear of loss but also
    fear of failing or fear of being cheated. It also means
    getting one's money's worth or, better, the most for one's
    money. Widely considered a national characteristic of
    Singaporeans in the late twentieth century, it is best
    described in Catherine Lim's short story masking as a
    scholarly paper, "Kiasuism: A Socio-Historico-Cultural
    Perspective," in her collection, *O Singapore!* (see in "Fic-
    tion" section under "Culture" in Bibliography). While
    most evident in assertive shopping behavior--which perva-
    sive, modern shopping centers provide ample opportunity
    to cultivate--it also provides an explanation for the separa-

tion of Singapore from Malaysia. Malaysians saw Singapore's merger as a balance in which the state retained special privileges (in the areas of education, finance, and labor) and thus could expect only limited equality with other states and citizens while Singapore's leadership expected open access to the Malaysian economic and political spheres in exchange for ceding control over defense, foreign affairs, and internal security to the national government. The reverse side of the term is marked risk aversion, which is more prevalent among younger Singaporeans than the first generation of leaders who gambled all in the struggle for power with the communists. With economic success, the electorate generally has been unwilling to risk material comforts for less tangible symbols of democracy, such as a free press and an effective opposition.

KOH THONG BEE, TOMMY (1937-). Past Ambassador to the United Nations and the United States. After graduating from the University of Malaya in Singapore, he earned a law degree from Harvard University and a diploma in criminology from Cambridge University. He joined the law faculty of the University of Singapore, rising to dean, before joining the diplomatic service. He was named to the nation's most prestigious posts, beginning as permanent representative to the United Kingdom and High Commissioner to Canada. In 1971, he was named the Ambassador to the United Nations and served four three-year terms. In this capacity, he achieved international distinction for his contributions to the international Law of the Seas Treaty. He then was named Ambassador to the United States (q.v.), during a time when Singapore was receiving strong criticism for its treatment of international, especially American, journalists and publications. At one point, he had to explain the government's professed respect for copyright protection while justifying a policy of photocopying regional news journals which it refused lawful entry. After returning to Singapore in mid-1990, he was named to head the government think tank, the Institute of Policy Studies.

KONGSI. Company, partnership, organization, association or society. While originally implying an economic or commercial endeavor, it was used for broader dialect and family organizations and also for secret societies. The dialect and family organizations frequently incorporated the idea of mutual help, offering assistance to poorer members and funeral arrangements.

KRETA AYER INCIDENT. Clash in the Kreta Ayer neighborhood between police and largely Hainanese *Kuomintang* (q.v.) supporters from Happy Valley in March 1927. At a ceremony to mark Sun Yat-sen's death, leftist *Kuomintang* members objected to anti-communist speeches. In the disturbances which ensued, police fired into the mobs, killing seven people.

KUOMINTANG (KMT; *pinyin*: *Guomindang*). Nationalist party of China, "National People's Party," founded by Sun Yat-sen and then controlled by his successor, Chiang Kai-Shek. Sun first visited Singapore in 1900 and returned in 1905, shortly before founding the *T'ung Meng Hui* (TMH; Revolutionary League) in Japan. In February 1906, he launched the first TMH chapter in Singapore, returning in July to complete the task. When the Manchus were overthrown in 1912, TMH chapters around the world were converted into the *Kuomintang*, with Lim Boon Keng (q.v.) and Lim Nee Soon as leaders. In the teens, the name was temporarily changed to the Chinese Revolutionary Party (CRP), following Yuan Shih-Kai's outlawing it in China. Its rise to power in China was paralleled by growth in the Straits Settlements (q.v.) and increasing British concern for its appeal. In 1925, it was outlawed--which had the effect of removing the moderating influence of the leadership and leaving the party to the radicals. One result was evident in the Kreta Ayer Incident (q.v.), as radical Hainanese (q.v.) KMT members ridiculed moderate leaders who tried to address them. In 1927, Chiang Kai-Shek purged the communist membership in China, a move echoed abroad. Through the 1930s and into the 1950s, Chinese leadership in Singapore was divided between KMT supporters and those sympathetic to the Chinese Communist Party. Issues in China more than those in Singapore determined the division.

-L-

LABOUR FRONT (LF). Political coalition which won the 1955 election and led the government until 1959. It was born as an election alliance between the Singapore Labour Party and the Singapore Socialist Party in 1954. The SLP later withdrew but a number of its leaders remained. Its leaders were surprised at the election success but then fell apart over the allotment of a limited number of ministries. In its first year in office, it lost half its membership when a number of leaders, including Lee Choon Eng, A. R. Lazaroo, and C.H. Koh resigned over leadership issues. When Marshall resigned as chief minister, Lim Yew Hock (q.v.), who had emerged in the forefront of the leadership contest, replaced him. Marshall's resignation from the party and its subsequent winning of only four of sixteen city council seats in 1957 were the beginning of the end. By the 1959 elections, even Lim Yew Hock had abandoned it to head a new party, the Singapore People's Alliance.

LAI TECK. Secretary-General of the Malayan Communist Party (MCP) (q.v.), 1939-1947, and double-agent for British and Japanese. Arriving in Singapore in 1934, he claimed to have been an agent of the Comintern and rose to party leadership. It has been revealed that he was brought from Saigon (hence, his alias, "the Annamese") by the British Special Branch, having previously worked for the French *Sûrêté* within the Vietnamese Communist Party. During World War II, he collaborated with the Japanese, including assisting with the killing or capture in September 1942 of most of the MCP central committee at a clandestine meeting in Batu Caves, north of Kuala Lumpur. The MCP continued to commemorate September 1st as Martyr's Day, for those who were lost. After the war, he was re-elected secretary-general of the party in January 1946, but evidence of his triple-dealing emerged. He was called to account at a party conference in March 1947, with his successor, Chin Peng, as a primary accuser. Rather than face his accusers, he fled with much of the party treasury, allegedly first to Hong Kong and then to Thailand. It has been reported but not confirmed that he was tracked down and executed by MCP agents.

LANGUAGE. Historically, English was the language of government and Malay (q.v.) and Chinese (q.v.) (actually a number of dialects) the languages of trade. Today, Malay, Chinese, Tamil, and English are official languages, with Malay as the national language and English as the administrative language. The preferred spoken Chinese is the national language of China, Mandarin (*pinyin*: *putonghua*), and distinct from the various dialects spoken by most Chinese residents in the country. The government has actively pursued a policy of multi-lingualism, encouraging students to learn at least two of the languages, and has promoted "Speak Mandarin" campaigns to encourage use of standard Chinese. All of the dialects and Mandarin share a common written language (today in the simplified form used by the People's Republic of China) but have distinct--and often unintelligible--differences in pronunciation. Despite promotion of Asian languages, English is the language of higher education and is seen as offering the greatest employment opportunities.

LAYCOCK, JOHN (1887?-). Colonial-era legislator and co-founder of the Progressive Party (q.v.). Born in England and educated at London University, he practiced law in Singapore and in the 1930s served as an unofficial member of the Legislative Council (q.v.). In the post-war period, he joined fellow lawyers in founding the Progressive Party in 1947 and won seats on the Legislative Council in 1948 and 1951 but was defeated in the 1955 general election. In the 1940s, he headed a legislative committee which recommended that two-thirds of the municipal commission (later the city council) be elected, which was effected in the 1949 election.

LEE HSIEN LOONG (1952-). Eldest son of Lee Kuan Yew (q.v.) and leading member of the "third" generation. After graduating with honors in mathematics and computer science from Cambridge University, he rose rapidly through the military to the rank of Brigadier General (accounting for his nickname, "the B.G.") and second in command before resigning in 1984 to enter politics. Winning his first Parliamentary contest, he was made a junior minister in 1985 and Minister for Trade and Industry in 1986. In February 1989, he was elected as second assistant secretary-general of the PAP. In the cabinet formed following his father's resignation in 1990, he was made Second Deputy Prime Minister--affirming his status as heir-apparent to Prime Minister Goh.

LEE KONG CHIAN (1893/4-1970). Prominent Chinese businessman, financier, and philanthropist. Born in China, he came to Singapore in 1903. He later studied engineering in Shanghai on a Chinese imperial government scholarship. He returned to Singapore as a translator for a Chinese paper and then a teacher and surveyor. He joined Tan Kah Kee's (q.v.) rubber company and, in 1920, married Tan Kah Kee's daughter. He formed his own companies in 1931 and, helping to reorganize Chinese banking, formed the Overseas Chinese Banking Corporation (OCBC), of which he served as chairman for many years. He shared his father-in-law's support for education, and in 1952 established the Lee Foundation, the nation's foremost philanthropic institution. In the 1960s, he was the first chancellor and a major economic supporter of the University of Singapore.

LEE KUAN YEW (1923-). Foremost statesman and Prime Minister, 1959-1990. Born to a Straits Chinese Hakka family, he was educated at Raffles College (q.v.), but his plans to study law in Britain were halted by World War II. In 1946 he entered the London School of Economics, transferring shortly afterward to Cambridge, from which he graduated with special distinction (a "double first") in 1949. The woman who would become his wife, Kwa Geok Choo, attended Cambridge at the same time and also won first class honors in just two years. In the newly formed Malayan Forum (q.v.) in London, he and other Raffles graduates--including Goh Keng Swee (q.v.) and Toh Chin Chye (q.v.)--began discussions of Malaya's future which culminated in their founding and leading the People's Action Party (PAP) (q.v.) five years later. Returning in 1950 to practice law, he served as Secretary of the Straits Chinese British Association (q.v.), joined the law firm of Laycock and Ong, and campaigned for the Progressive Party (q.v.) in the 1951 election. Leaving these arenas reserved for the English-educated elite, he increasingly associated with leftist and labor causes. In 1952, he represented postal workers, winning substantial concessions without a strike, and then supported protests against the special allowances provided European government officers but denied those from Singapore with the same qualifications. His union contacts also led to defending Chinese students arrested during the 1954 riots and the members of the University of Malaya Socialist Club (q.v.). In 1954, with his English-educated friends, he joined with leftist intellectuals and Chinese-educated labor leaders in founding the People's Action Party (q.v.) and became its first secretary general with Toh Chin Chye as President. The next five years were a struggle between his group and the others for control of the party. He realized that they needed the popular support which the unions and communists could mobilize and, especially after the Lim Yew Hock (q.v.) government arrested the leftist leaders who sought to dislodge his group from party leadership, the leftists needed the cover of the English-educated. That was the first of several occasions when his position was strengthened because others, usually political rivals, arrested his opponents. In the 1950s, he was viewed by many as a clandestine communist, a tool of the communists, or a fool. Yet, he and the PAP exploited the communists and far left to gain political dominance--

bringing the PAP to power in 1959 with Lee as Chief Minister--and then broke with them, leaving his group firmly in control of the party and the government. It was the last serious internal challenge to his leadership. The experience convinced him of the ruthlessness of the communists, and in the late 1970s and 1980s he saw dissident youth organizations as posing the same threat as those whom he had bested in the 1950s and 1960s. During the two years in Malaysia, his charisma and public speeches attracted people of all races (he previously had conscientiously learned Malay, Mandarin, and Tamil), but he and the PAP failed to dent the powerful electoral hold of the Alliance (q.v.) on the Peninsula. Faced with the choice of probable detention as a threat to national unity or separation, he reluctantly accepted the latter. August 1965 was a turning point in his life. His lifelong goal of independence within Malaya was shattered, and he publicly cried in describing separation. Afterward, as Prime Minister of the new nation, his populism increasingly gave way to remoteness mixed with statesmanship. Shirtsleeves yielded to business suits, and his speeches became more pedantic. Until stepping aside to become a senior minister in 1990, he led Singapore to a prosperity which few in the 1950s or even 1960s would have thought possible. Under his leadership, Singapore went from a turbulent colony to one of the most wealthy, stable, and productive countries in Asia. Beginning as a devoted socialist, both he and the PAP gingerly and then enthusiastically embraced capitalism--with a strong state presence--as offering the greatest social and economic benefits. From the late 1960s, he began testing and training potential successors and, after a trial in the mid 1980s when Goh Chok Tong and younger leaders made decisions and implemented policies without interference, he became a rarity among world leaders--someone who could step aside after thirty years at the helm. While he was respected more than loved, the nation felt dependent on his leadership, and many long for a Lee dynasty, believing his successor should have been his son, Lee Hsien Loong (q.v.).

LEE SIEW CHOH, DR. (1917-). *Barisan Sosialis* (q.v.) leader and 1990s appointed nonconstituency member of Parliament. Born in Kuala Lumpur, he graduated with distinction from the medical college. Recruited to the People's Action Party (q.v.) by Goh Keng Swee (q.v.), in 1960, he was appointed a party Parliamentary secretary. At the formation of the *Barisan Sosialis* in July 1959, he was the first chairman. In 1964, after the Hong Lim (q.v.) by-election defeat, he broke with the party over its accommodationist response to the draft but rejoined ten months later in March 1965. He favored the Parliamentary boycott in 1966 but repudiated it for the 1972 and subsequent elections. After the 1988 election, he was named as one of two nonconstituency members of Parliament

LEGISLATIVE ASSEMBLY. Domestic Parliament for Singapore, 1955-1965. Arising from the Rendel Commission (q.v.) consitution, the first Assembly was elected in 1955, with David Marshall's (q.v.) Labour Front (q.v.) winning a plurality. The Front was able to form a government with the votes of Alliance, the official members, and two of the unofficial members. By the 1959 election, official and appointed members were eliminated, leaving the enlarged fifty-one-member assembly entirely elected. In 1965, the assembly was replaced by the national Parliament of the newly independent Republic of Singapore (with members of the assembly made members of Parliament).

LEGISLATIVE COUNCIL (1867-1955). Singapore advisory council to governor of the Straits Settlements and colonial government. Established with the change to crown colony status, the Legislative Council consisted of the governor, members of the Executive Council (q.v.), the chief justice, and unofficial members nominated by the governor. When established in 1867, there were six officials plus the governor from the Executive Council and four unofficial (also called informal) members. Official members were required to support government policy and vote with the governor. In theory, each of the component states--

Penang (q.v.), Malacca (q.v.), and Singapore--were to be represented but, because the council met in Singapore, representatives of the other states were reluctant to serve and be away from their businesses. This led to resentment that the council was concerned only with Singapore. Gradually more unofficial members were added until, in 1924, there were equal numbers of official and unofficial members, with the governor having the deciding vote. The first Asian unofficial member was Hoo Ah Kay (q.v.), who was nominated in 1869. While the governor was to listen to the council's views, he retained ultimate authority, subject to Colonial Office approval, and responsibility for decisions. When the council was reformed in 1948, as the Singapore Legislative Council, it had nine official members and thirteen unofficial--four chosen by the governor, three by the chambers of commerce and six elected by British subjects residing in Singapore. In 1951, the elected members were increased to nine, and those nine could choose two members to serve on the Executive Council. With the implementation of the Rendel Commission recommendations, the Legislative Council was replaced by the Legislative Assembly (q.v.) in 1955.

LIBERAL SOCIALIST PARTY. Short-lived attempt by older political leaders to regain power in the mid-1950s. Formed by a merger of the Progressive Party (q.v.) and the Democratic Party (q.v.), both of which were considered too accommodationist and conservative, after they were defeated in the 1955 election, the party--despite its name--was too far removed from the radical popular sentiments. It still controlled six of twenty-five seats in the Legislative Assembly (q.v.) and a majority in the city council; however, in the 1957 city council election it captured only seven of the thirty-two seats, and none in the 1959 general election.

LIM BO SENG (1909-1943). Prominent Chinese businessman and *Kuomintang* (q.v.) supporter. He was a conspicuous agitator against the Japanese and, on the eve of invasion, led the Mobilization Council, which provided Chinese labor for defense construction, and formed the Chinese Liaison Committee for civil defense. He escaped to India before the surrender, but the *Kempeitai* (q.v.) captured many of his family members, who were not seen again. In India, he recruited *Kuomintang* colleagues for Force 136 (q.v.), the British guerrilla movement in Malaya. He was captured and tortured to death by the Japanese after joining Force 136 in 1943, betrayed by Malayan Communist Party (q.v.) leader Lai Teck (q.v.). After the war, his remains were recovered and given a hero's burial in Singapore.

LIM BOON KENG (1869-1957). Leading Straits Chinese. After graduating as the first Chinese Queen's Scholar from Raffles Institution (q.v.) and receiving a medical degree from the University of Edinburgh, he was a leader in educational and cultural reform, including crusading against the pigtail (queue)--a symbol of subservience to the Manchu--and opium usage. He founded the English-medium Singapore Chinese Girls' School, the Straits Chinese British Association (q.v.) in 1900, and the Singapore branch of the *Kuomintang* (q.v.) in 1912. He served as the first president of Amoy University (today Xiamen University) in China in 1921. As a writer, he edited the first issue of the *Straits Chinese Magazine* and authored *The Chinese Crisis from Within*. He was named to the Legislative Assembly (q.v.) in 1916. During World War II, he founded the Overseas Chinese Association (q.v.) to protect Chinese, although it was used by the Japanese to extract money from the Chinese.

LIM CHEE ONN (1944-). Technocrat ousted from National Trades Union Congress (NTUC) (q.v.) leadership. After graduating from the University of Glasgow and receiving a master's degree in public administration at Harvard, he entered public service in 1968 in the Marine Department. Seen as the prototypical technocrat, which characterized the second- and third-generation leaders, he was elected to Parliament in 1977 and joined the NTUC the same year. In March 1979 he was named Deputy Secretary

General of the NTUC and in May 1979 was elected Secretary General. In 1980, he named a Minister without Portfolio, demonstrating to labor that it had a voice in public policy. In April 1983, he was removed from his NTUC post and in July resigned from the cabinet.

LIM CHIN SIONG (1933-). PAP founder and leftist leader. A former cell leader in the Singapore Students' Anti-British League (q.v.), he was expelled from Chinese High School in 1952 for organizing class boycotts and became a clerk with a bus company. By 1954 he was an employee of the Singapore Bus Workers' Union and the following year became Secretary General of the Singapore Factory and Shop Workers' Union. He declined an invitation to serve as a founder of the People's Action Party (PAP) because of his notoriety following the May 1954 riots, suggesting Fong Swee Suan (q.v.) instead. In 1955, he was one of three PAP candidates elected to the Legislative Assembly (q.v.). In the 1956 PAP Central Executive Committee election, he out polled Lee Kuan Yew (q.v.) by more than one hundred votes but was arrested with other leftists following riots in October. He was released in 1959 when the detainees signed a commitment to democratic socialism demanded by Lee Kuan Yew. He led the failed attempt to oust Lee Kuan Yew in July 1961 and joined the dissidents who then formed the *Barisan Sosialis* (q.v.). He and other *Barisan* leaders were detained in "Operation Cold Store" (q.v.) in 1963. In 1969 he renounced politics and, on release from detention at Changi (q.v.), left to study in London, later returning to enter business.

LIM HONG BEE (1929?-). Co-founder of Malayan Democratic Union (q.v.) and spokesperson in London for communist causes. He won a prized Queen's scholarship in 1837, after being educated at Raffles Institution (q.v.), and studied law at Cambridge but was expelled for neglecting his studies for politics. He returned shortly before the Japanese occupation. He went into hiding following the invasion because of his efforts to support

China (q.v.). It is assumed that he joined the MPAJA during this time, but by the end of the war he was in the agricultural settlement of Endau. After the war, he actively promoted a united-front approach to opposing the British and was a founder of the Malayan Democratic Union. In 1947, he returned to London to further studies and was banned from entering Malaya or Singapore.

LIM KEAN CHYE. Leftist leader, lawyer, and a founder of the Malayan Democratic Union (MDU) (q.v.). He went to Cambridge University in 1935 (a schoolmate of Lim Hong Bee [q.v.]) where he received a B. A. degree and was active in the leftist student activities. He helped introduce Lim Hong Bee and Wu Tien Wang (q.v.) to his uncle, Philip Hoalim (q.v.), which resulted in Hoalim's leadership of the MDU. He was sympathetic to the Malayan Communist Party (q.v.) participation in the MDU and was described by Lee Kuan Yew (q.v.) as being absorbed by the communists. He avoided detention in 1951 by fleeing to China, and the British placed a S$5,000 reward for his capture. In 1960, he was allowed to return to Penang, where he was detained for three months and then resumed practicing law and abandoned political activity.

LIM YEW HOCK (1914-1984). Chief Minister of Singapore, 1956-1959. Lured from the Progressive Party (q.v.) in 1949, he became president of the Singapore Labour Party (q.v.). He had been a clerk and rose to become secretary-general of the Singapore Clerical and Administrative Workers Union, for which he was named to represent labor on the Legislative Council (q.v.) in 1948. In 1951 he helped found the Singapore Trade Union Congress (q.v.). In 1954, he helped form the Labour Front (q.v.) and was the only member of the Legislative Council to win a seat in the 1955 Legislative Assembly election. In June 1956, he succeeded David Marshall (q.v.) as Chief Minister. Confronted with strikes and riots, he arrested communist leaders (including a number of PAP cadre) and led the delegations to London which finalized arrangements for self-government. In 1969, he and other leaders of the

Labour Front took the name Singapore People's Alliance (q.v.) to contest the 1959 election and won four seats. His later Singapore Alliance (q.v.) failed to win seats in the 1963 election, and he declined to contest. He later served as Malaysia's High Commissioner to Australia but resigned after some embarrassing incidents. He later converted to Islam, with the name Hajji Omar Lim.

-M-

MACDONALD, MALCOLM (1901-1981). British cabinet member in 1930s; Governor-General of the Malayan Union and Singapore, 1946-1948, and Commissioner-General for Southeast Asia until 1955. Son of British Labour Party leader and first Labour Prime Minister Ramsay MacDonald, he served as Secretary of State for the Colonies and Colonial Secretary, 1935-1940. At the end of the British Military Administration, he was appointed Governor-General and assumed office in May 1946. In this position, he coordinated the policies of the Governor of Singapore and the High Commissioner of the Federation of Malaya. He also had great interest in the Borneo states of Sarawak and present-day Sabah. The late, former Prime Minister of Indonesia, Mohamed Hatta, contended that McDonald advised him in 1949 and 1952 of British plans to form the combined Borneo-Singapore-Malaya state of Malaysia.

MAJAPAHIT. Javanese empire of the fourteenth and fifteenth centuries. Centered in East Java and based on agriculture, its influence and possible hegemony spread through much of Indonesia and the Malay Peninsula. It emerged from the rivalry between the East Javanese kingdoms of Singosari and Kediri. Its peak influence, described in the court chronicle *Nagarakertagama*, was during the reign of Hayam Wuruk (1350-1389) and the chief ministership of Gajah Mada (1330-1364). Majapahit was the dominant force during the rise of Singapore (and sometimes credited with its destruction). Its decline late in the fourteenth century contributed to the emergence of the Malacca Sultanate (q.v.) as a regional power.

MALACCA. Portuguese, Dutch, and British colony and state in Malaya and Malaysia. From its capture in August 1511 by the Portuguese until the establishment of Penang (q.v.) in 1786, it was the only European colony on the peninsula and a major link in the Portuguese Empire between Goa and Macao. It was captured in 1641 by the Netherlands East Indies Company (VOC), which allowed it to stagnate, as the VOC made Batavia (Jakarta) the center of its colonial and trading empire. In 1795 it was taken by the British to deny it to the French after the conquest of the Netherlands but was returned in 1818 after the French defeat. With the settlement of Singapore, many Asian traders from Malacca opened operations in the new southern outpost. The Anglo-Dutch Treaty of 1824 (q.v.) returned Malacca to the British and, in 1826, with Penang and Singapore, it formed the Straits Settlements (q.v.).

MALACCA SULTANATE. Malay empire in the fifteenth century encompassing states on the peninsula and Sumatra. Tracing its roots to the Sumatran kingdom of Sri Vijaya, based in Palembang, and an interim regime in Singapore, it was founded at the beginning of the fifteenth century and became one of the busiest ports in the world, dominating the Straits of Malacca. Conquered by Portugal in 1511, the commander of the Malacca fleet (*Laksamana*) established a base at Singapura and the defeated sultan established himself on the Johore River, laying the basis for the Johore Kingdom (q.v.).

MALAY LANGUAGE (*Bahasa Melayu*). The language of the Malay people. Used in a broader sense, Malay was the language of indigenous and much international trade and commerce (*lingua franca*) throughout most of present-day Brunei, Indonesia, and Malaysia until the twentieth century. It is closely related to a number of Philippine

languages and is included as part of the larger Austrone-
sian (previously called Malayo-Polynesian) language
family--although with substantial imported vocabulary
from Sanskrit, Arabic, and Persian. It lost ground as the
language of government to Dutch and English under
colonial rule; however, independence has seen its reemer-
gence as the national languages of Indonesia (*Bahasa
Indonesia*), Malaysia (*Bahasa Malaysia*) and Brunei and
as one of the official languages of Singapore. Historically
and contemporarily, it has considerable local variation,
but its adoption as an official language has brought efforts
at standardization, internally and among the four nations.
These have emphasized rationalizing spelling because
historic Malay was written in Arabic script and separate
romanization schemes were followed by the British and
Dutch colonial establishments.

MALAY STATES. Collective term for the nine sultanates in
Malaya. Britain eventually convinced or coerced each of
the sultanates to accept British advisors. In 1896, the
system of advisors was consolidated into a structure of
Federated Malay States and Unfederated Malay States.
The former included Negeri Sembilan, Pahang, Perak, and
Selangor. The latter term was used for the remaining
five, including Johore. The Unfederated Malay States
were more individually ruled, while British authority was
centralized in a single individual as Governor of the
Straits Settlements and High Commissioner of the Federated Malay States, which continued until the Japanese
occupation and was dissolved with the establishment of
the Malayan Union (q.v.) in 1946. The nine later became
states in the Federation of Malaya (q.v.) and the Federation of Malaysia (q.v.).

MALAYA, FEDERATION OF. Political entity comprised of
peninsular Malay States plus Penang and Malacca, 1948 -
1963. When the Malayan Union (1946-1948) was rejected
by Malays and non-Malays, the Federation was imple-
mented--assuring some sovereignty to each sultan within
his state while offering greater citizenship rights to non-

Malays. The designation was retained when the Federation gained independence on August 31, 1957. After the creation of Malaysia in 1963, these eleven states have been referred to as Peninsular or West Malaysia.

MALAYAN ASSOCIATION OF INDIA. Organization of refugees from Malaya and Singapore during World War II. Formed in 1942, it attracted two-thirds of the refugees living in India as members but was dominated by Europeans. In 1943, many Chinese members--led by Tan Cheng Lock (q.v.)--broke away to form the Overseas Chinese Association (q.v.).

MALAYAN COMMUNIST PARTY (MCP). Primary communist organization opposing Malaya, Malaysia, and Singapore, which engaged in armed struggle against them, 1948-1989. Formed in Singapore in 1930, it set a pattern to be repeated two decades later in organizing strikes by Chinese student front groups; however, the arrest of a French communist leader--Joseph Ducroux--in 1931 led to discovery of much of the party's organization. In 1934, the party was reorganized with the arrival of Lai Teck (q.v.) as the comintern representative. Through the Malayan General Union, which succeeded the Nan Yang General Labour Union in 1930, and its affiliation with the comintern Pan-Pacific Trade Union Secretariat, the party sought to establish ties and influence the nascent trade union movement--an effort interrupted by the Japanese threat and invasion. Its members joined Dalforce and, after the surrender of Singapore, fled to the Malayan mainland, where they formed the Malayan People's Anti-Japanese Army (MPAJA) and engaged in guerrilla attacks on the occupation forces, despite the betrayal by Lai Teck (q.v.) which saw much of the party's and MPAJA's top leadership ambushed and killed in September 1942. At the end of the war, in the interim between the Japanese surrender and the British return, the MPAJA moved to assert its presence and settle grudges against people accused of collaboration--leading to armed clashes with Malays who felt personally as well as politically threatened. The antagonisms during this brief period removed any hope that the party might attract substantial support outside of the Chinese community. In the post-war celebrations, the MPAJA was recognized for its resistance, and the MCP was allowed to operate openly. At the same time, it developed front organizations not directly traceable to the party, such as the Malayan People's Anti-Japanese Ex-Service Comrades Association, and exerted influence over labor unions through the Singapore General Labour Union. To demonstrate its political muscle, it called a twenty-four-hour general strike on January 29, 1946, which was honored by at least 170,000 workers. A second strike was called for February 15 to memorialize the abandonment of Singapore to the Japanese in 1942, but arrests of party leaders two days before and the banning of processions prevented open confrontations, as occurred in Malaya. Ten of those arrested were banished to China. Following this experience, the party closed most of its open operations and relied increasingly on front organizations and labor unions. In Malaya, confrontations between unions and companies--especially plantations--were increasing, prompting a bill proscribing the Pan-Malayan Federation of Trade Unions (q.v.) in 1948. Violent strikes and attacks on plantation owners provoked a declaration of emergency on June 16 for some states and nationwide on June 18. The MCP was outlawed, and the guerrilla war known as the Malayan Emergency was begun--keeping most of the party leadership in the jungles. Still, through fronts and clandestine visits by party leaders (such as Fang Chuang Pi [q.v.], made famous by Lee Kuan Yew as the plenipotentiary of the MCP or "The Plen"), the MCP continued to exert its influence as late as the 1970s. The guerrillas in Malaya were increasingly isolated from the population and, after 1960, were largely limited to raids from bases in Thailand. In December 1989, with Thai mediation, the party finally agreed to end its armed struggle.

MALAYAN DEMOCRATIC UNION (MDU). First local political party in Singapore, formed in December 1945, chaired by Philip Hoalim (q.v.). Leading MDU members included radical lawyers Lim Kean Chye (q.v.) and John Eber (q.v.), both Cambridge-educated, and communists Wu Tian Wang (q.v.), Gerald De Cruz (q.v.), and Lim Hong Bee (q.v.). The MDU platform aimed at the inclusion of Singapore within the Malayan Union, steps toward self-government, a stronger representative Legislative Council, and multi-lingualism. Most of its estimated three thousand members were Chinese, with some Indians (q.v.) and Eurasians (q.v.). In early 1948, it lost the support of the communists and the Singapore Chinese Chamber of Commerce (q.v.)--depriving it of grassroots support and money. In March 1948, it boycotted the Legislative Council (q.v.) election and in June, with the outbreak of the Malayan Emergency, dissolved itself.

MALAYAN FORUM. Left-wing discussion group of Singapore and Malayan students in London in 1949-1950s. Formed in 1949 with Goh Keng Swee (q.v.) as first chair and including Abdul Razak (later deputy prime minister and prime minister of Malaysia), Maurice Baker, Mohamed Sopiee, Philip Hoalim, Jr., and F. Arulanandum, the forum sought to raise the consciousness of Malayan (including Singaporean) students about independence and to develop a dialogue with sympathetic British politicians. Indicative of later developments in Singapore, communist sympathizers such as Lim Hong Bee (q.v.) sought to gain control of the organization. He, with John Eber (q.v.), succeeded in 1954, but they were ousted by a group led by Goh Keng Swee, who had returned for Ph.D. study. In the early Forum meetings, Raffles College graduates Lee Kuan Yew, Goh Keng Swee, Toh Chin Chye (q.v.), and K. M. Byrne exchanged ideas. Five years later, they comprised the core leadership of the People's Action Party when it was formed.

MALAYAN NATIONAL LIBERATION LEAGUE (MNLL). Communist-linked organization opposed to the formation of Malaysia. It enjoyed close relations with the Indonesian Communist Party (PKI) and was led by communists such as P. V. Sharma (q.v.) and Eu Chooi Yip (q.v.), as well as a radical Malay unionist, Ibrahim Mohamad. An attempt to have a number of prominent Malay leftists join was thwarted when the Malaysian government detained them prior to their departure. Following the military seizure of control of Indonesia in late 1965, because of its ties with the PKI, its headquarters was closed and those operating it left the country for China or Vietnam.

MALAYAN NEW DEMOCRATIC YOUTH LEAGUE (MNDYL). Communist front organization in the 1970s. Described by the Singapore government as being formed in Perak by pro-communist students in February 1971, it spread to Singapore shortly afterward. Its alleged goals included subverting students, lower-level government employees, and soldiers as well as supporting and supplying the Malayan Communist Party's armed struggle. In 1976, the government arrested four student leaders (from Singapore Polytechnic and Ngee Ann Technical College) who confessed to being active in the organization.

MALAYAN PLANNING UNIT. Secret select body of Malayan Civil Service (MCS) veterans formed in World War II to plan for post-war government. Despite their experience, the plan they evolved--the Malayan Union (q.v.)--alienated nearly everyone, including the Asian residents of the Straits Settlements (q.v.) and Malay States (q.v.), as well as their former MCS colleagues.

MALAYAN UNION. Plan developed in Britain during World War II for post-war government. Initially conceived as uniting British interests in Borneo, Singapore, and Malaya, the Union replaced the British Military Administration (q.v.) on April 1, 1946. Singapore was excluded as a separate crown colony (with the Cocos-Keeling Islands and Christmas Island) but with the expectation that it would later join the union. Opposition to the union led to its replacement in 1948 by the Federation of Malaya.

MALAYS. From the Malay, *Orang Melayu*, or Malay people; indigenous people of the Malay peninsula and Sumatra. In practice, ethnically related peoples such as Javanese, Bataks, Bugis, and others are counted as Malays in Singapore. They are the largest minority and, because of religious and ethnic affinities with the majorities in Malaysia and Indonesia, the source of greatest concern. The government is anxious to prove to its neighbors that it does not discriminate against them. They look to the neighboring countries to protect their interests, just as Chinese minorities in Malaysia and Indonesia look to Singapore for support and, if needed, a place of refuge.

MALAYSIA, FEDERATION OF. Nation resulting from merger of Borneo states of Sabah and Sarawak, Singapore, and the Federation of Malaya on September 16, 1963. Singapore's entry was based on permitting it to retain control of its education and labor policies in exchange for receiving only 15 of 159 Parliamentary seats--12 for the People's Action Party (PAP) (q.v.) and 3 for *Barisan Sosialis* (q.v.). As the PAP sought to extend its influence and representation in the peninsular states, it was seen as a Chinese party (despite non-communal membership), eliciting strong reaction from Malays (q.v.) and the Malayan Chinese Association (MCA), which saw its representation of Chinese interests within the ruling Alliance threatened. Resulting racial tensions prompted the Malaysian government leadership to insist that Singapore leave the Federation. After separation on August 9, 1965, relations between the two nations remained cool; however, mutual dependency, shared interests, and membership in the Association of Southeast Asian Nations (q.v.) led to a positive working relationship in the 1980s.

MALAYSIAN SOLIDARITY CONVENTION (MSC). Alliance of Malaysian opposition parties led by the People's Action Party (PAP) (q.v.). Having failed to win more than one seat in the 1964 Malaysian election, Lee Kuan Yew (q.v.) and the PAP sought to strengthen the case of Singapore, the party, the Chinese, and multi-ethnicity through a public campaign for greater equality. This culminated in the formation of the convention on May 9, 1965, with the theme of a "Malaysian Malaysia." While the convention parties argued that this meant fairness for all Malaysians, it was interpreted by Malays as an attack on their constitutional special privileges. It was also seen as ethnically divisive and a threat to the non-Malay parties in the Alliance coalition which governed Malaysia. Only three months later, separation was demanded, and the MSC was an important step in precipitating it.

MANSOR, KASSIM ALI (1850-1915). Indian Muslim hanged for treason after the Indian Mutiny (q.v.) in 1915. He operated a coffee shop and was known to associate with Indians from the mutineer regiment and Sikhs from the Malay States Guides (who had refused to go to war in December 1914 and were returned to their base in Perak). Evidence against him consisted of a series of letters to his son in Rangoon, a number of which were for delivery to the honorary Turkish consul, an Indian, there (not knowing that the consulate had closed at the outbreak of World War I). Some letters were signed by Malay States Guides asking that a Turkish ship be sent so they could join in the fight against the British. A number of the letters asked why there had been no response to this request. He was found guilty in a court-martial--the only time a civilian was tried without regular judge and jury in the colonies--and sentenced to death. The prosecution argued that these actions must be considered part of the mutiny. For sending a letter to a non-existent consul requesting a warship (of which there were none in the area), he was hanged on May 31, 1915.

MARIA HERTOGH RIOT. First major riot against the British, especially supported by Malays and other Muslims. Maria Hertogh was a Eurasian girl in Indonesia who came under the guardianship of an Indonesian Muslim family in Bandung during World War II. In 1947, her adoptive Malay mother moved to Trengganu, Malaya. In 1950, her birth parents, living in Holland, sued in Singapore for her return. On May 19th the Chief Justice ruled that she had to be returned to her birth parents but stayed the decision to allow for an appeal. During the appeal process, the original decision was set aside, and on August 1st Maria--who was fourteen-and-one-half years old--was married in a Muslim ceremony. Although the marriage was legal under Islamic law, it was voided in a ruling that Maria was covered by Dutch law, despite never having lived in Holland. The appeal process generated wide public concern, and the decision on December 2nd to void the marriage and return her to her birth parents was viewed by Muslims as ignoring Islamic law in favor of European law. Rioting by angry Muslims broke out on December 11th and continued through the 13th, resulting in 18 people killed and 173 injured--mostly Europeans and Eurasians. The case and riots inspired two English-language novels: Han Suy.in's *Cast But One Shadow* and G. M. Glaskin's *Lion in the Sun* (for both, see in "Fiction" section under "Culture" in Bibliography).

MARSHALL, DAVID SAUL (1908-). Co-founder of Labour Front (q.v.), Chief Minister, 1955-1956, and founder and President of the Workers' Party (q.v.). Born in Singapore of Sephardic Jewish parents, at age six he was placed under house detention in Baghdad, which he was visiting with his mother, by the Turks during World War I. He completed his schooling in Singapore and earned a law degree in London before returning in 1937. During World War II, he was detained at Changi Prison and in 1943 was sent to northern Japan to work in coal mines. Pursuing his law career after the war, he became associated with the Progressive Party (q.v.) but resigned in 1952 over policy issues. Coming together with defectors from the Singapore Labour Party (q.v.), the Singapore Socialist Party (SSP) (q.v.) was formed in 1954 with Marshall as President, but failed to attract popular support. The SSP then forged an alliance, called the Labour Front (q.v.), with the Labour Party to contest the 1955 election under Marshall's leadership. The Front won ten of the twenty-five elected seats and negotiated sufficient additional support to form the government with Marshall as Chief Minister. Launched amid the turmoil of strikes and riots, he presided only fourteen months, resigning the chief ministership in 1956 when talks with Britain failed to secure full independence. After a mission the next year gained an agreement for self-government, he challenged Lee Kuan Yew (q.v.) to resign his seat and did so himself to test voter approval of agreement. Lee did so and won easily. Although Marshall resigned, he declined to contest the by-election. In 1957, he launched the Workers' Party which, with communist support, emerged as a political force in the December 1957 city council election but then faded, except as a vehicle for his winning a Parliamentary seat in a 1962 Anson by-election. In 1978, he accepted appointment as ambassador to France.

MELAKA. Present official Malay spelling for the southwestern coastal Peninsular Malaysian state formerly part of the Straits Settlements. For history, see under English spelling, MALACCA.

MERGER. Combining of the Borneo states of Sabah (British North Borneo) and Sarawak with Singapore and the Federation of Malaya to form Malaysia on September 16, 1963. Under the rubric "Battle for Merger," it was popularized in a number of speeches and broadcasts by Lee Kuan Yew in 1961.

MIDDLE ROAD (also MIDDLE ROADERS). Label for leftists and communists in the labor movement and the People's Action Party (PAP) in the mid-1950s and the unions with which they were associated. The designation referred to the headquarters of several labor unions associated with the Singapore Federation of Trade Unions (q.v.) located on the street, Middle Road, rather than to an ideological orientation. Associated with these unions were Lim Chin Siong (q.v.), Fong Swee Suan (q.v.), and others who broke with the PAP in the 1961 to form the *Barisan Sosialis* (q.v.).

MOHAMMED EUNOS BIN ABDULLAH (1876-1934). Malay community leader and pioneering journalist. Born in Sumatra, he grew up in Kampong Glam in Singapore and graduated from the Raffles Institution (q.v.). In 1907, William Makepeace, the owner of the *Singapore Free Press*, asked him to create a Malay edition of the paper, *Utusan Melayu*. It was the first national Malay newspaper and was primarily in *Jawi* (Malay in Arabic script) but contained one page in *Rumi* (Malay in Roman script). In 1814, he became editor of *Lembaga Melayu*, the Malay edition of the English *Malaya Tribune*. In 1922, he was named a municipal commissioner and, in 1924, became the first Malay member of the Legislative Council (q.v.). That same year he helped found the *Kesatuan Melayu Singapura* (KMS) (q.v.) which worked for the improvement of Malay life. He is considered the father of modern Malay journalism, and a street and an election constituency continue to bear his name (Eunos).

MONSOON (from Portuguese *monção*, and probably Arabic, *mausim* = season). Winds blowing predominantly from one direction for a number of months. In Singapore and the Malay Peninsula, there are two dominant monsoons, the northeast from late October through March and the southwest from June through September. The northeast monsoon is marked by increased rain. Historically, the monsoons account for the importance of Singapore and the Straits of Malacca. Ships engaged in the China trade would sail south from China during the northeast monsoon and return during the Southwest, following the reverse pattern from India and further west. This made a base or trans-shipment port at the southern end of the Straits of Malacca desirable.

-N-

NAIR, C[HENGARA] V[EETIL] DEVAN (1923-). Labor leader, co-founder of the People's Action Party (PAP), and president of Singapore, 1981-1985. As a teacher after World War II, he served as general secretary of the Singapore Teachers Union, 1949-1951, until he was detained by the British for seventeen months because of membership in the communist-front Anti-British League (q.v.). He returned to labor organizing with the Factory and Shop Workers Union and, in 1956, was detained for three more years. After four months as political secretary to the minister of education in the first PAP government, he resigned to return to teaching and union activities, becoming the first president of the National Trades Union Congress (NTUC) (q.v.). In 1964, he was the only victorious PAP candidate, out of 26, in Malaysian Parliamentary elections--a seat which he relinquished in 1969. He resumed leadership of the NTUC and was elected to the Singapore Parliament. In 1981, he was selected as President of the Republic but was asked to resign in 1985 for erratic behavior and was accused of alcoholism by Lee Kuan Yew (q.v.). After leaving office, he came to the United States and has become an outspoken critic of the government. As of 1991, he was living in Bloomington, Indiana, with his family.

NANYANG. Chinese term meaning "South Seas," referring to the South China Sea, used to identify the geographic area known as "Southeast Asia" in English.

NANYANG UNIVERSITY. Chinese-language university, 1956-1980 (also called *Nantah*, from the Chinese *Nanyang Ta Hsüeh* [*pinyin: Nanyang Daxue*]). In 1953, Tan Lark Sye (q.v.) attacked the value of English-language education and called for the establishment of a Nanyang university. With a gift of land from the Hokkien *Huay-kuan* (q.v.) and contributions from all levels of society, it was opened in 1956. An initial attempt to launch the university, under the chancellorship of Lin Yutang, failed when Lin and the entire staff resigned in April 1955, following public protests against Lin's anti-communist statements. In the 1950s and 1960s it was a hotbed of student agitation and a fertile source of leftist recruitment. After the

Chinese Middle Schools Students' Union was banned in 1956, many of its leaders formed the Nanyang University Students' Union. It included many distinguished scholars among its faculty and graduates but was continually criticized by the government for its low standards--a charge supported by the 1959 Prescott Commission, which recommended against government recognition of its degrees. In the 1970s, with English increasingly recognized as the language of economic opportunity and Chinese required as a second language for students of Chinese ancestry, the university began including English-medium instruction. Faced with declining enrollments, it increasingly shared programs with the English-medium University of Singapore, and in 1980 they were formally merged into the National University of Singapore (NUS).

NATIONAL IDEOLOGY.   Statement of principles for the Singapore nation promulgated in 1991.   In 1988, the government announced the desirability of identifying values (q.v.) which distinguished Singapore from the West.   In 1991, the government formally announced the national ideology--a step taken by Brunei just shortly before, Malaysia about twenty years prior with its *Rukunegara*, and Indonesia in 1945 with its *Pancasila*. Like the latter, the government discovered five principles, which it described as "Shared Values" in a January 5, 1991, White Paper. The five are: 1) nation before community and society above self, 2) family as the basic unit of society, 3) regard and community support for the individual, 4) consensus instead of contention, and 5) racial and religious harmony.

NATIONAL SERVICE. Compulsory military service for all male Singaporeans, introduced in March 1967. All males are required to register before age eighteen and face twenty-four to thirty-six months of active duty followed by a mandatory reserve requirement to age forty (fifty for officers), which includes up to forty days of training annually. The requirement also applies to Singapore citizens living abroad and carries jail sentences for failure to register or serve. Evidence of registration is required for employment and for permission to study abroad.

NATIONAL TRADES UNION CONGRESS (NTUC). Association of trade unions in Singapore, affiliated with the noncommunist International Confederation of Free Trade Unions (ICFTU). The 1961 split in the People's Action Party (PAP) also divided the labor movement, dissolving the Singapore Trade Union Congress (SATU) (q.v.). Supporters of the *Barisan Sosialis* (q.v.) formed the Singapore Association of Trade Unions (q.v.) and supporters of the People's Action Party, led by C. V. Devan Nair (q.v.), formed the far smaller NTUC. The eclipse of the *Barisan* by 1965 was accompanied by a similar decline in SATU, as the NTUC represented the majority of unions in that year. Since, the NTUC has maintained close ties with the PAP and the government, leading most unions to affiliate with the NTUC. The close ties have assured labor a voice in policies but have largely reduced the unions to social organizations as governmental bodies such as the National Wages Council (q.v.) determine most working issues, such as wages and working conditions.

NATIONAL WAGES COUNCIL (NWC). Recommends national wage and benefit guidelines. Established in 1972 with representatives of the government, employers, and unions, its purpose is to pre-empt industrial action (e.g., strikes and slow-downs) by setting the limits of collective bargaining. It has been chaired by the respected academician and economist, Lim Chong-Yah, since 1972. Its recommendations are subject to government approval. In the 1980s it spearheaded the government's effort to discourage labor-intensive industry by dramatically raising wages as well as contributions to the Central Provident Fund (q.v.).

NAVAL BASE. Key British military installation in Asia. Located in Singapore on the Johore Straits, it was projected as the Asian bastion of the British Empire between the World Wars, as the "Gibraltar of the East." Singapore's location between the monsoons, which had made it a vital port for sailing ships, was of minor importance for steamships; however, such ships required having their hulls thoroughly cleaned every six months, preferably in dry dock, as well as other repair and maintenance services. For the empire (including Hong Kong, Australia and New Zealand, and India) and its fleet in the East in the twentieth century, Singapore afforded a central site for such services; moreover, it lay outside the area in which naval forces were restricted under the Washington Treaty (q.v.) of 1922. Initially begun in 1923, it became a political football between Conservative and Labour governments in Britain, with the former pushing for development and the latter stopping or reducing building when it was in power. As a result, it was not completed until 1941 but was seen as an impregnable fortress--making its ineffectiveness against a Japanese assault from the mainland a devastating shock for Britain. After World War II, the base emerged as a major employer and, with related installations, supported the massive British efforts to suppress the communists during the Emergency and guerrilla activities in Borneo as well as repelling Indonesian incursions during Confrontation. By 1967, Britain announced a decision to withdraw its forces from "East of Suez," eliminating more than forty thousand jobs directly and 15 percent of the gross national product derived from British military spending. By the time the withdrawal was completed in 1971, activist government economic plans more than offset the loss.

NETHERLANDS EAST INDIES (N.E.I.). Name for Indonesia under Dutch rule (from *Nederlandsch Indië*). First used in 1815, the term designated the Dutch possessions in Indonesia until after Indonesian independence. Dutch claims to Singapore as a tributary of Rhio were rejected by the East India Company (q.v.) and formally excluded in the Anglo-Dutch Treaty of 1824 (q.v.).

NON-ELECTED MEMBERS OF PARLIAMENT (NEMP). Appointed, non-voting members of Parliament representing opposition viewpoints. The complete control of Parliamentary seats from the mid-1960s through 1981 by the People's Action Party (PAP) (q.v.) prompted concerns about the absence of any opposition representations. The election of J. B. Jeyretnam (q.v.) in 1981 was attributed by PAP leadership to growing public concern, and subsequent protest vote, that alternative views should be heard. As result, before the 1984 election, a law was enacted which allowed the appointment of up to three members of Parliament from the opposition parties. While the appointed seats were given rights to speak, debate motions, and raise questions, they were denied voting privileges and thus were considered second-class seats. Those appointed as NCMP have included Francis Seow (q.v.), who was subsequently tried *in absentia*, found guilty, and disqualified from Parliament because of the fine received, and Dr. Lee Siew Choh (q.v.)--both after the 1988 election.

-O-

ONG ENG GUAN. First mayor of municipal council and People's Action Party (PAP) maverick. Born in Johore, he earned an Australian degree in accountancy, then was a founder of the PAP and the first party treasurer. In the 1957 municipal election, he was elected mayor and, in the name of populism, transformed the staid council into a circus-like atmosphere. In March 1959, the government assumed many of the council's functions, leading Ong and other PAP members to resign in protest. In the first PAP government, he became the Minister of National Development (which assumed the responsibilities of the municipal council as well as overseeing the Housing and Development Board [q.v.] and harbor board) and was named to the powerful Internal Security Council (q.v.). Continuing his disruptive tactics, he was stripped of most responsibilities within a few months. He was stripped of the ministry and expelled from the party when he openly criticized the party executive council, prompting him to resign his

Parliamentary seat--Hong Lim (q.v.). In the April 1961 by-election, he won easily by attacking the PAP and championing Chinese issues. In June 1961, he formed the United People's Party (UPP) (q.v.) which allied with the *Barisan Sosialis* (q.v.) in opposing Malaysia (q.v.). In the 1963 election he won the only UPP seat. In 1965, he again resigned but was beaten easily in a July by-election, ending his wild, brief prominence on the national scene.

ONG TENG CHEONG (1936-). Government leader--Deputy Prime Minister since 1984. Graduating from the Chinese High School in 1955, he earned a degree in architecture from the University of Adelaide and a master's degree in civic design from Liverpool. He was elected to Parliament in 1972 (Kim Keat constituency) and entered the cabinet in 1975. He became Minister of Communications in 1978, later adding Labour, succeeded Toh Chin Chye (q.v.) as Chairman of the PAP central executive committee in 1981, and was named Second Deputy Prime Minister in 1984. In the 1990 cabinet, he was made First Deputy Prime Minister. Following the 1991 election, he and Lee Hsien Loong (q.v.) were each identified simply Deputy Prime Minister.

OPERATION COLD STORE. Detention of supporters of Brunei rebels and other leftists. In February 1963, the Internal Security Council authorized the detention of more than one hundred student, labor, and political leaders, including half of the *Barisan* central executive committee. Riots which followed prompted further detentions of middle-level leaders.

OPIUM. Drug made from the sap of a poppy (*Papaver somniferum*) and major source of government funds in Singapore's first century. In the eighteenth century, the East India Company's (q.v.) conquest of Bengal gave it control of a large opium-producing area. The company would collect the sap, allow it to putrefy, and shape it into balls weighing approximately three pounds each. Forty balls were packed in a wood crate, called a chest--which became a standard measure in the trade. By selling the opium in China, the company was able to cover the cost of tea purchased there. Chinese edicts prohibiting the importation and consumption were largely ignored by country traders (q.v.) willing to smuggle it. Markets also existed in Southeast Asia, with Singapore serving as a distribution center in addition to that consumed locally. Local supply was provided by opium revenue farms (q.v.), payment for which often provided more than half of government income into the 1920s. A suggestion by the Governor, Sir John Anderson, that consumption be prohibited and revenue raised instead through an income tax met strong resistance from the Asian and European business communities. In 1910, the opium farm was discontinued and distribution was provided directly by the government. For the workers in Singapore and even more in the tin mines in Malaya, opium smoking provided a means of easing the pain and monotony of daily labor. In 1908, a government commission found considerable false mythology about opium, observing that it was generally consumed in moderate amounts--with *Baba* (q.v.) increasingly becoming consumers--but, like alcohol, was subject to abuse by a few. It estimated annual per capita consumption among the male Chinese population over age fifteen at one to nearly one-and-one-half pounds of raw opium between 1898 and 1907. Per capita consumption among the same population in the Malay States, where the price was half that in the Straits Settlements, was estimated at one-and-one-half to two pounds. Nearly all of the consumption was in the form of *chandu* (q.v.) or dross therefrom--which could be scraped from the pipes and resold to poorer consumers. In the twentieth century, leaders in the Chinese community increasingly sought to discourage consumption; however, employers as late as the 1930s argued that opium was necessary to attract and keep Chinese laborers. Consumption and sale were outlawed in 1946. In the 1960s and 1970s, domestic consumption of heroin (an opium derivative) grew, with estimates ranging from two thousand to thirteen thousand addicts in the mid-1970s. Moreover, it was a convenient trans-shipment point between the "golden triangle" (in Burma, Laos, and Thailand) and Europe. In 1975, a mandatory death penalty was introduced for importing or exporting more than fifteen grams of heroin or thirty grams of morphine. While this threat and tight inspections decreased trafficking, in 1981 the first European (a Dutch woman) was arrested with more than a pound of heroin.

ORANG LAUT. Literally, sea people--also called sea gypsies and sea nomads. It was used to refer to a number of different peoples living in Singapore in 1819, including the *Orang Laut* of Riau-Lingga such as *Orang Galang* and the *Orang Gelam*, *Orang Selatar*, and *Biduanda Orang Kallang*. The only commonality they shared was some degree of Malay ethnicity and a preference for living on boats rather than land. The *Biduanda Orang Kallang* are considered the indigenous people of Singapore, inhabiting the swamps near the outlet of the Kallang River. The *Orang Galang* were associated with a large and active pirate fleet preying throughout the archipelago.

ORD, COLONEL SIR HARRY ST. GEORGE (1819-1885). First Governor of Straits Settlements (q.v.) as a colony, 1867-1873. Coming from West Africa to assume the new governorship, he faced a daunting task of reorganizing an administration which had deteriorated in the later years under the East India Company (q.v.). He was successful in increasing the honesty and efficiency of the government but alienated many of the most influential British residents by his manner as much as his policies. His other reform efforts, such as attempted reform of the coolie trade, were less successful. His reorganization was complemented by the opening of the Suez Canal in 1869 which saw trade grow 50 percent during his tenure and eliminated the government deficit.

OVERSEAS CHINESE ASSOCIATION (INDIA). Organization to advance interests of Malayan and Singapore Chinese who were refugees in India. Led by Tan Cheng Lock (q.v.) as president, Tan Chin Tuan (q.v.) as vice president, and Tan Siew Sin (Tan Cheng Lock's son and later president of the Malayan Chinese Association) as secretary, the organization was composed of members who broke with the Malayan Association of India in 1943. Its members unsuccessfully campaigned for a union of the Malay States and the Straits Settlements.

OVERSEAS CHINESE ASSOCIATION (*SYONAN*). Organization formed on Japanese initiative to exploit Chinese resources during World War II. With the reluctant leadership of Lim Boon Keng (q.v.), it arranged the release of Chinese business leaders shortly after the invasion. In return, the Japanese demanded that it make a gift of S$10 million to help Japan meet its expenses. It helped mediate between the Japanese occupiers and the Chinese community in an attempt to mitigate violence against the latter. As scarcities mounted in Singapore, with Japanese approval in 1944, it established an agricultural settlement at Endau, Johore, which accommodated about 12,000 Chinese, mostly Singaporeans, until the end of the war.

-P-

PAN-MALAYAN COUNCIL OF JOINT ACTION (PMCJA). Umbrella organization to oppose recommendations of the Anglo-Malay Working Committee (formally designated the Constitutional Working Committee of Twelve). With the uproar provoked by the precipitous adoption of the Malayan Union (q.v.), the Anglo-Malay Working Committee (including representatives of the colonial government, the Sultans of the Malay States [q.v.], and the United Malays National Organisation) met to address Malay concerns. Non-Malays feared its recommendations would reduce the rights of non-Malays and, led by Tan Cheng Lock (q.v.), formed a united front to counter them in December 1946. Initially a largely Straits Settlements (q.v.) organization called the Council of Joint Action, within a week, it was expanded and renamed. In August 1946, it was renamed the All-Malayan Council of Joint Action (AMCJA) (q.v.), because of Singapore Chinese Chamber of Commerce (q.v.) concerns that "Pan-Malayan" was a communist term. Membership in both organizations was a combination of chambers of commerce and communist-leaning, if not outright communist, labor unions.

PAN-MALAYAN FEDERATION OF TRADE UNIONS (PMFTU). Confederation of unions after World War II. Inaugurated on February 15, 1946, it was formed by General Labour Unions of Singapore and Malaya, with two parts: one for the mainland and the Singapore Federation of Trade Unions. Claiming 450,000 members, it was linked with the communists and dissolved when legislation in 1948 required that union officers have worked in the industry represented by the union and that federations be limited to related industries.

PARLIAMENT. Legislative body of the Republic of Singapore since 1965. With independence from Malaysia, the Legislative Assembly (q.v.) was renamed the Parliament. It is a unicameral (single house) system which must be reelected at least once each five years, or sooner at the discretion of the government and the president. It is presided over by a speaker, who is usually a member. The prime minister and ministers are appointed by the president, on the advice of the leader of the Parliamentary party enjoying the confidence of the majority. Its size has grown from 51 seats when it was created from the Legislative Assembly to 81 seats in the 1988 election and maintained at that level in the 1991 election.

PENANG (PINANG). Familiar name for the East India Company (q.v.) settlement in the Malay archipelago and the present Malaysian state of Pinang. The name is derived from the Malay *pulau pinang*--Island of the *pinang* (the areca palm). Established in 1786 by Francis Light (under a lease from the Sultan of Kedah) as a British base on the

Straits of Malacca to serve and protect shipping between Calcutta and Canton, it was the first component of the later Straits Settlements (q.v.). It was officially named Prince of Wales Island (in honor of the man who later became George IV) and its capital, Georgetown (in honor of the reigning George III). In 1800, the neighboring territory on the mainland was acquired from the Sultan of Kedah and added to the settlement as Province Wellesley. In 1805, it was raised to presidency status under the company. As a result of the war with France (which had conquered the Netherlands), the British seized Malacca (q.v.) in 1895 and administered it under Penang. At the time of Singapore's founding, the Penang administration and traders clearly saw the new settlement as a threat to Penang's primacy and campaigned unsuccessfully to have the company renounce Raffles's initiative. In 1826, to rationalize its settlements on the Straits of Malacca, the company combined Penang, Malacca, and Singapore to form the Straits Settlements as a presidency, reduced in 1830 to status of a residency under the Bengal presidency as an economy move. The combining of the three states was continued under the Colonial Office in 1867 until the formation of the Malayan Union (q.v.) in 1946, in which Malacca and Penang were incorporated with the Malay States (q.v.). This arrangement was carried forward in the 1948 Federation of Malaya (and subsequently Malaysia). Like Singapore, Penang was highly dependent on Chinese migrant workers and traders from its early years. Although it was unable to compete with Singapore, it remains one of the most Chinese cities in Malaysia.

PENINSULAR MALAYSIA. Term referring to the Malaysian states on the mainland of Asia. These are the states which formed the Federation of Malaya (q.v.). The remaining states in Malaysia, Sabah and Sarawak on the island of Borneo, are referred to as East Malaysia.

PEOPLE'S ACTION PARTY (PAP). Ruling political party in Singapore since 1959. Formed on November 21, 1954, the party was a coalition of young English- and England-educated intellectuals with leftist labor leaders, many of whom were communists or communist-sympathizers, dedicated to independence and socialism. Most notably, it brought together English-educated and Chinese-educated radicals. Toh Chin Chye (q.v.) was elected as the first chairman and Lee Kuan Yew (q.v.) as the secretary-general. In the 1955 election, it won three of four seats it contested and was widely seen as the most radical of the legal political parties but participated in the 1956 and 1957 all-party constitutional missions (q.v.) to London, which negotiated internal self-rule. Its early years were characterized by constant struggles between Lee's English-educated group and the intellectuals and Chinese-educated who were linked with the communists, called "Middle Roaders" (q.v.). None stood in the 1955 party election, but four were elected to the central executive committee (CEC) in 1956, including Lim Chin Siong (q.v.) who received the greatest number of votes. The 1957 party election was an open contest as the extremists attacked Lee's participation in the London talks. Lee and Toh Chin Chye resigned from the leadership, stripping the CEC of any veneer of moderation. Five of the newly elected CEC members and a number of other party officials were detained by the Lim Yew Hock (q.v.) government, convincing the left that the moderates were needed to shield their activities. Lee and Toh returned to office but extended the term to two years and restricted the voting for leadership through a cadre system (preventing packing party conferences). In the 1957 city council election, it won thirteen of fourteen seats contested. With the left mobilizing the masses, it won forty-three of the fifty-one seats in the 1959 election of a semi-independent Legislative Assembly (q.v.). Faced with a limited ability to control policy within the party, communists threw support in by-elections to dissidents such as Ong Eng Guan (q.v.) and David Marshall's (q.v.) Workers' Party (q.v.), producing embarrassing by-election defeats for the moderate party leadership. In 1961, the party split into two as the leftists unsuccessfully tried to oust Lee from leadership (using merger with Malaya as the issue), leaving the left faction to form the *Barisan Sosialis* (q.v.) as an opposition party. Although freed of internal opposition, the PAP also lost its grassroots organizers. In response, it established Citizens' Consultative Committees (q.v.) to force party leaders into greater contact with the populace and provide open communications channels for grievances. With the merger into Malaysia in 1963, the party assumed that it would join the ruling Alliance but was rebuffed by the Alliance-member Malayan Chinese Association, which rejected legitimating a rival for its Chinese constituency. As a result, the PAP formed branches in Peninsular Malaysia (q.v.) and contested the 1964 national election as a friendly opposition party. Despite enthusiastic receptions for the party leadership, the PAP won only one of eleven seats contested. With the 1965 separation, the Malaysian branches were separated to become the Democratic Action Party. Given its electoral dominance after separation, the PAP has become an instrument for recruiting and testing future leaders and for communication with constituents. While retaining the same leadership, the party evolved from a radical mass party to an elite organization and just one of many government communications channels.

PEOPLE'S ASSOCIATION (PA). Statutory board for community development. Formed by the government on July 1, 1960, the People's Association was intended as a means of reaching the grassroots and of skirting communist control of much of the People's Action Party (PAP) (q.v.) local party machinery. Following the mid-1962 PAP split, they were called on to provide basic education and recreational facilities, organize neighborhood social activity, combat communism, and increase loyalty to the government. By the 1963 legislative election, 130 PA community centers were built and 180 by 1965. While PA activities spread throughout the state, emphasis was given to areas of greatest *Barisan Sosialis* (q.v.) strength. The PA community centers were the positive side of the policy to erode communist influence by providing alternatives to traditional communist children's and youth activities. The negative side was represented the state security apparatus and the Internal Security Act (q.v.). In the 1980s and 1990s, the community centers extended beyond recreation to offer opportunities for developing new skills as well as day care and kindergartens.

PERANAKAN. Malay, literally "child of" or "native" but used before World War II for a non-Malay born in Malaya or Singapore who speaks Malay and follows some Malay customs. When used as a single noun, it usually refers to Straits-born Chinese. (In Indonesia, it refers to Indonesian-born Chinese.) With an ethnic modifier, it refers to non-Chinese non-Malays. *Peranakan Keling* (or *Kling*) identifies Muslim Indians, especially in Malacca, resident in the Straits for a number of generations. *Jawi Peranakan* also refers to Indian Muslims. *Peranakan* implies, even if not provable, that those described are of mixed race, usually by marriage with Malay women. See also *BABA*.

PERCIVAL, LIEUTENANT-GENERAL ARTHUR (1887-1966). General officer commanding in Malaya, May 1941-1945. A common misconception is that Singapore and Malaya fell so quickly to the Japanese invasion because they hadn't expected an invasion down the peninsula, but, in 1937, Percival--serving as a senior staff officer--described such an attack. When he returned in 1941, he was responsible for preventing it, but, faced with an absence of urgency, he frequently was thwarted by higher-ups in London and constant changes in command in Singapore. After the fall of Malaya, he was told to hold Singapore at any cost; however, the futility became evident. Barely more than two weeks after the evacuation of Malaya, he, with British Prime Minister Winston Churchill's permission, surrendered to General Yamashita (q.v.) and became a prisoner of war. Ironically, after release, he was in the Philippines and present at General Yamashita's surrender. "Who lost Singapore?" was a perennial argument, and he was often targeted as scapegoat.

PICKERING, WILLIAM (1840-1907). First Protector of the Chinese (1877-1888). He served in China and Taiwan for eight years before being invited by Sir Harry Ord (q.v.) to come to the Straits Settlements (q.v.) in 1872 as an interpreter. He was the only European official who could read and write Chinese. He discovered that the courts which relied on Chinese translators had been corrupted and mocked. In 1877, the Chinese Protectorate (q.v.) was established under his leadership, primarily to control the coolie trade (q.v.). Because of their heavy involvement, this eventually led to the control and suppression of secret societies (q.v.). Pickering argued against the latter course as ineffective because the societies would continue, but without government control. In 1887, he was attacked by an axe-wielding Teochew carpenter believed to be associated with the secret societies, leaving wounds which forced his retirement in 1888.

PILLAI, NARAYANA. First Indian settler of Singapore. He was a clerk in Penang who accompanied Raffles (q.v.) when he returned to Singapore in June 1819; however, when Raffles left soon afterward, he was left stranded. He temporarily served as "schroff" (chief clerk) to the treasury but was replaced soon afterward when Farquhar's schroff came from Malacca. Faced with the need to construct his own house, he asked friends in Penang to send some construction workers. He also started a brick kiln to meet the demands for building materials in the new settlement. He opened a cloth shop which grew to one of the largest retail establishments in the colony. As Indians increasingly moved to Singapore, he joined with other Indian leaders to establish a council to look after Indian affairs.

PINYIN. Fully *hanyu pinyin*; literally, Chinese spelling. The reformed system of romanization of Chinese characters in Mandarin (*putonghua*) adopted by the People's Republic of China and accepted as the standard in Singapore. Taiwan continues to use the older Wade-Giles romanization system.

PIRACY. Term applied by those claiming authority over an area to sea attacks by those who do not recognize that control. Since the increasing European presence in the eighteenth century, it was a recurrent theme in the area's history until late in the nineteenth century. Prior to the European presence, maritime empires and oversight from China facilitated trade in the region. The colonial empires claimed monopolies and disrupted traditional trading patterns for the purpose of enriching the colonial home, with little concern for those living in the region. They, further, claimed the right to attack any ship believed violating their restrictions, to confiscate the goods thereon, and to imprison the crew--evidenced in the British Navy's capture of the United States (q.v.) ship *Governor Endicott*. The colonial powers disrupted traditional trade, leaving seafarers to fall back on the historical legitimacy of privateering. Maritime empires would contract with *orang laut* (q.v.), Bugis (q.v.) or others with substantial fleets to provide naval and shipping resources for the realm. Seafaring peoples turned to the practice of attacking any ship unable to defend itself, taking the cargo, and enslaving the crew. Rather than see the symmetry, this prompted colonial powers to make restrictions more rigid. At the time Raffles (q.v.) landed in Singapore, many have contended that its population consisted nearly entirely of pirates operating on the fringe of Dutch control. Through the first half of the nineteenth century, several trading or disabled ships each year were attacked near Singapore. The British increasingly were able to control this as steam power provided them a decided edge. While piracy was gradually eradicated, sporadic attacks on ships in the South China Sea continued down to the 1980s.

POST OFFICE RIOTS (1876). Protest against government attempt to regularize remittances to China. Overseas Chinese regularly would send money to their families back in China. Up to 1876, remittances and letters had been handled by letter-shops who had treated them as cargo. They were shipped to agents in the port cities who, through sub-agents, arranged deliveries. The system offered many opportunities for currency manipulation and theft while affording the sender little protection. The government sought to assure proper handling by creating sub-post offices at which a sender would pay a fixed fee and have the letters delivered either by the government postal system or agents of the letter-shops. Just before the reform was implemented, a rumor spread that *Babas* (q.v.) from Penang would control the system and that the Teochew (q.v.) letter shops would lose out. When the first sub-post office opened on December 15, rioters attacked it and then a police station--resulting in some rioters being shot. A number of Teochew letter-shop owners plus the leaders of the Teochew *Ghee Hin* and the *Hai San* secret societies were implicated. The *Ghee Hin* leader was banished and the shop keepers placed aboard ship but, after posting one-thousand-dollar peace bonds, they were allowed to return. Three days later, the new sub-post offices opened without incident.

PRESIDENT. Head of state of the Republic of Singapore. With the 1965 separation of Singapore from Malaysia, the state's ruler--who had previously been identified as the *Yang di-Pertua Negara*--was redesignated as the President of the Republic of Singapore. The official powers have been largely ceremonial; however, they included such pro forma powers as the power to appoint the prime minister, dissolve Parliament, and ratify bills passed by Parliament. Based on discussions which began in the cabinet as early as 1982, a government white paper was issued in 1988 proposing an elected president and vice president with expanded powers, including a veto power over policies which would deplete the nation's financial reserves and over some appointments to high level public positions. As approved in 1990, a potential candidate will have to demonstrate past ministerial or executive experience to an impartial screening body to qualify as a candidate. The first election is planned at the end of President Wee Kim Wee's second four-year term in 1993.

PRESIDENTIAL COUNCIL. Advisory body to the president, 1970-1973. Created in 1969, it was composed of prominent political leaders and citizens, including a number of serving ministers and permanent secretaries. It was intended to advise the president on accepting bills passed by Parliament. A majority of its members present could require that a bill be reconsidered and approved by a two-thirds margin. Early, the government decided to limit the ability of the council to review bills on internal security and defense. Initial appointees included C. C. Tan (q.v.), Francis Thomas (q.v.), and David Marshall (q.v.), with the latter resigning after seven months to protest the council's closed discussions and limited powers. Since the People's Action Party controlled all of the Parliamentary seats, requiring a two-thirds vote meant little. In 1973, the council was reorganized as a smaller body and redesignated the Presidential Council for Minority Rights. Its new responsibilities were to analyze legislation and to identify any laws that appeared harmful to any ethnic group.

PRIVATIZATION. Transfer of public functions to private ownership. To reduce government expenses and presumably increase efficiency, the Singapore government has sought to sell shares in previously government-owned companies to private investors. The most successful divestment was Singapore Airlines (SIA). In the 1990s, the government plans to privatize telecommunications.

PROGRESSIVE PARTY (PP). First local party to win elected seats in Legislative Council (q.v.). Formed in August 1947 to compete in the election, the party leadership were western-educated lawyers. It enjoyed the support of the Straits Chinese British Association (q.v.). The founders were C. C. Tan (q.v.) as first Chairman, John Laycock, and N.A. Mallal. It won three of six seats (the others going to independents) in the 1948 election and six of nine seats in the 1951 election, but only four of twenty-five in the 1955 election. In the next year, it combined with the Democratic Party (q.v.) to form the Liberal

Socialist Party (q.v.), which won no seats in the 1959 election.

PULAU. Malay word for island. In Malay, it precedes the island name, such as Pulau Senang, Pulau Singapura (Singapore) or Pulau Pinang (Penang).

PULAU SENANG UPRISING (1963). Experiment in rehabilitation of secret society members which ended in a massacre. With a name that translates "island of ease," it was the site of a prison without walls for detained secret society members established in 1960. Under prison officer David Stanley Dutton, the scheme was to prepare detainees to return to society by teaching them hard work and proper behavior. Guards did not have guns and were ill-equipped to resist prisoners who attacked them with *cangkol*s (heavy, broad-bladed hoes) and *parang*s (machetes), July 12, 1963. A riot squad rushed to the island and suppressed the rioters within an hour but not before Dutton and three staff were killed. Charges were brought against 59 prisoners, of whom eighteen were convicted of murder and 29 of rioting. The eighteen were hanged October 29, 1965.

PUTHUCHEARY, JAMES J. (1924?-). Non-communist leftist intellectual and organizer in 1950s, of Keralan (Indian) ancestry. During World War II, he served in Burma in the Indian National Army (q.v.). He was first detained in 1951 for being a member of the Anti-British League (ABL) (q.v.) and, with Abdullah (Dollah) Majid, gained early release by confessing and renouncing it--leading to their expulsion from the ABL. Returning to school, they founded the University of Malaya Socialist Club (q.v.). In 1954, he chaired the editorial board of the club's publication, *Fajar*. He and other board members were arrested for publishing subversion in attacking the formation of the Southeast Asia Treaty Organization and calling Malaya a police state. Lee Kuan Yew (q.v.), the club's legal advisor, assisted D. N. Pritt in getting them acquitted. He also helped produce the communist organ, *Malayan*

Orchid. In the mid-1950s, he was involved in the discussions leading to the founding of the People's Action Party (PAP) and worked as a paid assistant secretary for the Singapore Factory and Shop Workers Union. In 1956, he was again detained for involvement in the Chinese schools strikes and released with other leftists before the PAP would consent to take power in June 1959. During his 1950s detentions, he wrote the seminal early study of the colonial economy, *Ownership and Control of the Malayan Economy* (see "Trade and Industry" section under "Economy" in the Bibliography). After release, he was active in the PAP and participated in the Eden Hall (q.v.) meeting to oust Lee Kuan Yew. He joined the *Barisan Sosialis* (q.v.) after the split and was again detained in Operation Cold Store (q.v.). After release, he retired from politics and moved to Malaysia, where he practiced law. Only in 1991 was he allowed to enter Singapore.

-R-

RAFFLES, SIR THOMAS STAMFORD (1781-1826). Founder of modern Singapore in 1819. Born at sea near Jamaica in the West Indies, he grew up in England and at fourteen joined the East India Company as a minor clerk. Ten years later, he was appointed assistant secretary to the Governor of Penang. In 1811, he joined in preparations for the invasion of Java and, after its capture from French-led Dutch forces, was named Lieutenant Governor of Java. He instituted a number of reforms but with the end of the Napoleonic Wars, it was returned to the Dutch in 1816. In 1818, he was made Lieutenant Governor of Bencoolen (q.v.) on Sumatra. In 1819, accompanied by William Farquhar (q.v.), he landed at the mouth of the Singapore River and negotiated an agreement for a British factory with Temenggong Abdul Rahman (q.v.). Although he spent little time in the settlement, October 1822 - June 1823 being the longest stretch, he defined its direction as a free port committed to liberal principles, clearly established in his 1823 proclamation. In it he recognized that the settlement would be predominantly Chinese (he estimated it would become over 90 percent) and tried to identify what he called "first principles." Included were protection of the property and liberty of the individual with the assurance of justice, "so that legal and moral obligation may never be at variance." He discussed problems such as intoxication and prostitution but determined that since they could not be eliminated, they were better controlled than outlawed. Overall, the vision was grander than the realization, but both were beyond his control as he left Singapore for the last time and returned to Bencoolen. On the eve of the cession of Bencoolen to the Dutch in 1824, he sailed for England. Unfortunately for historians, the ship caught fire and the hundreds of unique historic manuscripts, natural history collections, and notes that he had amassed during twenty years in the Indies were lost. Beyond founding Singapore, he is remembered for his massive study, *History of Java* (1817), and his name was given to the world's largest "flower," the Rafflesia, which produces blossoms three feet in diameter.

RAFFLES COLLEGE. Post-secondary school, 1921-1949. Faced with a proposal from the American Methodist Mission to open the colony's post-secondary college, British colonial authorities responded by establishing Raffles College in 1921; however, no students were enrolled until 1928. Featuring a curious blend of civil servants as instructors and administrators, the college offered a liberal arts course to which was added an economics course in 1933, which would enable students to sit for external degrees from the University of London. There was demand for affiliation with a British university, a step prevented by the outbreak of World War II. In 1947 a commission recommended that there was no need to be a college of a British university but that the Raffles College and the Medical College should be combined to create a University of Malaya. This was effected in 1949.

RAFFLES HOTEL. Archetype of colonial life. Opened in 1899, the Raffles has been featured in literature and history. In the 1930s it was a center of European social life in the colony and it continued to offer dancing nightly through the Japanese attack in January 1942. In the 1980s, an order assuring its preservation for another century was issued; however, despite renovations, it is now overshadowed by the high-rise Raffles City hotel, shopping, and office complex.

RAFFLES INSTITUTION. Leading and oldest secondary school. In 1823, Raffles selected a site for a school to educate the sons of native elite and others; however, formal launching had to wait a further eleven years. Classes were offered in English, Chinese, Malay, and Tamil. The latter was discontinued in 1836; Chinese (Hokkien and Teochew dialects) was dropped in 1841 and Malay in 1842. By 1844, enrollment had grown to 195 boys, and a separate Raffles Girls' School was started. Later some support was received from the East India Company (q.v.), but the institution remained under a private board of trustees until 1903, when it was absorbed as a government school. Through most of its history, it was a multi-ethnic school providing the elite with an English education, and its graduates (old Rafflesians or "old boys" in British parlance) have figured prominently in independent Singapore, including three of the four presidents and both prime ministers.

RAJAH, T. T. Temporarily replaced Lee Kuan Yew (q.v.) as Secretary-General of the People's Action Party in 1957. He was a pretentious Ceylonese lawyer who worked closely with leftist trade unions. In the showdown between the left and moderate wings of the PAP in August 1957, the left planned to seize control of the party executive committee while retaining a moderate leadership, including Lee Kuan Yew and Toh Chin Chye (q.v.) as a veneer. The stacked ballot ended up in an equal division between the moderates and the left. Lee and his colleagues refused to serve. With the visible split, the Lim Yew Hock (q.v.) Labour Front (q.v.) government detained five of the six leftist committee members, except Rajah, on August 22. Lest he appear to have betrayed his comrades, he resigned within days, for health reasons. He was arrested in 1963 when he tried to post bail for persons detained under Operation Cold Store (q.v.) and again briefly in the 1976 suppression of the Malayan New Democratic Youth League (q.v.).

RAJARATNAM, S[INNATHAMBY]. (1915-). Foremost People's Action Party (PAP) spokesman. Born in Ceylon and raised in Malaya, where his father worked on a rubber plantation in Negri Sembilan, he was educated at Raffles Institution and the University of London. He became associate editor of the *Singapore Standard,* and president of the Singapore Union of Journalists prior to joining in founding the PAP. In 1959, he left the *Straits Times* to become Minister of Culture, where he served as primary government spokesman. From 1965 through 1980, he was Minister of Foreign Affairs and, in 1980, was named Second Deputy Prime Minister, with responsibilities for foreign affairs. In 1988, he retired from politics but remained outspoken in political affairs, usually defending the government but also criticizing Lee Kuan Yew's (q.v.) emphasis on Chinese language and culture late in the 1980s.

READ, W[ILLIAM] H[ENRY] [MACLEOD] (1818-1907). Prominent businessman and public figure for more than forty-five years in the nineteenth century. Son of C. R. (Christopher Rideout) Read, who came to Singapore in 1822 from Bencoolen at Raffles's invitation, he took his retired father's place in a partnership in A. L. Johnston and Company in 1841. He was active in public affairs, a frequent submitter of letters to the newspapers, and even Dutch Consul for nearly thirty years--receiving knighthood from the Dutch government. He was the first "unofficial" (non-government servant) member of the Legislative Council after transfer to the Colonial Office in 1867. In 1887, he retired to England.

RENDEL, SIR GEORGE (1889-1979). Chairman, Commission
on Constitutional Development in Singapore, 1953-1954.
After graduating from Oxford, he entered the diplomatic
corps and worked extensively with refugee issues. After
retiring in 1950, he was invited back to undertake special
tasks and negotiations, which included drafting a transi-
tional constitution for greater self-government in Singapore. The constitution substantially revised the Legislative Assembly (q.v.) and the electoral franchise but was
sufficiently vague as to allow interpretation and negotiations during its life. His name usually is linked with both
the commission and the constitution.

RENDEL COMMISSION. Created the constitution implemented in 1955. In 1953, Sir George Rendel (q.v.) was appointed to head a commission to review the constitution
of the colony. Members included representatives of the
Chinese, Malay, and Indian communities as well as a
European and the attorney-general and president of the
city council. It called for a separate city government and
a central government with a single Legislative Assembly
composed of 25 elected members, three ex-officio members, and four nominated members. The British accepted
the commission's recommendations for a central government and the April 1955 election were to implement its
provisions.

RHIO-LINGGA ISLANDS. Island groups (archipelagos) south
of Singapore, incorporated into the Netherlands East
Indies in the late eighteenth century and then into Indonesia. For historical importance, see JOHORE KING-
DOM.

RIDLEY, HENRY (1855-1956). Director of the Singapore
Botanic Gardens and "father" of the rubber industry.
Rubber seeds were collected in the Amazon in an 1876
expedition and sent to Kew Gardens, from which three
thousand were sent to Ceylon, and from there twenty-two
plants arrived in Singapore in 1877. There was some
experimentation with the plants, which accelerated when

Ridley was named director of the Gardens in 1888--a post he held until 1911. He began research on rubber the following year, making his most important discovery in 1895--a means of tapping which did not seriously damage the trees. This made plantations practical, and his evangelism for the crop--coupled with a sharp increase in demand as the auto industry developed--made rubber key to the twentieth century prosperity of Malaya and Singapore.

RIAU. State in Indonesia consisting of the islands south and west of Singapore. It was transliterated Rhio by the British and Riouw by the Dutch.

RUBBER. Product from congealing and processing tree sap. Introduced into the Straits Settlements (q.v.) and the Malay States (q.v.) late in the nineteenth century and promoted by Henry Ridley (q.v.), it grew to become Malaya's largest export commodity, for which Singapore was a major processing and market center. Singapore also processed and marketed crude rubber from Sumatra. Spurred by demand for rubber for automobile tires, exports grew rapidly--from 522 tons in 1912 to 31,003 tons in 1918. With independence, both Indonesia and Malaysia (earlier Malaya) increasingly sought to process and directly export their own production rather than depend on Singapore. By the 1980s, rubber processing produced less than three percent of exports.

-S-

SAMSUI WOMEN. Cantonese female construction workers. In nineteenth and twentieth century Kwangtung, substantial numbers of women (q.v.) took vows to abstain from marriage and formed sisterhoods. The vows were often made in a sor hei ceremony (Cantonese, meaning to comb up the hair in the fashion of married women), which was a declaration of independence from one's family. Many women from these sisterhoods migrated to Southeast Asia. A good portion sought employment as amahs (domestic servants). In Singapore, those desiring work in road and other construction industries were known as *Samsui* women (after their origin in Sanshui district). In the second half of the twentieth century, they were a striking sight, each carrying a pole on her shoulder with a basket of dirt or rock suspended each end, and engaging in heavy construction.

SANG NILA UTAMA. Formal name for Sri Tri Buana (q.v.), quasi-mythical founder of Singapore.

SEAH EU CHIN (1805-1883). Early Teochew (q.v.) settler and leading merchant. Coming to Singapore from Swatow in 1823, he became engaged in indigenous trade but by the mid-1930s had accumulated sufficient wealth to buy large tracts of land for agriculture and to become active in the pepper and gambier trade. His close ties with the Europeans helped him market local products, especially pepper and gambier, to Europe. He was respected by the European community, a contributor of articles on the Chinese to Logan's *Journal*, and one of the first Chinese to be named a justice of the peace (JP). He married the daughter of the senior Chinese official (Captain China) of Perak--making the opium and spirit farmer Tan Seng Poh his brother-in-law--and, following her death, her younger sister. His sons, Seah Song Seah and Seah Pek Seah, also served as leaders of an opium farm syndicate.

SECRET SOCIETIES. Also called triads or the Hung League-- referring primarily to the Heaven and Earth Society--as well as individual names. Predominantly Chinese organizations intended to resist political oppression but degenerating into gangster brotherhoods comparable to the Mafia in the West. The secrecy referred to is in the rituals rather than membership or the society itself (a trait shared with Freemasonry). China had a tradition of wandering gangs which would avenge injustice and rob from the rich to give to the poor, which are believed to be the beginnings of the secret societies. As formal organizations, they date from at least the mid-thirteenth century but increased in importance as means of resisting the foreign Manchu (*Ch'ing*; *pinyin*: *Qing*) Dynasty, 1644-1911, especially in the south, the homeland of most Singapore Chinese. They are first mentioned in Singapore in the mid-1820s as consisting of thousands of plantation operators and bandits living in the interior of the island, identified as the *T'in Tei Wui*. This society was later known as the *Ghee Hin* Society and figured in the first secret society riot in 1846 against the rival *Kuan Tec Hoey* as well as the Anti-Catholic riots in 1851. The 1854 Hokkien-Teochew riots were also intensified by the massive influx of refugees arising from the abortive "small sword" rebellion in Amoy, which provided new secret society armies. A new Teochew society, the *Ghee Hok*, emerged as the largest and most criminally inclined. During the nineteenth century, the secret societies were linked closely with the revenue farms (both with holders and competitors), involved in much of the migration, especially the coolie trade, and the pervasive illegal gambling. Like the Mafia, the secret societies were also subject to internal conflicts, often triggered between dialect groups. Outlawing the societies in the 1890s reduced the visibility of the societies but did not eliminate them. Banishment proved the most effective means of dealing with society leaders. In the twentieth century, the societies were used as facades for gangster gangs which engaged in robbery, gambling, protection, prostitution, kidnapping rich Chinese for ransom, illegal opium, and fighting each other--earning Singapore the reputation as the Chicago of the East in the 1920s. After World War II, they increasingly were involved with the political struggle as well. An international society, the *Hung Mun Chi Kung Tong*, supported in Singapore by the Chinese Consul and the *Kuomintang* (q.v.), tried to capitalize on the societies and turn them from crime to anti-communism, attempting to register as a political party while retaining secret society rituals. Mass arrests in 1950 and 1951 revealed many secret society members were also members of the communist-front Anti-British League (q.v.). The secret societies were active in the riots of the mid-1950s, but it is unclear whether this was sympathy with the leftist aims or simply opportunism. When the PAP came to power in 1959, it made gang eradication a high priority. An attempt at rehabilitation ended in failure in 1963 when a riot in a camp destroyed the camp at Pulau Senang and killed the superintendent. The government blamed secret societies for involvement in the racial riots of July and September 1964 and claimed that Indonesia had trained some secret society members to foment disorder and engage in sabotage. Since the 1970s, the societies have been suppressed, if not fully eliminated.

SEET AI MEE (1943-) . First female member of cabinet, 1991. Born in Malacca, she earned advanced degrees in clinical biochemistry and operated her own medical laboratory. In 1988, she became the third woman in the nation's history to be elected to Parliament and, in the July 1991 cabinet reorganization, was named Acting Minister for Community Development. In the 1991 election, she narrowly lost to Ling How Doong of the Singapore Democratic Party, thereby becoming the first cabinet member to lose a parliamentary seat since independence.

SEH (XING). Chinese family name; derivatively, a family-name organization. For example, the Tan Seh or Chua Seh would refer to the mutual support organization of people with the surname Tan or the surname Chua.

SEOW, FRANCIS (1928-). Lawyer and past president of the Singapore Law Society and former solicitor general. He was elected president of the Law Society in 1985; however, when it was critical of government policies on human rights, he came under close government scrutiny. After the society criticized proposed restrictions on foreign news publications in 1986, he was asked to submit tax information for the previous twelve years. His accountants withdrew their representation of him and his bank withdrew his overdraft credits. When he sought financial assistance from his fiance, a Malaysian who had resided in Singapore for ten years, her entry permit was revoked, and she was prohibited from entering Singapore. In May 1988, he was detained and put through an extended interrogation. This was after the American diplomat Mason Hendrickson was expelled for what the government described as encouraging lawyers to run as opposition candidates. The implication was also made that the Americans had paid Seow to cover his debts. In July, he was released and then charged with tax evasion in August. Prior to his scheduled trial, he was given permission to go to the U.S. for medical treatment and human rights hearings. When his return was delayed, he was tried in absentia, convicted, and fined. He had been selected as a non-constituency member of Parliament after the 1988 election, but the fine levied disqualified him from serving. He has remained in the U.S. since the verdict, fearing arrest on return, but has been watched by hired detectives.

SHARMA, P. V. Communist and labor leader. As general secretary of the Singapore Teachers Union after World War II, he recruited future president C. V. Devan Nair (q.v.) into the Anti-British League (ABL) (q.v.). Before World War II, he was active in organizing dock workers and after, was on the executive committee of the Malayan Democratic Union (MDU) (q.v.) from 1946. He helped organize the Singapore Teachers' Union (STU) and pushed its support for the MDU as well as its membership in the Federation of Government and Municipal Servants Unions. He was one of the ABL leaders detained in 1951 and was the party organizer among detainees. After release, he was repatriated to India in 1953 but then went on to China, where he became a representative of the Malayan National Liberation League (q.v.).

SHEARES, DR. BENJAMIN HENRY (1907-1981). Prominent People's Action Party (PAP) leader and President of Singapore, 1970-1981. After an education at Raffles

Institution and a medical degree from the King Edward VII College of Medicine in Singapore, he received a Queen's Fellowship but was unable to use it because of World War II. In 1951-1952, he used the fellowship to observe medical practice in the U.S. While serving as a professor of obstetrics and gynecology at King Edward VII College and the University of Malaya in Singapore, he developed a gynecological operation which was adopted internationally and bears his name. He was active in the PAP, serving two terms as a member of Parliament prior to becoming president, and he was a close associate of Lee Kuan Yew (q.v.).

SIAM. Historic name for present-day Kingdom of Thailand. It refers to Thai regimes prior to 1939, including the Kingdom of Ayudhya (also spelled Ayutthaya; 1351-1767). The country briefly was again called Siam between 1946 and 1949. For a period in the fifteenth century, Singapore and the early Sultanate of Malacca (q.v.) were tributaries of Ayudhya. In the eighteenth century, the threat posed by Siam encouraged the Sultan of Kedah to lease Penang to Francis Light, acting on behalf of the East India Company (q.v.).

SINGAPORE ALLIANCE. Opposition coalition formed to contest 1963 election. Lim Yew Hock's (q.v.) Singapore People's Alliance (q.v.) joined with the Singapore branches of the United Malays National Organisation (UMNO), the Malayan Chinese Association (MCA), and Malayan Indian Congress (MIC), replicating the Alliance in Malaya. It won only 8.4% of the popular vote and failed to win a seat. Following that defeat, it reorganized as the Alliance Party Singapura (q.v.).

SINGAPORE ASSOCIATION OF TRADE UNIONS (SATU). Short-lived leftist labor union federation. The acronym SATU literally means "one," signifying unity in Malay. With the 1961 split in the People's Action Party (PAP), the Middle Roaders (q.v.) who joined the Barisan Sosialis (q.v.) dominated most of the labor movement through their control of the Singapore Trade Union Congress (STUC) (q.v.) secretariat by Lim Chin Siong (q.v.), Fong Swee Suan (q.v.), Sandra Woodhull (q.v.), Dominic Puthucheary (brother of James Puthucheary [q.v.]), S. T. Bani, and Jamit Singh. This prompted the government to deregister (in effect, outlaw) the STUC. In response, in mid-August 1961, they formed SATU--led by S. T. Bani--with most but not all of the unions following, while the PAP launched the National Trade Unions Congress (q.v.). Much of SATU's leadership were arrested in Operation Cold Store (q.v.). When it declared strikes in October 1963, Malaysia--which was responsible for internal security--deregistered it and arrested the few remaining *Barisan* assemblymen not in detention.

SINGAPORE CHINESE CHAMBER OF COMMERCE. Also called the Singapore Chinese Chamber of Commerce and Industry (SCCCI). Organization of Chinese businessmen. Established in 1906, on the recommendation of the Consul General of China, Penang and Medan millionaire Thio Thiauw Siat (known in Mandarin as Chang Chen-hsun), it enjoyed the support of most businesses and was able to help mediate disputes within the Chinese community. Begun as the Singapore Chinese Commercial Association, it changed to the Singapore Chinese Chamber of Commerce in 1917. Its initial charter prescribed that it should have a president and vice-president, one a Hokkien and the other a Cantonese, with the top office rotated between the two dialect groups. Reflecting the society, it was organized along *bang* (q.v.) (dialect group) lines as these usually represented trade or occupational distinctions within the community. In 1921, it was allowed to nominate two members as municipal commissioners. Before World War II, it encouraged Chinese nationalism, culture and, after the Japanese invasion of China, a boycott of Japanese goods and formation of the Singapore Chinese General Association for the Relief of Refugees in China. After the war, it supported efforts to increase Chinese rights, such as the Malayan Democratic Union, but was fearful of the growing power of communists and labor organizations. In 1955, it launched the unsuccessful Democratic Party (q.v.) to oppose the Labour Front (q.v.) and the People's Action Party (PAP) (q.v.). After the PAP came to power, it remained a voice for Chinese interests--calling for greater expenditures on Chinese schools in 1963--but accommodated itself to government policy.

SINGAPORE DEMOCRATIC PARTY (SDP). Major opposition party, with only elected opposition member of Parliament, Chiam See Tong (q.v.) between 1986 and 1991. Chiam, who founded it in 1980, was elected to Parliament in 1984 and reelected in 1988. While it fields other candidates, it largely has been Chiam's party and has aimed at airing government shortcomings and misguided policies rather than challenging for power. In the 1991 election, it won three seats, becoming the first opposition party since independence to win more than one seat.

SINGAPORE LABOUR PARTY (SLP). Party patterned after the British Labour Party. Formed September 1, 1948, after the election, it was led by M. A. Majid, president of the Singapore Seamen's Union, M. P. D. Nair, Francis Thomas (q.v.), and Peter Williams. Lim Yew Hock (q.v.) was won over from the Progressive Party (q.v.) and named its president in 1949. In the early 1950s, it split into moderate and radical wings, led by Thomas and Williams respectively. Lim Yew Hock was expelled in 1952, and while the party still existed in 1955, most of its members and leaders had deserted.

SINGAPORE PEOPLE'S ALLIANCE. Opposition Party. Organized by Lim Yew Hock (q.v.) with associates from the Labour Front (q.v.), it won four seats in the 1959 election. In 1962, it provided the decisive votes to pre-serve Lee Kuan Yew's People's Action Party government following the formation of the *Barisan Sosialis* (q.v.). In the 1963 election, it reorganized as the Singapore Alliance (q.v.).

SINGAPORE SOCIALIST PARTY (SSP). Short-lived party which helped form the Labour Front (q.v.) coalition for the 1955 general election. Formed in April 1984 and led by Lim Yew Hock (q.v.), David Marshall (q.v.), and Francis Thomas (q.v.), within months it began negotiations with the Singapore Labour Party (q.v.) to cooperate in the election as the People's United Front--which at registration was called the Labour Front.

SINGAPORE TOWN COMMITTEE. Malayan Communist Party (MCP) (q.v.) core organization in Singapore. With the outlawing of the MCP in 1948, it went from an organization coordinating trade unions and special organizations to a hierarchical cellular organization with itself at the top, reporting to the MCP's South Malayan Bureau in Johore. In December 1950, it was decimated with the arrest of nearly its entire membership--two escapees were Eu Chooi Yip (q.v.) and Fang Chuang Pi (q.v.)--crippling the party in Singapore until 1954.

SINGAPORE TRADE UNION CONGRESS (STUC). Also called Trade Union Congress (TUC). Trade Union Federation. To counter communist influence in the labor movement, the colonial government passed a series of measures which effectively dissolved the Pan-Malayan Federation of Trade Unions (PMFTU) (q.v.). The PMFTU had been formed in 1946 by the General Labour Unions (GLU) of Singapore and Malaya, with its Singapore division known as the Singapore Federation of Trade Unions. It was dominated by the communists and was affiliated with the World Federation of Trade Unions. The STUC enjoyed government encouragement in 1949 as a non-communist alternative for labor and was formally established in 1951, growing to twenty-three thousand largely white-collar members; however, by 1953 it was divided and moribund. In 1959, the moderates within the People's Action Party revived it as an alternative to the militant unions associated with the communists and leftists and as a way of harnessing labor unrest; however, leftist leaders among the existing unions also joined the secretariat. These included the left wing of the PAP, which was expelled from the party in 1961, at which time the STUC split into the National Trades Union Congress (q.v.) and the Singapore Association of Trade Unions (q.v.).

SINGAPORE VOLUNTEER CORPS (SVC). Civilian self-defense corps. Following the Hokkien-Teochew riots (q.v.) in 1854, European and Eurasian residents formed the Singapore Volunteer Rifle Corps. In 1901, following requests by leading Straits Chinese (q.v.), a companion Chinese Singapore Volunteer Company was added. The Volunteer Rifle Corps was dissolved in 1904 but a Singapore Volunteer Artillery was formed in 1914. In 1915, the Volunteers assisted in putting down the Indian Mutiny. In the late 1930s, the Corps consisted of two European companies (one for British and West Europeans and one for Eastern Europeans and others), a Scottish company, a Eurasian company, a Chinese company, and a Malay company. These were also known as the Straits Settlements Volunteer Corps (SSVC) and Straits Settlements Volunteer Force (SSVF) Recognizing the growing threat posed by the Japanese, the Volunteers were expanded in 1940-1941 but equipment was largely leftover from the First World War. Asian volunteers were sought actively only in late 1941. Given the Japanese momentum, it was too little too late.

SINGAPURA. Name of Singapore in Malay, derived from Sanskrit, meaning Lion City (*singa* = lion and *pura* = city). The name is derived from a story in the *Malay Annals* about Sri Tri Buana (q.v.), a prince from Sumatra who observed an animal said to resemble a lion (although lions are not found in Asia), which led him to change the name of the settlement from Temasek (q.v.) to Singapura. The name today is represented by the national symbol, a stylized drawing of a lion's head, and by a modern imaginary symbol, a merlion--having the tail of a fish and the head of a lion. Small statues of the latter are sold as tourist souvenirs.

SINGKEH. Chinese born in China, literally "new man" or "new friend" in Hokkien, also used to distinguish between China-born and local born. In the later nineteenth century, Chinese society was strongly divided between them and the *Baba* (q.v.) (Straits-born).

SINGLISH. Colloquial form of English in Singapore. Drawing on constructions from the various Chinese dialects and other Asian languages, this patois is a frequent target of scholarly and humorous studies, including *The Story of English* (a book by Robert McCrum, William Cran, and Robert MacNeil and a 1980s BBC television mini-series), which featured a section on programs by Singapore Airlines to teach employees not to use it. Examples include "my one" for "mine" and the suffix "*-lah*" (from Malay) added to many words and sentences for emphasis, exemplified in an often heard complaint by children over the red envelope (*ang pao*) at Chinese New Year, "My one coins only-lah!"

SLAVERY. Involuntary bondage or servitude, usually as a chattel or property of another. Various forms of slavery had existed in the Malaysian/Indonesian archipelago from earliest history, often as a result of capture or conquest; moreover, the absorption of slaves into the family of the owner created a continuous demand for new slaves. During his last stay in Singapore, Raffles (q.v.) sought to outlaw slavery--arguing that it had been abolished by the British Parliament--and cited Farquhar's (q.v.) lax enforcement as a justification for dismissal. Raffles also sought to limit debt slavery. In 1830, the Governor noted that debt-slavery was being used as a cover for slavery and declared it illegal. In 1842, Governor Bonham declared that the last remnant of slavery "had been forever abolished." Still, later in the century, the coolie trade (q.v.) flourished for many years, and indentured Chinese coolies passed through Singapore on their way to mines in Malaya and to other territories in the East and West Indies. The Chinese Protectorate (q.v.) sought to assure that the indentured received some protection. Well into the twentieth century, a peculiar Chinese form of slavery, *mui tsai* (Cantonese, meaning "little younger sister"), in which parents would sell a daughter into total servitude, continued to exist--vividly described in Janet Lim's *Sold for Silver* (see in "Biographies and Memoirs" section under "History" in the Bibliography).

SMITH, SIR CECIL CLEMENTI (1840-1916). Governor of the Straits Settlements (1887-1893). He had long service in Asia before becoming governor, first coming to Hong Kong in 1864 where he learned Chinese and became a scholar of Chinese culture. In 1878, he came to Singapore as Colonial Secretary and served as acting Governor in 1884-85. Following two years in Ceylon, he returned as Governor. With Pickering's (q.v.) retirement, he was able to pass a law outlawing secret societies and forcing registration on other Chinese societies.

SMUGGLING. Illegal import of materials. In the nineteenth century, smuggling focused on those products which were subject to revenue farms (q.v.), such as opium, in an otherwise free port. Frequently, rivals for a farm would seek to undermine the profits of the successful bidder by smuggling in the product and underselling the farmer's price. After independence, smuggling was given an official cover for products from Indonesia. Until the late 1980s, Singapore did not publish trade statistics for Indonesia to avoid embarrassing a powerful neighbor by revealing how many traders and producers opted to bring products to Singapore markets from neighboring islands and Sumatra rather than using Indonesian markets or complying with Indonesian export procedures. Not tolerated has been smuggling of cheaper gasoline (due to lower taxes) from Johor by driving across the Causeway (q.v.) for a fill-up. A 1989 law required that persons leaving Singapore have at least half a tank of gasoline and, in 1991, the requirement was raised to three-fourths of a tank.

SOCIAL DEVELOPMENT UNIT. Governmental dating and match-making agency. Government concern over the nation's limited population and gene pool as well as the large number of better-educated women who remained unmarried prompted the introduction of the SDU in 1983, under Deputy Prime Minister Goh Keng Swee. Consistent with Lee Kuan Yew's emphasis on genetics, the SDU seeks to encourage marriage among the better educated. The SDU sponsors events, such as parties and outings, which enable unmarried government officers to become better acquainted. Mate selection and marriage decisions are left to the individuals involved.

SOCIALISM. Public ownership of the means of production. The People's Action Party (PAP) (q.v.) began as an avowedly socialist party but, through its governing history, has given great latitude to capitalism and free enterprise. In a form of democratic socialism, the government encourages public-/private-sector partnerships and in the late 1980s embraced the international trend toward privatization. Its social security system, the Central Provident Fund (CPF) (q.v.), makes contributors' funds available for the purchase of apartments as well as retirement. Its historic rival, the *Barisan Sosialis* (q.v.), was committed to a more doctrinaire and Marxist socialism. Criticism of the government's human rights, political and economic policies by member parties of the Socialist International prompted the PAP to withdraw in 1976.

SONG ONG SIANG, SIR. Author and Chinese community leader. He studied law in England and was admitted to the bar, as well as earning a master's degree and a doctorate of letters from Cambridge. He helped to found the Straits Chinese British Association (q.v.) and to force the inclusion of Chinese in the Singapore Volunteer Corps (q.v.). He also launched the first romanized Malay newspaper, *Bintang Timor*, especially for Straits Chinese (q.v.) readers. He was the first Chinese to be knighted.

SRI TRI BUANA. Legendary founder of Singapore. According to the legend in the *Malay Annals*, he was a Sumatran prince who settled in Singapore, renaming it *Singapura* (q.v.) and founding a royal line that extended into the Malacca Sultanate (q.v.) or, according to the Portuguese, until the reigning sultan was murdered by the founder of Malacca, Sultan Iskandar Shah (see under "Temasek and Singapura" in Overview).

SRIVIJAYA. Maritime empire based in Sumatra which dominated the Straits of Malacca from the seventh to the eleventh century. Heirs to Srivijaya in Palembang were credited with founding Singapore and thence the Malacca Sultanate (q.v.).

STRAITS CHINESE. Chinese born in Straits Settlements. They saw themselves as the elite and identified more with the British than with the Chinese newcomers or the Malays--evidenced in the name of their organization, the Straits Chinese British Association. In Penang (q.v.), they called themselves the King's Chinese. See also *BABA* and *PERANAKAN*.

STRAITS CHINESE BRITISH ASSOCIATION (SCBA). Social and political organization of Straits-born Chinese. Founded in 1900, it was committed to both parts of its name, loyalty to the queen and interest in the British Empire coupled with promotion of the welfare of the Chinese, especially Chinese British subjects. In the 1930s, under the leadership of Tan Cheng Lock (q.v.), it led in the advocacy of governmental reform to provide greater public representation. After the war, its members participated in forming the Progressive Party (q.v.), after debating if the SCBA should become a party. Even in the early 1950s, it provided an early platform for Lee Kuan Yew's (q.v.) ambitions as he served as its secretary, after returning from London in 1950.

STRAITS CIVIL SERVICE (SCS). Staffing system for the crown colony. Beginning with nominated candidates in 1867, an examination system was added in 1869, and the system was opened to the British public in 1882. Candidates were recruited in England and sent to the Straits

Settlements (q.v.) as cadets where they learned Malay or, for the Chinese Protectorate (q.v.), Chinese after the 1880s. With the combining of the Federated Malay States (q.v.) under the governor and high commissioner, the civil services were unified as the Malayan Civil Service (MCS). In 1934, the SCS designation was revived to provide administrative opportunities for Asians with British degrees; however, members of the revived SCS were not allowed to transfer to the MCS. A Straits Medical Service was established in 1932 and a Straits Legal Service in 1837 to attract Asians to specialized public service.

STRAITS SETTLEMENTS (SS). British possessions on the Straits of Malacca (Penang, Malacca, and Singapore), under the East India Company (q.v.) and then the Colonial Office. In 1826, the company combined its settlements at Penang (q.v.), Malacca (q.v.) and Singapore together as a presidency but later placed them under the Bengal presidency in Calcutta. In 1836, Singapore replaced Penang as the seat of government. Because of distance from India and the limited customs revenues, resulting from the commitment to free trade, the SS were a peripheral concern to company servants in Calcutta. In 1867, the SS received crown colony status under the British colonial office. The office of Governor was expanded in 1896 to include designation as High Commissioner to the Federated Malay States. The Governor was advised by an Executive Council (q.v.) and a Legislative Council (q.v.), with the latter including representatives of the private sector--one or more of whom would be a Chinese. The Straits Settlements were not officially abolished until April 1, 1946, when Penang and Malacca were incorporated into the Malayan Union (q.v.) and Singapore remained a crown colony.

STRAITS SETTLEMENTS ASSOCIATION. Organization to promote Straits Settlements (q.v.) interests. Formed by former residents of the Straits Settlements in Britain who had agitated for transfer to colony status in 1868. John Crawfurd (q.v.) was elected first president, and chapters were established in Singapore and Penang. The organization was active in opposing government policies in the early years as a colony. Amid fears of Anglo-Russian war over Afghanistan, in 1885 the association petitioned for bases to defend the colony. In Britain, it was replaced by a broader Association of British Malaya (ABM) (q.v.) in 1920, but the Singapore chapter declined to join. In the 1920s, the Singapore organization nominated members to the municipal commission and continued until after World War II, when it became the Singapore Association.

SULTAN HUSSAIN ORDINANCE (1991). Law to limit claims by heirs to Sultan Hussein (q.v.) (also spelled Hussain), who was acknowledged as Sultan of Johore (q.v.) by Raffles (q.v.) in 1819. When Sultan Hussein signed a treaty in 1824 ceding Singapore to the British, he was given the district of Kampong Glam for his residence. Although a court of appeal ruled in 1897 that there were no claimants to succeed the Sultan (who died in 1835), in 1904 the Straits Settlements enacted a law to provide income to his descendants. Under the law, the descendants would receive up S$750 and 90 percent of any revenue produced annually by the land in exchange for giving the land to the government. In 1974/75 the payment was S$64,590 and S$254,749 in 1886/87. Because the 1904 law siphoned off money that might be used to develop the land, it had remained relatively undeveloped in a land-scarce nation. Under the ordinance, the descendants can receive no more than S$250,000 per year.

SWETTENHAM, SIR FRANK ATHELSTANE (1850-1946). Long-time British Resident in the Malay States and Governor and Commander in Chief of the Straits Settlements (1901-1904). Coming to the Malay States in 1875, he was involved in the full duration of the advance of British influence and control, from the Perak Expedition in 1875-76 to serving as Resident of both Selangor and Perak to serving as the first Resident General of the Federated Malay States (1896-1901) prior to becoming Governor.

SYONAN. Japanese name for Singapore, meaning "light of the South," used during Japanese Occupation (q.v.), 1942 - 1945. The suffix *"to,"* meaning island, was sometimes added, making it *Syonanto.*

-T-

TAN, C[HYE] C[HENG] (1911?-1991). Co-founder and first president of the Progressive Party. He practiced law in Singapore after graduating from London University and being called to the bar. He joined in founding the Progressive Party (q.v.), became its first president, and was elected to the Legislative Council (q.v.) in 1948. In 1951, he became one of two councilors named to the Executive Council (q.v.). He lost in the 1955 and 1959 general elections and retired from politics. In 1970, he was named to the Presidential Council (q.v.). From 1974 to 1982, he served as chairman of the Straits Times Press. He was also active in the Straits Chinese Association (q.v.) and the Singapore Olympics and Sports Council, serving as president of the latter, 1951-1962.

TAN CHENG LOCK, SIR (1883-1960). Prominent Straits Chinese leader and founder of the Malayan Chinese Association (MCA). Born in Malacca of Hokkien ancestry (his forebearers had resided in Malacca for a century), he graduated from Raffles Institution (q.v.) but could not afford a university education abroad. After he taught at Raffles for six years, his mother convinced him to return to Malacca in 1908, where he became involved in the booming rubber industry. Two years later, he started his own company. In 1913, he married the daughter of the Hokkien leader in Malacca, and her inheritance saved his company--which eventually yielded him substantial wealth. In 1923, he was appointed as an unofficial member of the Legislative Council, where he supported a united, self-governing Malaya until resigning in 1935. He took his family to Europe for his wife's health--1935-

1939--and spent the war-years with them in India. After World War II, he served as Chairman of the Pan-Malayan Council of Joint Action and the All-Malaya Council of Joint Action, which organized the successful 1947 hartals (q.v.) to demand greater rights from the British. In 1949, he was elected the first president of the MCA. His son, Tan Siew Sin, also led the MCA and served as finance minister of Malaya and Malaysia in the 1950s and 1960s.

TAN CHIN TUAN (1908-). Prominent businessman and Straits Chinese leader. Joining the Chinese Commercial Bank in 1925, he became manager of the newly formed Overseas Chinese Banking Corporation (OCBC) in 1933, managing director in 1942, and chairman after 1973. He served as municipal commissioner, 1939-1941, and as vice president of the Overseas Chinese Association (India) (q.v.) when he lived in India during the war. After the war, as member of the Singapore Progressive Party (q.v.), he served as a member of the Executive Council (q.v.), 1948-52 and the Legislative Council (q.v.), 1948-1955 -- serving as deputy Council president after 1951.

TAN JIAK KIM (1859-1917). Businessman and government advisor. Son of Tan Beng Swee and grandson of Tan Kim Seng (q.v.), he continued the family business, which he joined as an apprentice when he was eighteen. He was one of the founders of the Straits Steamship Company. After the passage of the municipal ordinance, he was elected a municipal commissioner in 1886. In 1889, he began a three-year term on the Legislative Council (q.v.) and was again appointed in 1902, a seat which he held until 1915.

TAN KAH KEE (1873-1961). Famous Hokkien (q.v.) entrepreneur and philanthropist. Born near Amoy (*pinyin*: Xiamen), he came to Singapore at age seventeen without money and worked in a shop. Beginning by opening a small rice shop, he moved into pineapple canning and rubber processing, both of which his companies dominated, as well as journalism (publishing the *Nanyang Siang*

Pau) and rubber-growing in Singapore and Johore. From early in his career, he championed education, founded primary schools, generously supported the Raffles Institution (q.v.), and established a kindergarten-to-university school system in Amoy--culminating in Amoy University. He went bankrupt during the Depression, in 1933, but left it to his son-in-law, Lee Kong Chian, to restore the businesses while he committed himself to helping China. During the Sino-Japanese War, he was a leader of the Nanyang Chinese National Salvation Movement--which was closely associated with the *Kuomintang* (q.v.)--and was president of the Singapore Chinese General Association for the Relief of Refugees in China. In 1940/41 he visited China, following which--appalled by the treatment of Nanyang (q.v.) volunteers and corruption among Chiang Kai-Shek's associates--he broke with the *Kuomintang*. With Japanese invasion imminent, he helped to mobilize Chinese to assist the British. At the beginning of the Occupation, he fled to Sumatra and then to East Java, where he hid throughout the war. In the post-war era, he supported the Chinese Communist Party as China's best hope, and, when he visited China in 1950 to help restore his educational institutions, the British refused to allow him to return. He settled in Fujian Province and died there.

TAN KENG YAM, DR. TONY (1940-). Leading cabinet minister. One of the best-educated younger leaders, he graduated from the University of Singapore in physics in 1962, and then earned an M. S. in operations research from the Massachusetts Institute of Technology in 1964, and a Ph.D. in applied mathematics in 1967 from the University of Adelaide. After briefly teaching at the University of Singapore, he joined the Overseas-Chinese Banking Corporation (OCBC) and in nine years rose to chairman. Recruited as among the potential "successor generation" to Lee Kuan Yew (q.v.), he won a Parliamentary seat in 1978. He since has held a number of important ministries, including education, trade and industry, and finance. In accepting an appointment as Minister of

Education following the 1991 election, he announced that he would relinquish the post on December 31, 1991, to return to the private sector.

TAN KIM CHING (1829-1892). Head of the Hokkien *Huay Kuan* (q.v.) in 1850s. Son of Tan Tock Seng (q.v.), he continued his father's business and involvement in community betterment, especially the hospital built and named in his father's honor. In 1863, he was one of the promoters of the Tanjong Pagar Dock Company. He was named Justice of the peace in 1865 and served as consul general for Siam (q.v.) for many years.

TAN KIM SENG (1805-1864). Chinese business and civic leader. Born in Malacca, he built one of the largest Chinese firms, Kim Seng & Co., and was an influential advisor to the government on Chinese concerns. He succeeded Tan Tock Seng (q.v.) as justice of the peace in 1850. He was active in the community, building a bridge and serving as president of a temple in Malacca as well as building and endowing the Singapore Chinese Free School. He helped improve the water supply through a private donation in 1857 which gave rise to the Singapore Waterworks. His son, Tan Beng Swee, continued his father's legacy in business and civic activity.

TAN LARK SYE (1896-1972) Hokkien (q.v.) entrepreneur and Chinese community leader. Born in Fukien in China, he founded the firm of Aik Hoe Co. in 1825 with his brother, building the biggest rubber factory in Singapore. He served as president of the Singapore Chinese Chamber of Commerce (q.v.) and as head of the Hokkien *Huay kuan* (q.v.). Attacking English education for "increasing taxes" and "turning out fools," in 1953 he helped found the Chinese-medium Nanyang University, which attracted donations from the richest to the poorest. He provided significant funding to the Democratic Party (q.v.), which was closely linked to the Singapore Chinese Chamber of Commerce in the 1955 assembly election, and later financially supported the *Barisan Sosialis* (q.v.).

TAN SENG POH (1830?-1879). Leading opium farmer. Brother-in-law of Seah Eu Chin (q.v.) and also a Teochew (q.v.), he came to Singapore when his sister married Seah. When Seah retired in 1864, he, with Seah's two sons, took over the family business. In 1870, he became the first Chinese to serve on the municipal commission, and was made a justice of the peace in 1871 and an honorary magistrate in 1872. He controlled the opium farm during 1863-1868, was a partner in the farm from 1870-1879, and at various times, held the farms in Johore (q.v.) and Rhio.

TAN TOCK SENG. (1798-1850) Early Hokkien (q.v.) entrepreneur and philanthropist. He came to Singapore from Malacca shortly after its founding and began selling vegetables, fruit, and fowl. He became wealthy from speculations with J. H. Whitehead, of Shaw, Whitehead & Co. He is listed among the early Chinese landowners, and the firm bearing his name (until his death in 1850) was among the early businesses. He was the first Asian appointed justice of the peace and well known for his charity. He usually provided the burial costs for poor Chinese and, in 1844, led in the establishment of the hospital for the poor which bore his name for more than a century.

TAN WAH PIOH (1952-). Radical former student leader living in exile in London. In 1974, he was elected president of the University of Singapore Students' Union (USSU). Singapore's economy suffered in the international economic slump in the early 1970s, and Tan and USSU sought closer ties between students and workers, including establishing a Retrenchment Research Center. He was arrested for allegedly rioting at the Pioneer Industries Employees' Union and, in 1975, was convicted and sentenced to one year in jail. When he was released in February 1976, he was given three days to report for national service (q.v.). Claiming that he feared for his safety, he fled to Europe. In England, he was active in the now defunct Federation of United Kingdom and Eire Malaysian and Singaporean Students' Organization (FU-

KEMSSO). In 1987, the government accused him of leading a Marxist plot to subvert the government and accused Vincent Cheng (q.v.) of being his subordinate. Cheng and fifteen persons were detained in May 1987. Tan has denied the charges and regularly publishes letters to the editor to refute government allegations. He also responded to the 1987 and 1988 detentions with a book, *Let the People Judge* (see in "Politics and Administration" section under "Politics and Government" of Bibliography).

TEH CHEANG WAN (1928-1986). Disgraced Cabinet Minister. He was an architect working with public housing in Australia and Malaya, prior to joining public service in Singapore in 1959. He rose to head the Housing and Development Board from 1970 until 1979, when he retired to enter politics, and served as Chairman of the Jurong Town Corporation from 1976 to 1979. He was elected to Parliament in a 1979 by-election and named Minister of National Development in 1979. Confronted by evidence of corruption from the Corrupt Practices Investigation Bureau (CPIB), he committed suicide in December 1986. His death prevented a trial which would have established his guilt or innocence, but a public Commission of Inquiry concluded that he twice received bribes of five hundred thousand dollars.

TEMASEK. Early name for Singapore. A settlement of this name is identified in 1365 in the Javanese *Nagarakerta-gama*. Other reports indicated that it probably existed through most of the fourteenth century.

TEOCHEW(S). People and dialect from area around the port city of Swatow (Shantou) in northern Kwangtung (Guang-dong) in China. They were the secondmost influential dialect group in the nineteenth and early twentieth centuries, having started and prospered in gambier and pepper cultivation (q.v.), later moving into other export agriculture, such as rubber and pineapple canning.

THOMAS, FRANCIS (1912-). Founder of Singapore Labour Party (SLP) (q.v.) and minister in Labour Front (LF) (q.v.) government. Born in England, after graduate education at Cambridge, he began teaching in Singapore in 1934, eventually becoming principal and warden. He was interned by the Japanese, working on the "death railway" in Thailand and then in Japan. He attended the first meeting of the SLP and was elected as an officer, serving briefly as party president in 1949. In 1953, having abandoned the SLP, he worked with Lim Yew Hock (q.v.) to form a new Democratic Labour Party (q.v.), later renamed--with the addition of David Marshall--the Singapore Socialist Party, and soon thereafter was absorbed in the LF. When the LF formed the government after the 1955 election, he was named Minister of Communications and Works, a post which he held until resigning in 1959 in protest of Lim Yew Hock's election methods. In the LF split at the end of 1955, he was elected secretary-general of the party. In 1970, he was named to the Presidential Council (q.v.).

THOMAS, SIR SHENTON THOMAS WHITLEGGE (1879-1962). Governor, 1934-1942, until interned by Japanese. After twenty-five years in the colonial service in Africa, including serving as Governor of Nyasaland (present-day Malawi) and of the Gold Coast, he was named Governor of the Straits Settlements. He arrived in 1934 and oversaw the recovery from the worldwide depression. Like most others in positions of responsibility in Singapore in 1941, he is frequently included among the scapegoats blamed for losing Singapore, even though the defense was a military matter over which he had little authority. He and his wife were imprisoned at Changi during the war although he later was moved to prison camps in Formosa (Taiwan) and then Manchuria. His advice on post-war policy was largely ignored by the colonial office.

THOMPSON, JOHN TURNBULL (1821-1884). Surveyor, builder, author, and artist. Having worked as a surveyor for a number of years in Penang (q.v.) and the Malay

States (q.v.), in 1841 he was appointed Government Surveyor for the Straits Settlements (q.v.). For twelve years, he was engaged in mapping the settlement and designing and constructing public buildings and facilities, including the first lighthouse in Asia. At the same time, he recorded mid-nineteenth century life on the island and surrounding areas in articles, sketches, and paintings. The exertion of the lighthouse construction sapped his health, and he returned to England in 1853. Having recovered, he unsuccessfully attempted to obtain a new position in 1855 and ended up in New Zealand where he authored books on his experiences in the colony and a translation of extracts from Munshi Abdullah's *Hikayat Abdullah* while serving as the first Surveyor General of New Zealand.

TOH CHIN CHYE, DR. (1921-). Former Deputy Prime Minister and People's Action Party chairman. He was educated at Raffles College and received his Ph.D. in physiology from the University of London, where he succeeded Goh Keng Swee (q.v.) as chair of the Malayan Forum (q.v.). He was a co-founder of the PAP, which he chaired 1954-1981, served in Parliament 1959-1988, and served in the cabinet 1959-1980. Always unafraid to assert his opinions, he kept his criticisms within the cabinet until leaving it and then aired his reservations in Parliament as a back-bencher.

TOWKAY. Hokkien, literally head of household, term for a wealthy Chinese businessman. It is sometimes used to refer to entrepreneurs or bosses from other ethnic groups but usually with the connotation that they share characteristics with the wealthy Chinese.

TRANSPORTATION. Despite its small size, transportation has been a perennial Singapore concern. From the nineteenth and early twentieth century and from rickshaws through the bus companies which figured prominently in the turbulence of the 1950s, getting to work and around the island has attracted public attention. With the prosperity which followed independence, the increasing number of cars threatened to overwhelm the parking and road network. In response, the government sought initially to discourage automobile use and finally ownership. This was accomplished through heavy duties, taxes, and fees-- so much so that a Japanese automobile would cost three or four times as much as in the U.S. in the early 1980s. A preferential additional registration fee (PARF) accelerates as a car ages, promoting sale of an automobile after two or three years. Under an area licensing scheme (ALS), most of the central business district (CBD) was designated as a restricted zone (RZ), meaning that automobiles were prohibited from entering the area during morning rush hour (7:30-10:30 a.m.) unless they were carrying at least four people or had purchased a special daily or monthly permit. As an alternative, a mass rapid transit (MRT) system of fast above- and below-ground trains was constructed to provide the backbone for an extensive bus system. In 1990, a new measure required purchasing a license to buy an automobile to further discourage automobile ownership. Under the system, a designated number of licenses are available each month and these are sold at auctions. In 1991, a "weekend car" system was introduced offering substantial reductions to those who do not drive to work. This was announced as a transition to an electronically monitored highway system later in the decade which will be able to record travel and charge for use by distance and time of day.

-U-

UMNO-MCA-MALAY UNION ALLIANCE. Parliamentary coalition in the 1955 Legislative Assembly (q.v.) election. Based on the Alliance in the Federation of Malaya, in which the United Malays National Organization (UMNO) and the Malayan Chinese Association (MCA) cooperated, this Singapore version added a local Malay party. It won three seats in the election and provided the decisive votes enabling the Labour Front to form a government (although the Malay Union declined to participate). UMNO leader Abdul Hamid bin Haji Jumat was made Minister of Local Government, Lands, and Housing. By the next election, the coalition reemerged as the Singapore People's Alliance (q.v.).

UNITED KINGDOM OF GREAT BRITAIN AND NORTHERN IRELAND (UK). Official name for political entity including England and the dominant political power in Singapore and Malaya prior to independence. Since Singapore was under the UK from 1819 to 1963, references to its representatives and policies are found throughout the Dictionary. Even since independence, national leaders have retained ties and affection for the UK, where most of them were educated. Singaporeans increasingly are undertaking higher and graduate education in Australia and North America, but the best and brightest graduates each year are usually directed toward higher education in the UK.

UNITED PEOPLE'S PARTY (UPP). Opposition party led by Ong Eng Guan (q.v.) in 1960s. After Ong Eng Guan was ousted from the cabinet and the People's Action Party (PAP) in 1960, he resigned from his seat in the Legislative Assembly, forcing a by-election in his constituency, Hong Lim (q.v.), in April 1961. Ong won easily as an independent and, in June 1961, formed the UPP to compete against the PAP. With the Workers' Party (q.v.) and the *Barisan Sosialis* (q.v.), it asked the United Nations to reject the merger to form Malaysia, an effort which failed following the successful merger referendum in 1962. In the 1963 general election, Ong retained his seat but the party won no others. In 1964, he again resigned his seat, forcing another Hong Lim by-election. The party was largely a vehicle for Ong's political ambitions, and, with the second resignation, ceased to be a political factor.

UNITED STATES. Major trading partner and world power. Under the July 3, 1815, Treaty of London, signed at the end of the War of 1812, Britain agreed that Americans would "be admitted and hospitably received at the principal settlements of the British dominions in the East Indies"; however, the treaty also identified those dominions including Penang. Because Singapore was not yet a British dominion, the East India Company (q.v.) claimed that the treaty did not apply to it, and Americans were excluded. Indeed, in 1825, the American ship *Governor Endicott* was captured in the vicinity of Singapore and taken to India (where the charge of trading with Singapore was dismissed since the ship had not arrived in Singapore). As a result, the first American consul resident in Singapore (from 1834) was actually accredited to Rhio. American vessels would anchor near Batam, outside British territory, and have cargos carried to and from Singapore on smaller boats. Only in 1836 was the American consul recognized by the company's Court of Directors in London, and in June 1837 he was acknowledged as consul in Singapore, with trade opened to Americans. In 1834, a mission was also established by the American Board of Commissioners of Foreign Missions (ABCFM). In addition to the evangelical efforts, they played an important role in developing Asian education, including having one of their members serve as the second headmaster of the Singapore Institution. In the 1840s, most of the American and British missionaries departed, as China--for which they had been preparing--was opened following the first Opium War. Later in the nineteenth century, the Methodists began opening schools--usually identified as Anglo-Chinese Schools for Boys and Methodist Girls Schools. The U.S. became an increasingly important purchaser of Singapore exports, a trend which jumped dramatically with the growth of the rubber industry. In the 1980s, the U.S. remained the number one purchaser of exports and was second to Japan as a source of imports. Under Lee Kuan Yew (q.v.), relations between the two nations were generally cordial; however, in speeches immediately following separation from Malaysia, he indicated that he lacked faith in the U.S. His opinion was based, in part, on frustrated efforts to obtain medical treatment in the U.S. for his wife and distrust over the capture of Central Intelligence Agency (CIA) officers in a hotel in 1960. Lee did appreciate the special role of the U.S. as a great power and was generally supportive of the U.S. involvement in Vietnam. Many servicemen from the Vietnam War undertook rest and relaxation (R & R) in Singapore, contributing economically in the late 1960s and early 1970s, deprecatingly memorialized in Paul Theroux's novel and the movie based on it, *Saint Jack* (see in "Fiction" section under "Culture" in Bibliography). In May 1988, Singapore demonstrated that it retained doubts about American intentions as it expelled an embassy political officer, Mason Hendrickson, for contacts with opposition party members. In 1989, the U.S. determined that Singapore (as well as Hong Kong, South Korea, and Taiwan) no longer qualified for special tariff concessions under the Generalized System of Preferences (GSP). Continuing to believe in the importance of the U.S. in balancing Russia and China, in 1990 Lee volunteered the use of Singapore shipping and repair facilities as alternatives to the Philippines (where base negotiations were stalled). With the U.S. withdrawal from the Philippines, it likely will make increasing usage of Singapore's facilities.

UNIVERSITY OF MALAYA. Established in Singapore in 1949 with the merger of Raffles College and the King Edward College of Medicine. It was an English-medium institution to serve Singapore, the Federation of Malaya, and British Borneo. In 1962, the name was moved to the new campus in Kuala Lumpur and the Singapore campus was renamed the University of Singapore.

UNIVERSITY OF MALAYA SOCIALIST CLUB. Organization of leftist intellectuals accused of publishing sedition. In 1953, the recently released detainees James Puthucheary (q.v.), Abdullah (Dollah) Majid, and S. Woodhull (q.v.) organized it to oppose colonialism. In 1954, eight club members, including Puthucheary and Edwin Thumboo (presently Singapore's foremost academic literary voice and poet), were charged with sedition for an editorial in the club's organ, *Fajar*. With the assistance of Lee Kuan Yew (q.v.), Queen's Counsel D. N. Pritt won them an acquittal.

-V-

VALUES. Concern over morality and world outlook of younger Singaporeans. The People's Action Party (PAP) (q.v.) government and especially past Prime Minister Lee Kuan Yew (q.v.) have long been concerned that Singaporeans lacked a core of beliefs which made them a nation and which would prevent them from uncritically embracing a vacuous Western materialism. Because of its size and prosperity, the citizenry of Singapore were subject to much greater British and Western influence than Malaya. With the embracing of English by the government, in part as a counter to radical opponents who courted the Chinese-educated, by 1985 97 percent of the students were in English-medium schools. In such a context, the nation--like its English-educated leadership--risked being described as bananas (yellow on the outside and white on the inside). To counter this, the government has regularly sought alternative values, pointing to Japan as a model rather than the West. While religion has traditionally provided such a moral core, the nation's ethnic and religious diversity required a more secular response. In introducing values to the educational curriculum, provision was made for Hindus (Indians), Muslims (Malays and Indians), and Christians (Chinese, Eurasians, and Indians) to have the instruction based on these religions; however, for the majority Chinese, no such easy option existed. Chinese religious tradition is syncretic in embracing elements of Buddhism, folk religion and Taoism, and Confucianism (q.v.) (the latter two being more philosophies than religions). For the majority, Confucian ethics were introduced. But this was moral education rather than shared values. For the latter, the National Ideology (q.v.) was identified.

-W-

WASHINGTON TREATY FOR THE LIMITATION OF NAVAL ARMAMENTS (Signed February 4, 1922). International agreement limiting the size and growth of naval forces in the wake of World War I. Faced with replacing ships damaged in war, orders in the postwar period stimulated a naval arms race that threatened to consume the budgets of the naval powers. Beginning in 1921, Britain, France, Italy, Japan, and the United States undertook negotiations to control the growth of fleets, and to avoid a massive escalation of forces in the Pacific. The agreement which defined the sizes of ships and fleets of the signatories was in effect until 1936. The restrictions specifically prohibited British fortification of Hong Kong; however, Singapore was seen as sufficiently distant from Japan as to pose no threat and thus was outside the controlled area. While the treaty proved ineffective in preventing another world war, it did cause Britain to look to Singapore as the site for its major naval base in Asia.

WEE KIM WEE (1915-). President of Singapore (1985-). A former journalist who rose to Editorial Manager of the *Straits Times*, he later followed a diplomatic career beginning with his appointment as High Commissioner (title for an ambassador to a country which is a member of the Commonwealth) to Malaysia in 1973. In 1980, he was named as Ambassador to Japan and, concurrently, as Ambassador to South Korea in 1981. In 1984, he returned to Singapore and was made chairman of the Singapore Broadcasting Corporation in May. In 1985, he was selected as the nation's fourth President and given a second term in 1989.

WOMEN. Historically, from 1830 until World War II, women--especially Chinese and Indian--were a small minority of the society (outnumbered 3:1 by men in the nineteenth century). In the 1930s, female immigration was allowed and the gap began narrowing, approaching 1:1 only in the 1980s. Escaping from a culturally mandated dependency on their fathers and husbands, Singapore women in the last half of the twentieth century have excelled in higher education and a variety of professions. Their success and independence has caused concern for the government as many are unwilling to fulfill the traditional role of dependent or subservient wife. Consistent with the belief of senior governmental leaders in genetic determinacy, programs were introduced to encourage the brightest and best-educated to wed and have children. It was feared that, without intervention, future generations would come disproportionately from the poorest and least-educated segments of the society. Measures have included government-sponsored socials for single male and female government officials and tax incentives for having children. While women comprised over 40 percent of the work force in the 1980s, only late in the decade did they begin gaining a presence in politics. In 1980, no women held Parliamentary seats and only four out of eighty-one seats were held by women after the 1988 election. In that year, the first woman was named to a non-cabinet ministerial post, and in 1989 the first woman ambassador was selected.

WOMEN'S CHARTER. Legal protection of married women. Passed in 1961 and occasionally amended since, it prohibited men from taking more than one wife, except Muslims, whose religious belief allows up to four wives under certain conditions, and required registration of marriages. It also outlined the rights of women in marriage and permitted divorce only by court order or, for Muslims, only after attempting reconciliation.

WOODHULL, SANDRA[SEGARAM] (1933?-). Leftist organizer of Ceylonese (Sri Lankan) descent. An earlier leader of the University of Malaya Socialist Club (q.v.), Lee Kuan

Yew helped him become paid secretary of the Naval Base Labour Union in 1953. He was a founder of the People's Action Party (PAP) (q.v.) but, with Devan Nair (q.v.) and Lim Chin Siong (q.v.), he was prevented from running for the Central Committee in 1955 to avoid the appearance of strong communist influence on the party. In 1957, he was detained with Devan Nair and others associated with Middle Road (q.v.) unions, who were released after the PAP came to power in 1959. He was appointed political secretary for health in the new government. With James Puthucheary (q.v.), Lim Chin Siong, and Fong Swee Suan (q.v.), he participated in the Eden Hall Tea Party (q.v.) and the split from the PAP to form the *Barisan Sosialis* (q.v.) in 1961. He became vice chairman of the *Barisan* as well as assistant secretary general of the Singapore Association of Trade Unions (q.v.). With most of his colleagues, he was again detained in Operation Cold Store (q.v.) in 1962. Like Puthucheary, he renounced politics and, after release, moved to Malaysia to practice law. He was prohibited from returning to Singapore until 1991.

WORKERS' PARTY (WP). Leading opposition party in 1980s. Founded on November 7, 1957, by David Marshall (q.v.), with the principles of *Merdeka* (independence), democracy, and socialism, the party was clandestinely adopted by the Malayan Communist Party (MCP) (q.v.) as offering an alternative to the People's Action Party (PAP) (q.v.) in case its supporters were purged from the latter. The party won four out of five city council seats which it contested in December 1957. Seeking to placate the PAP, the communists abandoned it and, to demonstrate their sincerity (and power) to Lee Kuan Yew (q.v.), had the vice-chairman, Chang Yuen Tong, resign from the city council and the party. In a July by-election in Kallang, without communist support, it polled only 304 votes where it had received 2,704 only months before. Following this embarrassment, remaining party leaders deserted to join the Singapore People's Alliance (q.v.). Remaining party loyalists entered the 1959 election, with no success as even Marshall was defeated by Lim Yew Hock (q.v.).

By 1961, the communists again were disenchanted with the PAP moderate leadership and backed Marshall as WP candidate in winning the Anson by-election. In the 1962 merger referendum, Marshall learned that the party vice chairman, Sum Chong Heng, and others were twisting his words in Chinese reports to appear to oppose merger. Unable to oust the left, Marshall resigned from the party in January 1963, and it faded in importance. Following the 1968 PAP sweep of parliamentary seats, Marshall's law partner, J. B. Jeyaretnam (q.v.), and others revived the Workers' Party in 1971. Failing to win seats in the 1970s, Jeyaretnam became the first opposition member of Parliament in fifteen years in 1981 after winning an Anson by-election. He defended the seat in 1984 but was ousted from Parliament in 1986 and disqualified because legal penalties levied against him made him ineligible. In the 1988 election, the party unsuccessfully worked with the *Barisan Sosialis* (q.v.) and the Singapore Democratic Party (q.v.). In the 1991 election, it won one seat.

WU TIEN WANG. Communist leader. Born in Perak about the time of World War I, he was active in labor organizing and opposing the Japanese, leading to his arrest for sedition in 1939. He was released before the war in the amnesty for communists and was a leader in the Malayan People's Anti-Japanese Army during World War II. He was a member of the first Malayan Democratic Union (q.v.) executive committee but contributed little, probably because of his open communist affiliation. He was a correspondent for the *Daily Worker*, newspaper of the British Communist Party, and composed the only official history of the Malayan Communist Party (MCP) (q.v.). With the outbreak of the Emergency (q.v.) in 1948, he went underground and joined his MCP colleagues in the jungle.

-Y-

YAMASHITA, LIEUTENANT-GENERAL TOMOYUKI (1885-1946). Commander of the 25th Japanese Army which conquered Malaya and Singapore, earning him the appellation "Tiger of Malaya." His concern to eliminate resistance led him to order the commander of *Syonan* (q.v.), Major-General Saburo Kawamura, to severely punish Chinese resisters, leading--under the *Kempeitai*--to indiscriminate torture and murder of thousands of Chinese. In July 1942, he was reassigned to Manchukuo (Manchuria) and then to the Philippines in 1944 to resist the American reconquest. For atrocities committed by his troops during the latter, he was the first Japanese general to face a war-crime trial. He was convicted and hanged in February 1946. It has been cogently argued that he had no control over the actions of his troops for which he was convicted, but the behavior of his forces in Singapore--for which he was responsible--would have justified the verdict and sentence.

YAP PHENG GEK (1901-). Teochew commander of the Chinese Company of the Singapore Volunteer Corps (q.v.) before World War II and prominent businessman. After an education at the Anglo-Chinese School, a degree from the University of Hong Kong, and thirteen years of teaching, he joined a Chinese bank. Shortly afterwards, in the midst of the worldwide depression, his and two other Chinese banks merged to form the Overseas Chinese Banking Corporation (OCBC), which remains one of Singapore's premier financial institutions. After the war, he sought reconciliation among the English- and Chinese-speaking Chinese communities through participation in the Straits Chinese British Association (q.v.), by virtue of his Volunteers office as he was born in Johore, and the Singapore Chinese Chamber of Commerce (q.v.). In 1963, he unsuccessfully ran for a seat in the Legislative Assembly (q.v.) as a Malayan Chinese Association candidate in the Singapore Alliance (q.v.). He also was called to serve on a number of delegations to international organizations.

YEO YONG-BOON, BRIGADIER-GENERAL (RES.) GEORGE (1954-). Among brightest members of the cabinet in the 1990s. After graduating as a top student from secondary school, he studied engineering at Cambridge University as a President's Scholar and as a Singapore Armed Forces Scholar. In 1976, he graduated with a Double First Honours Degree and won the UK Institution of Civil Engineer's Prize for Management Studies. He then served in the armed forces and in 1979 graduated at the top of his class from the Singapore Command and Staff College. While still in the military, he graduated from Harvard University with an MBA Degree with High Distinction. After rising as a staff officer, he was named Director of Joint Operations and Planning in the Ministry of Defence. In August 1988, he resigned from the military and September 3rd was elected to Parliament. Ten days later, he was then named Minister of State for Finance and Minister of State for Foreign Affairs. In 1990, he was named Acting Minister of Information and the Arts and Second Minister of Foreign Affairs. In July 1991, he was made a full Minister in the same posts and was renamed to those posts in September 1991. He is widely respected for his intellect and analytical abilities and is considered a strong candidate to become Prime Minister in the future.

YOUNG, CAPTAIN SIR ARTHUR HENDERSON (1854-1938). Governor of Straits Settlements and High Commissioner for the Malay States, 1911-1919. After a lengthy career in Cyprus, he was appointed Colonial Secretary for the Straits Settlements in 1906, followed by the governorship. His term spanned the tension of World War I and the Indian Mutiny (q.v.); however, it was mostly a period of economic growth.

YUSOF BIN ISHAK (1910-1981). Second head of state, with titles of *Yang di Pertua Negara* and President (q.v.).

After schooling at Raffles Institution, he became a journalist and founded the Malay-language *Utusan Melayu* in 1938, which he revived after World War II. As a modernist Muslim, he was committed to a multi-racial and progressive nation. His brothers, Rahim Ishak and Abdul Aziz Ishak, were active in politics, the former as a leader in the People's Action Party (q.v.) and cabinet minister, and the latter as a member of UMNO and cabinet minister in Malaya (detained by the Malaysian government, 1965-1966).

APPENDICES

Heads of Government[1]

Residents (under East India Company), 1819 - 1826.

William Farquhar, Colonel, February 6, 1819 - May 27, 1823
John Crawfurd, Dr., June 9, 1823 - August 14, 1826.

Resident Councillors of Singapore, 1826 - 1867
(under East India Company)

John Prince, August 15, 1826 - November 18, 1827.
Kenneth Murchison, November 29, 1827 - December 1833.
Samuel George Bonham, December 1833 - 1836.
Thomas Church, March 4, 1837 - 1856
Henry Somerset MacKenzie, 1856 - 1859
Ronald MacPherson, Colonel, 1860 - 1867

Governors of the Straits Settlements

Robert Fullerton, November 27, 1826 - 1830.
Robert Ibbetson, 1830 - December 6, 1833.
Kenneth Murchison, December 7, 1833 - November 17, 1836
Samuel George Bonham, Sir, Nov. 18, 1836 - January 1843

---

[1]   Most of the information in this appendix is based on original research reported in Saran Singh: *The Encyclopaedia of the Coins of Malaysia, Singapore and Brunei, 1400-1986.* Kuala Lumpur: Malaysia Numismatic Society, 1986. Copyright © by Saran Singh and used with his permission.

William John Butterworth, Colonel, August 1845 - March 20, 1855

Edmund Augustus Blundell, March 21, 1855 - August 1859

Orfeur Cavenagh, Colonel Sir, August 6, 1859 - March 16, 1867.

Harry St. George Ord, Colonel Sir, March 17, 1867 - November 3, 1873

Andrew Clarke, Major General Sir, November 4, 1873 - May 7, 1875

William Francis Drummond Jervois, Major General Sir, May 8, 1875 - April 3, 1877.

William Cleaver Francis Robinson, August 1877 - February 10, 1879.

Frederick Aloysius Weld, May 6, 1880 - October 17, 1887

Cecil Clementi Smith, Sir, October 17, 1887 - August 30, 1893

Charles Bullen Hugh Mitchell, Colonel Sir, February 1, 1894 - December 7, 1899.

Frank Althelstane Swettenham, Sir, February 18, 1901 - October 12, 1903

John Anderson, Sir, April 15, 1904 - April 9, 1911

Arthur Henderson Young, Sir, September 9, 1911 - August 24, 1919.

Laurence Nunns Guillemard, Sir, February 3, 1920 - May 5, 1927.

Hugh Charles Clifford, Sir, June 3, 1927 - October 20, 1929.

Cecil Clementi, Sir, February 5, 1930 - February 16, 1934.

Thomas Shenton Whitelegge Thomas, November 9, 1934 - March 31, 1846 (Prisoner of Japanese, February 15, 1942 - August 15, 1945).

British Military Authority, 1945-1946

Louis Mountbatten, Lord, September 5 - March 31, 1946

Governors of Singapore, 1946-1949

Franklin Gimson, Sir, April 1, 1946 - March 20, 1952.

John Fearns Nicoll, Sir, April 23, 1952 - June 3, 1955.

Robert Brown Black, Sir, June 30, 1955 - December 4, 1957.

William Goode, Sir, December 9, 1957 - June 2, 1959.

Chief Ministers, 1956-1959

David Marshall, April 6, 1955 - June 7, 1956
Lim Yew Hock, June 3, 1956 - June 1, 1959

Head of State (Yang di Pertua Negara), 1959 - 1965

William Goode, Sir, June 3, 1959 - December 2, 1959.
Yusof bin Ishak, December 3, 1959 - December 21, 1965.

Presidents, 1965 -

Yusof bin Ishak, December 22, 1965 - November 23, 1970.
Benjamin Henry Sheares, January 2, 1971 - May 12, 1981.
C. V. Devan Nair, October 24, 1981 - March 29, 1985.
Wee Kim Wee, August 30, 1985 -

Prime Ministers, 1959 -

Lee Kuan Yew, June 3, 1959 - November 28, 1990
Goh Chok Tong, November 28, 1990 -

Cabinets of Singapore

CABINET FOLLOWING MAY 30, 1959, GENERAL ELECTION

Lee Kuan Yew, Prime Minister
Toh Chin Chye, Deputy Prime Minister
Ahmad bin Ibrahim, Minister for Health
Goh Keng Swee, Minister for Finance
K. M. Byrne, Minister for Labour and Law
S. Rajaratnam, Minister for Culture
Ong Pang Boon, Minister for Home Affairs
Yong Nyuk Lin, Minister for Education
Ong Eng Guan, Minister for National Development (expelled from PAP in 1960)

CABINET FOLLOWING SEPT. 21, 1963, GENERAL ELECTION

Lee Kuan Yew, Prime Minister
Toh Chin Chye, Deputy Prime Minister
Goh Keng Swee, Minister for Finance
S. Rajaratnam, Minister for Culture
Ong Pang Boon, Minister for Education
Yong Nyuk Lin, Minister for Health
Lim Kim San, Minister for National Development
Othman bin Wok, Minister for Social Affairs
E. W. Barker, Minister for Law
Jek Yuen Thong, Minister for Labour

CABINET FOLLOWING AUG. 9, 1965, SEPARATION FROM MALAYSIA

Lee Kuan Yew, Prime Minister
Toh Chin Chye, Deputy Prime Minister
Goh Keng Swee, Minister of Defence
S. Rajaratnam, Minister for Foreign Affairs
Ong Pang Boon, Minister for Education
Yong Nyuk Lin, Minister for Health
Lim Kim San, Minister for Finance
Jek Yeun Thong, Minister for Labour

Othman bin Wok, Minister for Culture and Social Affairs
E. W. Barker, Minister for Law and National Development

CABINET FOLLOWING APR. 13, 1968, GENERAL ELECTION

Lee Kuan Yew, Prime Minister
Toh Chin Chye, Minister for Science and Technology
Goh Keng Swee, Minister for Finance
S. Rajaratnam, Minister for Foreign Affairs and Labour
Ong Pang Boon, Minister for Education
Yong Nyuk Lin, Minister for Communications
Lim Kim San, Minister for Interior and Defence
Othman bin Wok, Minister for Social Affairs
E. W. Barker, Minister for Law and National Development
Chua Sian Chin, Minister for Health
Jek Yeun Thong, Minister for Culture

CABINET FOLLOWING SEPT. 2, 1972, GENERAL ELECTION

Lee Kuan Yew, Prime Minister
Goh Keng Swee, Deputy Prime Minister and Minister of Defence
Toh Chin Chye, Minister for Science and Technology
S. Rajaratnam, Minister for Foreign Affairs
Ong Pang Boon, Minister for Labour
Yong Nyuk Lin, Minister for Communications
Lim Kim San, Minister for the Environment
Jek Yeun Thong, Minister for Culture
Othman bin Wok, Minister for Social Affairs
E. W. Barker, Minister for Law and National Development
Chua Sian Chin, Minister for Health and Home Affairs
Hon Sui Sen, Minister for Finance
Lee Chiaw Meng, Minister for Education

CABINET FOLLOWING DEC. 23, 1976, GENERAL ELECTION

Lee Kuan Yew, Prime Minister
Goh Keng Swee, Deputy Prime Minister and Minister of Defence

Toh Chin Chye, Minister for Health
S. Rajaratnam, Minister for Foreign Affairs
Ong Pang Boon, Minister for Labour
Lim Kim San, Minister for National Development and
  Communications
Jek Yeun Thong, Minister for Culture and Science and Technology
Othman bin Wok, Minister for Social Affairs
E. W. Barker, Minister for Law and the Environment
Chua Sian Chin, Minister for Home Affairs and Education
Hon Sui Sen, Minister for Finance

CABINET FOLLOWING DEC. 23, 1980, GENERAL ELECTION

Lee Kuan Yew, Prime Minister
Goh Keng Swee, 1st Deputy Prime Minister and Minister for
  Education
S. Rajaratnam, 2nd Deputy Prime Minister (Foreign Affairs)
Hon Sui Sen, Minister for Finance
Ong Pang Boon, Minister for the Environment
E. W. Barker, Minister for Law
Chua Sian Chin, Minister for Home Affairs
Ong Teng Cheong, Minister for Communications and Minister for
  Labour
Howe Yoon Chong, Minister of Defence
Teh Cheang Wan, Minister for National Development
Goh Chok Tong, Minister for Health and 2nd Minister of Defence
S. Dhanabalan, Minister for Foreign Affairs and Minister for
  Culture
Tony Tan Keng Yam, Minister for Trade and Industry
Lim Chee Onn, Minister without Portfolio (resigned 7/22/83)
Ahmad Matter, Minister for Social Affairs (Acting)

CABINET REORGANIZATION, SEPTEMBER 1983

Lee Kuan Yew, Prime Minister
Goh Keng Swee, First Deputy Prime Minister and Minister of
  Education
S. Rajaratnam, Second Deputy Prime Minister (Foreign Affairs)
Hon Sui Sen, Minister of Finance (died, October 1983)

Ong Pang Boon, Minister for the Environment
E. W. Barker, Minister for Law
Chua Sian Chin, Minister for Home Affairs
Ong Teng Cheong, Minister without Portfolio
Howe Yoon Chong, Minister for Health
Teh Cheang Wan, Minister for National Development
Goh Chok Tong, Minister of Defence and Second Minister for
    Health
S. Dhanabalan, Minister for Foreign Affairs and Minister for
    Culture
Tony Tan Keng Yam, Minister for Finance (after Oct. 1983) and
    Minister for Trade and Industry
Ahmad Mattar, Minister for Social Affairs
Yeo Ning Hong, Minister for Communications and Second Minister
    for Defence
S. Jayakumar, Minister for Labour and Second Minister for Law
    and Home Affairs

CABINET FORMED AFTER DEC. 22, 1984, GENERAL ELECTION

Lee Kuan Yew, Prime Minister
S. Rajaratnam, Senior Minister (Prime Minister's Office)
Goh Chok Tong, First Deputy Prime Minister and Minister for
    Defence
Ong Teng Cheong, Second Deputy Prime Minister
E. W. Barker, Minister for Law
Teh Cheang Wan, Minister for National Development
S. Dhanabalan, Minister for Foreign Affairs and Minister for
    Community Development
Tony Tan Keng Yam, Minister for Finance, Minister for Education,
    and Minister for Health
Ahmad Mattar, Minister for the Environment
Yeo Ning Hong, Minister for Communications and Information,
    Second Minister for Defence, and Second Minister for National
    Development
S. Jayakumar, Minister for Home Affairs and Second Minister for
    Law
Richard Hu Tsu Tau, Minister for Trade and Industry
Lee Yock Suan, Senior Minister of State for Labour and Acting
    Minister of Labour

CABINET FOLLOWING SEPT. 1, 1988, GENERAL ELECTION

Lee Kuan Yew, Prime Minister
Goh Chok Tong, First Prime Minister and Minister for Defence
Ong Teng Cheong, Second Deputy Prime Minister
S. Dhanabalan, Minister for National Development
Tony Tan Keng Yam, Minister for Education
Ahmad Mattar, Minister for the Environment
Yeo Ning Hong, Minister for Communication and Information and
    Second Minister for Defence (Policy)
S. Jayakumar, Minister for Law and Minister for Home Affairs
Richard Hu Tsu Tau, Minister for Finance
Lee Yock Suan, Minister for Labour
Wong Kan Seng, Minister for Foreign Affairs and Minister for
    Community Development
Lee Hsien Loong, Minister for Trade and Industry and Second
    Minister for Defence (Services)
Yeo Cheow Tong, Acting Minister for Health

CABINET FOLLOWING GOH CHOK TONG PRIME MINISTERSHIP, NOV. 28, 1990

Goh Chok Tong, Prime Minister and Minister of Defence
Lee Kuan Yew, Senior Minister (PM's office)
Ong Teng Cheong, Deputy Prime Minister
Lee Hsien Loong, Deputy Prime Minister and Minister of Trade and
    Industry
S. Dhanabalan, Minister for National Development
Tony Tan Keng Yam, Minister for Education
Ahmad Mattar, Minister for the Environment and Minister in-
    charge-of Muslim Affairs
Yeo Ning Hong, Minister for Communications and Second Minister
    for Defence
S. Jayakumar, Minister for Law and for Home Affairs
Richard Hu Tsu Tau, Minister for Finance
Lee Yock Suan, Minister for Labour
Wong Kan Seng, Minister for Foreign Affairs and for Community
    Development
Yeo Cheow Tong, Minister for Health
George Yeo, Acting Minister for Information and the Arts, and
    Senior Minister of State for Foreign Affairs

CABINET REORGANIZATION, JULY 1, 1991

Goh Chok Tong, Prime Minister

Lee Kuan Yew, Senior Minister (PM's office)

Ong Teng Cheong, Deputy Prime Minister

Lee Hsien Loong, Deputy Prime Minister and Minister of Trade and Industry

S. Dhanabalan, Minister for National Development

Tony Tan Keng Yam, Minister for Education

Ahmad Mattar, Minister for the Environment and Minister in-charge-of Muslim Affairs

Yeo Ning Hong, Minister for Defence

S. Jayakumar, Minister for Law and for Home Affairs

Richard Hu Tsu Tau, Minister for Finance

Lee Yock Suan, Minister for Labour

Wong Kan Seng, Minister for Foreign Affairs

Yeo Cheow Tong, Minister for Health

George Yeo, Minister for Information and the Arts, and Second Minister for Foreign Affairs

Lee Boon Yang, Minister in PM's Office and Second Minister of Defence

Mah Bow Tan, Acting Minister for Communications and Minister of State for Trade and Industry

Seet Ai Mee, Acting Minister for Community Development

CABINET FOLLOWING AUG. 31, 1991, GENERAL ELECTION

Goh Chok Tong, Prime Minister

Lee Kuan Yew, Senior Minister (PM's office)

Ong Teng Cheong, Deputy Prime Minister

Lee Hsien Loong, Deputy Prime Minister and Minister of Trade and Industry

S. Dhanabalan, Minister for National Development

Tony Tan Keng Yam, Minister for Education (announced resignation effective at end of 1991)

Ahmad Mattar, Minister for the Environment and Minister in-charge-of Muslim Affairs

Yeo Ning Hong, Minister for Defence

S. Jayakumar, Minister for Law and for Home Affairs

Richard Hu Tsu Tau, Minister for Finance

Lee Yock Suan, Minister for Labour and Second Minister for

Education (to succeed Tony Tan at end of 1991)

Wong Kan Seng, Minister for Foreign Affairs

Yeo Cheow Tong, Minister for Health and for Community Development

George Yeo, Minister for Information and the Arts, and Second Minister for Foreign Affairs

Lee Boon Yang, Minister in PM's Office and Second Minister of Defence

Mah Bow Tan, Minister for Communications

General Elections Since 1955

Date	No. of Seats	No. of Parties	Winning Party	No. of Seats Won	Percent of Vote
Legislative Assembly					
2 Apr 55	25	5	Labour Front	10	26.7
30 May 59	51	10	PAP	43	53.4
21 Sep 63	51	8	PAP	37	40.5
Parliament					
13 Apr 68	58	2	PAP	58	84.4
2 Sep 72	65	6	PAP	65	69.0
23 Dec 76	69	7	PAP	69	72.4
13 Dec 80	75	8	PAP	75	75.6
22 Dec 84	79	9	PAP	77	62.9
3 Sep 88	81	8	PAP	80	61.8
31 Aug 91	81	6	PAP	77	61.0

Source: Election Board, reported in *Singapore 1990* (Singapore: Psychological Defence and Publicity Division, Ministry of Communications and Industry, 1990), p. 226.

Population by Ethnicity

Year	Total	Chinese	Malays	Indians	Others
1821[1]	4,727	1,159	2,851	132	585
1824[2]	10,683	3,317	6,431	756	179
1830[2]	16,634	6,555	7,640	1,913	526
1836[2]	29,984	13,749	12,538	2,932	765
1840[2]	35,389	17,704	13,200	3,375	1,110
1849[2]	52,891	27,988	17,039	6,284	1,580
1860[2]	81,734	50,043	16,202	12,973	2,516
1871[2]	94,816	54,572	26,141	10,313	3,790
1881[2]	137,722	86,766	33,012	12,086	5,858
1891[2]	181,602	121,908	35,956	16,009	7,727
1901[2]	226,842	164,041	35,988	17,047	9,768
1911[2]	303,321	219,577	41,806	27,755	14,183
1921[2]	418,358	315,151	53,595	32,314	17,298
1931[2]	557,745	418,640	65,014	50,811	23,280
1947[2]	938,144	729,473	113,803	68,967	25,901
1957[2]	1,445,929	1,090,595	197,060	124,084	34,190
1970[3]	2,074,500	1,579,900	311,400	145,100	38,100
1980[4]	2,413,900	1,856,200	351,500	154,600	51,600
1990[4]	3,002,800	2,239,700	406,200	230,000	126,900

[1]M. V. Del Tufo, *Malaya, Comprising the Federation of Malaya and the Colony of Singapore: A report on the 1947 Census of Population* (London: Crown Agents, 1949), p. 588.

[2]Saw Swee-Hock, *Singapore Population in Transition* (Philadelphia: University of Pennsylvania Press, 1970), p. 57. Used with permission of the publisher.

[3]Rounded to 100s. *Yearbook of Statistics, Singapore, 1984/85.*

[4]Rounded to 100s. *Census of Population, 1990: Advance Data Release.* Singapore: Department of Statistics, 1991.

Percentage Distribution of Chinese by Dialect Group

(in 1,000s)

Year	Hok-kien	Teo-chew	Canton-ese	Hainan-ese	Hakka	Other
1848[1]	25.0	47.5	15.0	1.8	10.0	0.8
1881[2]	39.8	26.1	17.1	9.6	7.1	0.3
1891[2]	48.1	19.5	19.2	7.1	6.1	0.0
1901[2]	45.4	16.8	18.8	5.8	5.2	8.0
1911[2]	41.7	17.1	22.2	4.9	6.6	7.5
1921[2]	43.0	16.8	24.9	4.6	4.6	6.1
1931[2]	43.0	19.7	22.5	4.7	4.6	5.5
1947[2]	39.6	21.6	21.6	7.1	5.5	4.6
1957[2]	40.6	22.5	18.9	7.2	6.7	4.1
1970[2]	42.2	22.4	17.0	7.3	7.0	4.1
1980[2]	43.1	22.0	16.5	7.1	7.4	3.9
1990[3]	43.1	22.1	16.5	7.1	7.4	3.8

[1]Siah U Chin, "The Chinese in Singapore," *The Journal of the Indian Archipelago and Eastern Asia*, II (1848), p. 290. Evidently an estimate by Siah, himself a Teochew.

[2]Cheng Lim-Keak, *Social Change and the Chinese in Singapore: A Socio-Economic Geography With Special Reference to Bang Structure.* Singapore: Singapore University Press, 1985. Used with permission.

[3]*Census of Population, 1990.*

BIBLIOGRAPHY

Bibliographical Note

In the 172 years since its modern founding, the small state of Singapore has produced or been the subject of an imposing number of publications--a majority of which have been in English. With this magnitude, this bibliography is necessarily highly selective. Value to a non-specialist and English medium were primary criteria in winnowing, with preference given to books over articles or reports. This note highlights a few of the most important volumes among those identified.

Titles in the Bibliographies section which follows provide a more complete guide to the full body of material dealing with Singapore. That section, however, does not include the best bibliography: the thirty-five page bibliographical essay at the end of C. M. Turnbull's *A History of Singapore, 1918-1988* (see in "General" section under "History"). Its value lies in the author's judgements and comments, even more than its comprehensiveness. The recent annotated compilation by Stella and Jon Quah, *Singapore* (see under "Bibliographies") and the compilation by Patricia Lim Pui Huen, *The Malay World of Southeast Asia: A Select Cultural Bibliography* (see under "Bibliographies"), also are useful.

Special mention needs be made of three relatively contemporaneous volumes which provide summations of primary or newspaper sources on the history: Charles Burton Buckley's *An Anecdotal History of Old Times in Singapore, 1819-1867* (see in "Founding and East India Company Rule" section under "History"); Walter Makepeace, Gilbert E. Brooke, and Roland St. J. Braddell, eds., *One Hundred Years of Singapore*, two volumes, and its companion, Song Ong Siang's *One Hundred Years' History of the Chinese in Singapore* (see both in "General" section under "History"). For the sesquicentennial, Donald and Joanna Moore drew on the approaches of Buckley and of Makepeace et al. in providing primary reportage linked by a narrative in *The First 150 Years of Singapore* (see in "General" section under "History") and Mubin Shepherd compiled articles which had appeared in the *Journal of the Straits Branch of the Royal Asiatic Society* and its successor, the *Journal of the Malayan Branch of the Royal Asiatic Society* in the reprint, *Singapore 150 Years* (see in "General" section under "History").

For general histories, C. M. Turnbull's volume (noted above) is unparalleled and her *The Straits Settlements, 1826-67* (see in "Founding and East India Company Rule" section under "History") is equally valuable for that period; however, the new compilation by Ernest Chew and Edwin Lee, *A History of Singapore*, (see in "General" section under "History") offers a collection of interpretations of Singapore's history in articles by the nation's leading scholars.

Modern scholarship increasingly has focused on narrower periods. Especially notable have been the studies of the Chinese, including Lee Poh Ping's *Chinese Society in Nineteenth Century Singapore*, Yen Ching-hwang's *A Social History of the Chinese in Singapore and Malaya, 1800-1911* (see both in "General" section under "History"), as well as his *The Overseas Chinese and the 1911 Revolution, with Special Reference to Singapore and Malaya* and *Coolies and Mandarins: China's Protection of Overseas Chinese during the Late Ch'ing Period (1851-1911)* (both in "Crown Colony" section under "History"), and C. F. Yong and R. B. McKenna's *The Kuomintang Movement in British Malaya, 1912-1949* (see in "Crown Colony" section under "History"). Notable for focusing on the Chinese interaction with Europeans are James C. Jackson's *Planters and Speculators: Chinese and European Agricultural Enterprise in Malaya, 1786-1921* (see in "Founding and East India

Company Rule" section under "History") and Carl Trocki's *Opium and Empire: Chinese Society in Colonial Singapore* (see in "General" section under "History").

The selection knife has been wielded most ruthlessly in the sections treating the Japanese Occupation and in the Memoirs. Reference to Turnbull's essay (cited above) is recommended for elaboration and titles in these categories. As a result of a flood of what would be called "coffee-table books" in the West, the section "Neighborhoods and Pictorial Works" offers only a representative sample of this recent emphasis in Singapore publishing. For the most part, these are attractive, well-produced books which offer photographic referents for the printed word. In conveying bygone eras and present modernity, they evidence that a picture is worth a thousand words.

For analyses of the contemporary Republic of Singapore, Kernial Singh Sandhu and Paul Wheatley's huge (over 1,150 pages) compilation, *Management of Success: The Moulding of Modern Singapore* (see in "General" section under "Economy") should be a title of first resort for many years; however, its neglect of history (except for Edwin Lee's introductory essay, "The Colonial Heritage") is regrettable and probably symptomatic of younger Singaporeans' atemporal view of their nation.

Two bibliographical sections, which may appear incongruous, are included: "Fiction" and "The Lighter Side" (see each under "Culture"). Under the former are included a sampling of creative writing on and from Singapore; however, the emphasis is on fictional works which illustrate historical events or society. Spared the rigors of scholarship, fictional authors often are able to explore the emotions of participants and afford greater insight into social and historical developments than researchers and reporters bound to facts. Moreover, at their best, they are able to so do more entertainingly. "The Lighter Side" reflects the ability of at least some Singaporeans to reflect on themselves and their society and see the humor therein. Humor is an important if often unremarked-on characteristic of the Singapore personality. The titles included in this section are worthy and human antidotes to dry social scientific reportage and statistics.

Bibliographies

Abdul Majid bin Nabi Baksh. "Malaysia and Singapore--A Regional Bibliography of Literature in English." In *Asian/Pacific Literatures in English: Bibliographies*, edited by Robert E. McDowell and Judith H. McDowell, pp. 47-54. Washington: Three Continents Press, 1978.

Brown, B. J., and E. Srinivasagam. *Malaysia and Singapore*. Bruxelles: Institut de Sociologie, Université Libre de Bruxelles, 1967.

Communities of Singapore: A Catalogue of Oral History Interviews. Singapore: Oral History Department, 1989.

Cheeseman, Harold Ambrose Robinson. *Bibliography of Malaya, Being a Classified List of Books Wholly or Partly in English Relating to the Federation of Malaya and Singapore*. New York: Longmans, Green for the British Association of Malaya, 1959.

Chen, Peter S. J., and Tai Ching Ling, comps. *Social Development in Singapore: A Selected Bibliography*. Singapore: Chopmen Enterprises, 1976.

Corfield, Justin J. *A Bibliography of Literature Relating to the Malayan Campaign and the Japanese Period in Malaya, Singapore and Northern Borneo*. Bibliography and Literature Series, Paper No. 5. Hull: University of Hull, Centre for Southeast Asian Studies, 1988.

Cumulative Bibliography of Asian Studies, 1941-1965, 1966-1970. Boston: G. K. Hall. Annual volumes published as *Bibliography of Asian Studies*. Ann Arbor: Association for Asian Studies.

Ee, George C. H. *Bibliomed-SM: A Comprehensive Bibliography of Medicine and Related Sciences in Singapore and Malaysia*. Tokyo: Southeast Asian Medical Information Center, 1976. *Supplement, 1974-1979*. SEAMIC Publication, No. 30. Tokyo: Southeast Asian Medical Information Center, 1982.

Giam, Diana. *Education in Singapore: A Select Bibliography*. Singapore: Ministry of Education, Library and Information Centre, 1986.

Franke, Wolfgang. *Sino-Malaysiana: Selected Papers on Ming & Qing History and on the Overseas Chinese in Southeast Asia, 1942-1988*. Singapore: South Seas Society, 1989.

Herbert, Patricia, and Anthony Miller. *Southeast Asia Languages and Literatures: A Select Guide*. Honolulu: University of Hawaii Press, 1989.

Heussler, Robert. *British Malaya: A Bibliographical and Biographical Compendium*. Garland Reference Library of Social Science, Vol. 79. New York: Garland Pub., 1981.

Hill, Lewis. *A Checklist of English-Language Fiction Relating to Malaysia, Singapore and Brunei*. Bibliography and Literature Series, No. 2. Hull: University of Hull, Centre for South-East Asian Studies, 1986.

Guide to the Sources of History in Singapore. Guide to the Sources of Asian History, No. 10. Singapore: Published under the auspices of UNESCO by National Archives of Singapore, 1989.

Inglis, Christine, and Rita Nash. *Education in Southeast Asia: A Select Bibliography of English Language Materials on Education in Indonesia, Malaysia, Philippines, Singapore and Thailand, 1945-1983*. Brookfield, Vt.: Gower, 1985.

Karni, Rahadi S. *Bibliography of Malaysia and Singapore*. Kuala Lumpur: Penerbit Universiti Malaya, 1980.

Lim How Seng (Lin Hsiao Sheng). *Singapore Chinese Huiguan Publications: A Bibliography*. Singapore: Singapore Federation of Clan Associations, 1989.

Lim Pui Huen, Patricia. *The Malay World of Southeast Asia: A Select Cultural Bibliography*. Singapore: Institute of Southeast Asian Studies, 1986.

Our Literary Heritage, History and Criticism: A Select Bibliography. Singapore: National Library, 1989.

Pelzer, Karl J. *West Malaysia and Singapore: A Selected Bibliography*. Behavior Science Bibliographies. New Haven: Human Relations Area Files Press, 1971.

Pioneers of Singapore: A Catalogue of Oral History Interviews. Singapore: Archives and Oral History Department, 1984.

Quah, Stella R., and Jon S. T. Quah. *Singapore*. World Bibliographical Series, Vol. 95. Oxford: Clio, 1988.

Sbrega, John J. *The War against Japan, 1941-1945: An Annotated Bibliography*. New York: Garland, 1989.

Singapore National Bibliography. 1967-   . Annual. Singapore: National Library.

Syonan, Singapore under the Japanese: A Catalogue of Oral History Interviews. Singapore: Oral History Department, 1986.

Tay Lian Soo. *Classified Bibliography of Chinese Historical Materials in Malaysia and Singapore*. Singapore: Nan-yang Hsueh Hui, 1984.

Traditional Drama: A Select Bibliography. Singapore: National Library, 1988.

University of Singapore Library. *Catalogue of the Singapore/Malaysia Collection*. Boston: G. K. Hall, 1968. *Supplement, 1968-1972*. Singapore: Singapore University Press, 1974.

Yeh, Stephen H. K., and Margaret W. N. Leong, comps. *Annotated Urban Bibliography of Singapore*. Singapore: Housing and Development Board Statistics and Research Dept., and University of Singapore Economic Research Centre, 1972.

History

General

Barber, Noel. *The Singapore Story: From Raffles to Lee Kuan Yew*. London: Fontana, 1978.

The Best of Times: Singapore in Newspictures, 1940-1980. Singapore: Times Books International, 1980.

Buchanan, Iain. *Singapore in Southeast Asia: An Economic and Political Appraisal.* London: G. Bell, 1971.

Chew, Ernest C. T., and Edwin Lee, eds. *A History of Singapore.* New York: Oxford University Press, 1991.

Fernandez, George Joseph. *The Singapore Saga.* Singapore: F. J. George, 1985.

Josey, Alex, and Eric Jennings. *Singapore Panorama: 150 Years in Pictures.* Singapore: Straits Times Press, 1969.

Lee Poh Ping. *Chinese Society in Nineteenth Century Singapore.* Kuala Lumpur: Oxford University Press, 1978.

Makepeace, Walter E., Gilbert Edward Brooke, and Roland St. John Braddell, eds. *One Hundred Years of Singapore, Being Some Account of the Capital of the Straits Settlements from Its Foundation by Sir Stamford Raffles on the 6th February 1819 to the 6th February 1919.* London: J. Murray, 1921.

Moore, Donald, and Joanna Moore. *The First 150 Years of Singapore.* Singapore: Donald Moore Press, 1969.

Ooi Jin Bee, and Chiang Hai Ding, eds. *Modern Singapore.* Singapore: University of Singapore, 1969.

Quahe, Yvonne. *We Remember: Cameos of Pioneer Life.* Singapore: Landmark Books, 1986.

Road to Nationhood: Singapore 1819-1980. Singapore: Archives and Oral History Dept., 1984.

Sheppard, Mubin, ed. *Singapore 150 Years; 150th Anniversary of the Founding of Singapore.* Singapore: Malaysian Branch of the Royal Asiatic Society (MBRAS), 1982.

Singh, Daljit, and V. T. Arasu, eds. *Singapore, An Illustrated History, 1941-1984.* Singapore: Information Division, Ministry of Culture, 1984.

Song Ong Siang. *One Hundred Years' History of the Chinese in Singapore*. Singapore: Oxford University Press, 1984.

Tan Ding Eing. *A Portrait of Malaysia and Singapore*. Singapore: Oxford University Press, 1975.

Tate, D. J. M., comp. *Straits Affairs: The Malay World and Singapore, Being Glimpses of the Straits Settlements and the Malay Peninsula in the Nineteenth Century as Seen through the Illustrated London News, and Other Contemporary Sources*. Hong Kong: J. Nicholson, 1989.

Trocki, Carl A. *Opium and Empire: Chinese Society in Colonial Singapore, 1800-1910*. Ithaca, N.Y.: Cornell University Press, 1990.

Turnbull, Constance Mary. *A History of Singapore, 1819-1988*. 2d ed. New York: Oxford University Press, 1989.

Yen Ching-hwang (Yen Ch'ing-huang). *A Social History of the Chinese in Singapore and Malaya 1800-1911*. New York: Oxford University Press, 1986.

Pre-colonial History

Braddell, Roland St John. *A Study of Ancient Times in the Malay Peninsula and the Straits of Malacca, and Notes on Ancient Times in Malaya*; and *Notes on the Historical Geography of Malaya*, by F. W. Douglas. MBRAS Reprint No. 7. Kuala Lumpur: Malaysian Branch of the Royal Asiatic Society, 1989.

Brown, C. C., tr. *Sejarah Melayu or Malay Annals*. An Annotated translation by C. C. Brown. With a new introduction by R. Roolvink. Kuala Lumpur: Oxford University Press, 1970.

Choo, Alexandra Avieropoulou. *Report on the Excavation at Fort Canning Hill, Singapore*. Singapore: National Museum, 1986.

Colless, B. E. "The Ancient History of Singapore." *Journal of Southeast Asian History*, Vol. 10, No. 1 (1969), pp. 10-24.

Crawfurd, John. *History of the Indian Archipelago: Containing an Account of the Manners, Arts, Languages, Religions, Institutions and Commerce of the Inhabitants*. London: F. Cass, 1967; reprint of 1820 ed.

Gibson-Hill, C. A. *Singapore Old Strait and New Harbour, 1300-1870*; and *The Tanjong Pagar Dock Company, 1864-1905*, by G. Bogaars. Memoirs of the Raffles Museum, No. 3. Singapore: Govt. Print. Off., 1956.

Miksic, John N. "Archaeological Research on Fort Canning Hill, November 1987." *Journal of the History Society*, 1987/88, pp. 25-33.

Ng Chin Keong. *Trade and Society: The Amoy Network on the China Coast 1683-1735*. Singapore: Singapore University Press, 1983.

Raja Ali Haji Ibn Ahmad. *The Precious Gift (Tuhfat al-Nafis)*. Annotated translation by Virginia Matheson and Barbara Watson Andaya. Kuala Lumpur: Oxford University Press, 1982.

Wheatley, P. *The Golden Khersonese: Studies in the Historical Geography of the Malay Peninsula before A.D. 1500*. Kuala Lumpur: University of Malaya Press, 1961.

_____. *Impressions of the Malay Peninsula in Ancient Times*. Singapore: Donald Moore for Eastern Universities Press, 1964.

Winstedt, Richard O. *A History of Johore (1365-1895)*; and *The Kangchu System in Johore*, by A. E. Coope; and *Hikayat Negeri Johor: A Nineteenth Century Bugis History Relating Events in Riau & Selangor*, by Ismail Hussein. MBRAS Reprint, No. 6. Kuala Lumpur: Malaysian Branch of the Royal Asiatic Society, 1979.

Wolters, O. W. *The Fall of Srivijaya in Malay History*. Ithaca: Cornell University Press, 1970.

Founding and East India Company Rule

Abdullah bin Abdul Kadir, Munshi. *The Hikayat Abdullah*. Annotated translation by A. H. Hill. Oxford in Asia Historical Reprints.

Kuala Lumpur: Oxford University Press, 1970; reprint of 1955 ed.

Anderson, John. *Political and Commercial Considerations Relative to the Malayan Peninsula, and the British Settlements in the Straits of Malacca.* Singapore: MBRAS, 1965; reprint of 1824 ed.

Bassett, D. K. *The British in South-East Asia during the Seventeenth and Eighteenth Centuries.* Hull: University of Hull, Centre for South-East Asian Studies, 1990.

Buckley, Charles Burton. *An Anecdotal History of Old Times in Singapore, 1819-1867: From the Foundation of the Settlement under the Honourable the East India Company on February 6th, 1819 to the Transfer to the Colonial Office as Part of the Colonial Possessions of the Crown on April 1st, 1867.* With an introduction by C. M Turnbull. New York: Oxford University Press, 1984; reprint of 1902 ed.

Cameron, John. *Our Tropical Possessions in Malayan India, Being a Descriptive Account of Singapore, Penang, Province Wellesley and Malacca, Their Peoples, Products, Commerce and Government.* Kuala Lumpur: Oxford University Press, 1965; reprint of 1865 ed.

Cowan, Charles Donald. *Nineteenth Century Malaya: The Origins of British Control.* London: Oxford University Press, 1967.

Crawfurd, John. *A Descriptive Dictionary of the Indian Islands and Adjacent Countries.* New York: Oxford University Press, 1971; reprint of 1856 ed.

Earl, George Windsor. *The Eastern Seas, or Voyages and Adventures in the Indian Archipelago, in 1832-33-34, Comprising a Tour of the Island of Java--Visits to Borneo, Malay Peninsula, Siam, etc., Also an Account of the Present State of Singapore, with Observations on the Commercial Resources of the Archipelago.* New York: Oxford University Press, 1971; reprint of 1837 ed.

Hall-Jones, John. *The Thomson Paintings: Mid-Nineteenth Century Paintings of the Straits Settlements and Malaya.* New York: Oxford University Press, 1983.

_____, and Christopher Hooi. *An Early Surveyor in Singapore: John Turnbull Thomson in Singapore, 1841-1853.* Singapore: National Museum, 1979.

Hancock, T. H. H. *Coleman's Singapore.* Monograph of the Malaysian Branch of the Royal Asiatic Society, No. 15. Singapore: The Society in association with Pelanduk Publications, 1986.

Harrison, Brian. *Waiting for China: The Anglo-Chinese College at Malacca, 1818-1843, and Early Nineteenth-Century Missions.* Hong Kong: Hong Kong University Press, 1979.

Hooi, Christopher. *The Revere Bell and the Balestiers.* Singapore: National Museum, 1976.

Jackson, James C. *Planters and Speculators: Chinese and European Agricultural Enterprises in Malaya 1786-1921.* Kuala Lumpur: University of Malaya Press, 1968.

Marks, Harry J. *The First Contest for Singapore: 1819-1824.* Verhandelingen van het Koninklijk Instituut voor Taal-, Land- en Volkenkunde, No. 27. 's-Gravenhage: Nijhoff, 1959.

Mills, Lennox A. *British Malaya 1824-67.* With an introductory chapter by D. K. Bassett and a bibliography by C. M. Turnbull. Oxford in Asia Historical Reprints. New York: Oxford University Press, 1966; reprint of 1925 ed.

Newbold, T. J. *Political and Statistical Account of the British Settlements in the Straits of Malacca, viz. Penang, Malacca and Singapore on the Peninsula of Malacca.* Kuala Lumpur: Oxford University Press, 1971; reprint of 1839 ed.

Syed Hussein Alatas. *Thomas Stamford Raffles, 1781-1826: Schemer or Reformer.* Singapore: Angus and Robertson, 1971.

Tarling, N. *Anglo-Dutch Rivalry in the Malay World, 1780-1824.* Cambridge: Cambridge University Press, 1962.

_____. *Piracy and Politics in the Malay World: A Study of British Imperialism in the Nineteenth Century.* Melbourne: F. W. Cheshire, 1963.

190 \ Bibliography

(remaining)

Teo, Marianne, Chong Yu Chee, and Julia Oh. *Nineteenth Century Prints of Singapore*. Singapore: National Museum, 1987.

Tregonning, Kennedy G. *The British in Malaya: The First Forty Years, 1786-1826*. Association for Asian Studies Monographs and Papers, No. 18. Tucson: University of Arizona Press, 1965.

Trocki, Carl A. *Prince of Pirates: The Temenggongs and the Development of Johor and Singapore, 1784-1885*. Singapore: Singapore University Press, 1979.

Turnbull, Constance Mary. *The Straits Settlements, 1826-67: Indian Presidency to Crown Colony*. London: Athlone Press, 1972.

Crown Colony

Akashi, Y. *The Nanyang Chinese National Salvation Movement, 1937-1941*. Lawrence, Kansas: University of Kansas, Center for East Asian Studies, 1970.

Begbie, P. J. *The Malayan Peninsula*. With an introduction by Diptendra M. Banerjee. Kuala Lumpur: Oxford University Press, 1967; reprint of 1834 ed.

Braddell, Roland St. John. *The Lights of Singapore*. Kuala Lumpur: Oxford University Press, 1982; reprint of 1934 ed.

Butcher, John Glover. *The British in Malaya, 1880-1941: The Social History of a European Community in Colonial South-East Asia*. New York: Oxford University Press, 1979.

Chen Ta. *Emigrant Communities in South China: A Study of Overseas Migration and Its Influence on Standards of Living and Social Change*. New York: Institute of Pacific Relations Secretariat, 1940.

Chiang Hai Ding. *A History of Straits Settlements Foreign Trade, 1870-1915*. Memoirs of the National Museum, No. 6. Singapore: National Museum, 1978.

Davenport-Hines, R. P. T., and Geoffrey Jones, eds. *British Business in Asia since 1860*. New York: Cambridge University Press, 1989.

Dixon, A. *Singapore Patrol*. London: G. G. Harrap, 1935.

Godley, Michael R. *The Mandarin-Capitalists from Nanyang: Overseas Chinese Enterprise in the Modernization of China 1893-1911*. New York: Cambridge University Press, 1981.

Harper, R. W. E., and Harry Miller. *Singapore Mutiny*. Kuala Lumpur: Oxford University Press, 1984.

Ku Hung Ting. *Kuomintang's Mass Movement and the Kreta Ayer Incident (1927) in Malaya*. Occasional Paper, No. 13. Singapore: Nanyang University, Institute of Humanities and Social Sciences, 1976.

Lee, Edwin. *The British as Rulers: Governing Multiracial Singapore, 1867-1914*. Singapore: Singapore University Press, 1991.

McKie, Ronald C. H. *This Was Singapore*. Sydney: Angus & Robertson, 1942.

Onraet, R. H. de S. *Singapore: A Police Background*. London: Dorothy Crisp and Co., 1947.

Rimmer, Peter J. "Hackney Carriage Syces and Rikisha Pullers in Singapore: A Colonial Registrar's Perspective on Public Transport, 1892-1923." In *The Underside of Malaysian History: Pullers, Prostitutes, Plantation Workers*, edited by Peter J. Rimmer and Lisa M. Allen, pp. 129-160. Singapore: Singapore University Press for the Malaysia Society of the Asian Studies Association of Australia, 1990.

Roff, William R. *The Origins of Malay Nationalism*. Yale Southeast Asia Studies, 2. New Haven: Yale University Press, 1967.

Sardesai, D. R. *British Trade and Expansion in Southeast Asia, 1830-1914*. New Delhi: Allied, 1977.

Stenson, Michael R. *Industrial Conflict in Malaya: Prelude to the Communist Revolt of 1948*. New York: Oxford University Press, 1970.

Warren, James F. *Rickshaw Coolie: A People's History of Singapore (1880-1940)*. Singapore: Oxford University Press, 1986.

Wright, Arnold, and H. A. Cartwright. *Twentieth Century Impressions of British Malaya: Its History, People, Commerce, Industries and Resources*. London: Lloyd's Greater Britain Pub. Co., 1908.

Wright, C. *Cameos of the Old Federated Malay States and Straits Settlements, 1912-24*. Ilfracombe: Stockwell, 1972.

Yen Ching-hwang (Yen Ch'ing-huang). *Coolies and Mandarins: China's Protection of Overseas Chinese during the Late Ch'ing Period (1851-1911)*. Singapore: Singapore University Press, 1985.

_____. *The Overseas Chinese and the 1911 Revolution: With Special Reference to Singapore and Malaya*. Kuala Lumpur: Oxford University Press, 1976.

Yong, C. F., and R. B. McKenna. *The Kuomintang Movement in British Malaya, 1912-1949*. Singapore: Singapore University Press, 1990.

Syonan

Allen, Louis. *Singapore, 1941-1942*. London: Davis-Poynter, 1977.

Barber, Noel. *Sinister Twilight: The Fall and Rise Again of Singapore*. Boston: Houghton Mifflin, 1968.

Bennett, Henry Gordon, Lt.-Gen. *Why Singapore Fell*. London: Angus and Robertson, 1944.

Chin Kee Onn. *Malaya Upside Down*. 3d ed. Singapore: Federal Publication, 1976.

Deacon, Richard. *Kempei Tai: The Japanese Secret Service Then and Now*. Tokyo: Charles Tuttle Co., 1990.

Donnison, F. S. V. *British Military Administration in the Far East, 1943-46*. London: H. M. Stationery Office, 1956.

Falk, Stanley L. *Seventy Days to Singapore: The Malayan Campaign, 1941-1942*. New York: Putnam, 1975.

Fujiwara, Iwaichi. *F. Kikan: Japanese Army Intelligence Operations in Southeast Asia during World War II*. Transl. by Y. Akashi. Hong Kong: Heinemann Asia, 1983.

Glover, Edwin Maurice. *In 70 Days: The Story of the Japanese Campaign in British Malaya*. 2d ed. rev. and enl. London: Muller, 1949.

The Japanese Occupation, Singapore, 1942-1945. Singapore: Archives & Oral History Dept: Singapore News & Publications, 1985.

Kemp, Anthony, and Richard Holmes. *The Bitter End: The Fall of Singapore, 1941-42*. Chichester: Anthony Bird, 1982.

Kennedy, Joseph. *When Singapore Fell: Evacuations and Escapes, 1941-42*. New York: St. Martin's Press, 1989.

Kirby, S. Woodburn. *Singapore: The Chain of Disaster*. London: Cassell, 1971.

_____, ed. *The War Against Japan*. Vol. 1, *The Loss of Singapore*. London: H. M. Stationery Off., 1957.

Leasor, James. *Singapore: The Battle that Changed the World*. Garden City, N.Y.: Doubleday, 1968.

Lebra, Joyce C., ed. *Japan's Greater East Asia Co-Prosperity Sphere in World War II: Selected Readings and Documents*. New York: Oxford University Press, 1974.

_____. *Jungle Alliance: Japan and the Indian National Army*. Singapore: Donald Moore for Asia Pacific Press, 1971.

Middlebrook, Martin, and Patrick Mahoney. *Battleship: The Sinking of the Prince of Wales and the Repulse*. New York: Scribner, 1979.

Percival, A. E. *The War in Malaya*. London: Eyre & Spottiswoode, 1949.

Pownall, Henry. *Chief of Staff: The Diaries of Lieutenant-General Sir Henry Pownall*. Vol. 2, *1940-44*. Edited by Brian Bond. Hamden, Conn.: Archon Books, 1974.

Reel, A. Frank. *The Case of General Yamashita*. Chicago: University of Chicago Press, 1949.

Robertson, Eric. *The Japanese File: Pre-War Japanese Penetration in Southeast Asia*. Hong Kong: Heinemann Asia, 1979.

Shinozaki, Mamoru. *Syonan - My Story: The Japanese Occupation of Singapore*. Singapore: Asia Pacific Press, 1975.

Simson, I. *Singapore: Too Little, Too Late*. London: Leo Cooper, 1970.

Sleeman, Colin, and S. C. Silkin, eds. *The Trial of Sumida Haruzo and Twenty Others (The "Double Tenth" Trial)*. London: W. Hodge, 1951.

Smyth, John. *Percival and the Tragedy of Singapore*. London: Mac-Donald & Co., 1971.

Swinson, Arthur. *Defeat in Malaya: The Fall of Singapore*. New York: Ballantine Books, 1969.

Tsuji, Masanobu. *Singapore: The Japanese Version*. New York: Oxford University Press, 1988; reprint of 1960 ed.; first published in Japanese in 1952.

Weller, G. A. *Singapore Is Silent*. New York: Harcourt, Brace and Co., 1943.

Toward Independence

Allen, James de V. *The Malayan Union*. Monograph Series, No. 10. New Haven: Yale University, Southeast Asia Studies, 1967.

Ampalavanar, Rajeswary. *The Indian Minority and Political Change in Malaya, 1945-1957*. East Asian Historical Monographs. Kuala Lumpur: Oxford University Press, 1981.

Bellows, Thomas J. *The People's Action Party of Singapore: Emergence of a Dominant Party System*. Monograph Series, No. 14. New Haven: Yale University, Southeast Asia Studies, 1970.

Cheah Boon Keng. *Red Star over Malaya: Resistance and Social Conflict During and After the Japanese Occuption of Malaya 1941-1946*. Singapore: Singapore University Press, 1983.

Clutterbuck, R. *Conflict and Violence in Singapore and Malaysia, 1945-1983*. Rev., updated and enl. ed. Boulder, Colo.: Westview Press, 1985.

Gilmour, Andrew. *My Role in the Rehabilitation of Singapore, 1946-1953*. Singapore: Institute of Southeast Asian Studies, 1973.

Hanrahan, G. Z. *The Communist Struggle in Malaya*. Kuala Lumpur: University of Malaya Press, 1971.

Jackson, Robert. *The Malayan Emergency: The Commonwealth Wars, 1948-1966*. London: Routledge, 1991.

Lau, Albert. *The Malayan Union Controversy, 1942-1948*. Singapore: Oxford University Press, 1991.

Marshall, David. *Singapore's Struggle for Nationhood, 1945-1959*. Singapore: University Education Press, 1971.

Miller, Harry. *Menace in Malaya*. London: Harrap, 1954.

Mills, Lennox A. *Malaya: A Political and Economic Appraisal*. Westport: Greenwood Press, 1958.

Mohamed Noordin Sopiee. *From Malayan Union to Singapore Separation: Political Unification in the Malaysia Region, 1945-65*. Kuala Lumpur: Universiti Malaya, 1974.

Moore, Donald. *We Live in Singapore*. London: Hodder & Stoughton, 1955.

Short, Anthony. *The Communist Insurrection in Malaya, 1948-1960*. London: Frederick Muller, 1975.

Tregonning, Kennedy G. *Home Port Singapore: An Australian Historian's Experience, 1953-67*. Australians in Asia Series, No. 4. Nathan: Griffith University, Center for the Study of Australia-Asia Relations, 1989.

Merger and Independence

Backhouse, Sally. *Singapore*. London: Newton Abbot, 1972.

Bedlington, Stanley S. *Malaysia and Singapore: The Building of New States*. Ithaca, N.Y.: Cornell University Press, 1978.

Bloodworth, Dennis. *The Tiger and the Trojan Horse*. Singapore: Times Books International, 1986.

Brackman, A. C. *Southeast Asia's Second Front: The Power Struggle in the Malay Archipelago*. New York: Praeger, 1966.

Chan Heng Chee. *Singapore: The Politics of Survival, 1965-1967*. Singapore: Oxford University Press, 1971.

Fletcher, Nancy McHenry. *The Separation of Singapore from Malaysia*. Data Paper, No. 73. Ithaca, N.Y.: Cornell University, Southeast Asia Program, 1969.

George, Thayil Jacob Sony. *Lee Kuan Yew's Singapore*. London: Andre Deutsch, 1973.

Hanna, W. A. *The Formation of Malaysia*. New York: American Universities Field Staff, 1964.

_____. *Sequel to Colonialism*. New York: American Universities Field Staff, 1965.

Josey, Alex. *David Marshall's Political Interlude*. Singapore: Eastern Universities Press, 1982.

_____. *Lee Kuan Yew*. Singapore: Times Books International, 1980; first published in 1968.

McKie, Ronald C. H. *Singapore*. Singapore: Angus and Robertson, 1972.

Nair, C. V. Devan. *Not by Wages Alone: Selected Speeches and Writings of C.V. Devan Nair, 1958-1981*. Singapore: NTUC, 1982.

Osborne, Milton E. *Singapore and Malaysia*. Ithaca, N.Y.: Southeast Asia Program, Dept. of Asian Studies, 1964.

Rajaratnam, S. *The Prophetic and the Political: Selected Speeches and Writings of S. Rajaratnam.* Edited by Chan Heng Chee and Obaid ul Haq. New York: St. Martin's Press, 1987.

Sweeney, George. "Singapore, 1945-57." in *Malaya: The Making of a Neo-Colony*, edited by Mohamed Amin and Malcolm Caldwell, pp. 199-215. Nottingham, Eng.: Spokesman, 1977.

Wilson, Dick. *East Meets West: Singapore.* 2d ed. revised by Zainul Abidin Rashid. Singapore: Times Printer, 1975.

Biographies and Memoirs

Anderson, Patrick. *Snake Wine: A Singapore Episode.* London: Chatto & Windus, 1955.

Boulger, Demetrius C. de Kavanagh. *The Life of Sir Stamford Raffles.* London: Knight, 1973; reprint of 1897 ed.

Chan Heng Chee. *A Sensation of Independence: Biography of David Marshall.* New York: Oxford University Press, 1984.

Chia, Felix. *Reminiscences.* Singapore: Magro International, 1984.

Corner, E. J. H. *The Marquis: A Tale of Syonan-to.* Singapore: Heinemann Asia, 1981.

Enright, Dennis Joseph. *Memoirs of a Mendicant Professor.* London: Chatto & Windus, 1969.

Flower, Raymond. *Raffles: The Story of Singapore.* Singapore: Eastern Universities Press, 1984.

Fong Sip Chee. *The PAP Story: The Pioneering Years, November 1954-April 1968: A Diary of Events of the People's Action Party: Reminiscences of an Old Cadre.* Singapore: Times Periodicals, 1979.

Gilmour, Andrew. *An Eastern Cadet's Anecdotage.* Singapore: University Education Press, 1974.

Gilmour, O. W. *With Freedom to Singapore*. London: Ernest Benn, 1950.

Gwee Thian Hock. *A Nonya Mosaic--My Mother's Childhood*. Singapore: Times Books International, 1985.

Hahn, E. *Raffles of Singapore*. Garden City, N.Y.: Doubleday, 1968; reprint of 1946 ed.

Hon, Joan. *Relatively Speaking*. Singapore: Times Books International, 1984.

Hughes, Tom Eames. *Tangled Worlds: The Story of Maria Hertogh*. Local History and Memoirs, No. 1. Singapore: Institute of Southeast Asian Studies, 1980.

Jackson, Robert Nicholas. *Pickering: Protector of Chinese*. Kuala Lumpur: Oxford University Press, 1965.

Lim, Janet. *Sold for Silver: An Autobiography*. New York: Oxford University Press, 1985; reprint of 1958 ed.

Lim Yew Hock. *Reflections*. Kuala Lumpur: Pustaka Antara, 1986.

Low Ngiong Ing. *Chinese Jetsam on a Tropic Shore*. Singapore: Eastern Universities Press, 1974; reprint of 1958 ed.

Menon, K. R. *East Asia in Turmoil: Letters to My Son*. Singapore: Educational Publications Bureau, 1981.

Montgomery, Brian. *Shenton of Singapore: Governor and Prisoner of War*. London: Leo Cooper in association with Secker & Warburg, 1984.

Parkinson, Cyril Northcote. *A Law unto Themselves: Twelve Portraits*. Boston: Houghton Mifflin, 1966.

Peet, George L. *Rickshaw Reporter*. Singapore: Eastern Universities Press, 1985.

Phua, Edward. *Sunny Days in Serangoon*. Singapore: Pan Pacific Book Distributors in association with Manhattan Press, 1981.

Raffles, Sophia. *Memoir of the Life and Public Services of Sir Thomas Stamford Raffles*. London: Murray, 1830.

Siew Fung Fong. *To My Heart, With Smiles: The Love Letters of Siew Fung Fong and Wan Kwai Pik, 1920-1941*. Singapore: Landmark Books, 1988.

Sim, Victor (Shen Wei Tse). *Biographies of Prominent Chinese in Singapore*. Singapore: Nan Kok, 1950.

Tan Beng Luan, ed. *A Battle to Be Remembered: Oral History Extracts of War-Time Singapore*. Singapore: Oral History Dept., 1988.

Tan Kok Seng. *Son of Singapore: The Autobiography of a Coolie*. Singapore: University Education Press, 1972.

Thio Chan Bee. *Extraordinary Adventures of an Ordinary Man*. London: Grosvenor Books, 1977.

Thomas, Francis. *Memoirs of a Migrant*. Singapore: University Education Press, 1972.

Van Cuylenburg, John Bertram. *Singapore - Through Sunshine and Shadow*. Singapore: Heinemann Asia, 1982.

Wurtzburg, C. E. *Raffles of the Eastern Isles*. New York: Oxford University Press, 1984; reprint of 1954 ed.

Yap Pheng Geck. *Scholar, Banker, Gentleman Soldier: The Reminiscences of Dr. Yap Pheng Geck*. Singapore: Times Books International, 1982.

Yeo Siew Siang. *Tan Cheng Lock: The Straits Legislator and Chinese Leader*. Petaling Jaya: Pelanduk Publications, 1990.

Yong Ching Fatt. *Tan Kah-Kee: The Making of an Overseas Chinese Legend*. Singapore: Oxford University Press, 1987.

Politics and Government

General

Bloodworth, Dennis. *The Eye of the Dragon: Southeast Asia Observed, 1954-1986*. Singapore: Times Books International, 1987.

Brimmell, J. H. *Communism in South East Asia: A Political Analysis*. New York: Oxford University Press, 1959.

Emerson, Rupert. *Representative Government in Southeast Asia*. Cambridge, Mass.: Harvard University Press, 1955.

_____, Lennox A. Mills, and Virginia Thompson. *Government and Nationalism in Southeast Asia*. New York: Institute of Pacific Relations, 1942.

Thompson, Virginia and R. Adloff. *The Left Wing in Southeast Asia*. New York: Sloane, 1950.

Government and Administration

Busch, Peter A. *Legitimacy and Ethnicity: A Case Study of Singapore*. Lexington, Mass.: Lexington Books, 1974.

Chong, Alan. *Goh Chok Tong: Singapore's New Premier*. Petaling Jaya: Pelanduk Publications, 1991.

Drysdale, John. *Singapore: Struggle for Success*. Singapore: Times Books International, 1984.

Emerson, Rupert. *Malaysia: A Study in Direct and Indirect Rule*. Kuala Lumpur: University of Malaya Press, 1964; reprint of 1937 ed.

Heussler, Robert. *British Rule in Malaya: The Malayan Civil Service and Its Predecessors, 1867-1942*. Westport: Greenwood Press, 1981.

_____. *Completing a Stewardship: The Malayan Civil Service 1942-1957*. Westport: Greenwood Press, 1983.

Ismail Kassim. *Problems of Elite Cohesion: A Perspective from a Minority Community.* Singapore: Singapore University Press, 1974.

Jones, S. W. *Public Administration in Malaya.* New York and London: Royal Institute of International Affairs, 1953.

Lee Boon Hiok. "Leadership and Security in Singapore: The Prevailing Paradigm." In *Leadership Perceptions and National Security: The Southeast Asian Experience,* edited by Mohammed Ayoob and Chai-Anan Samudavanija, pp. 160-180. Singapore: Institute of Southeast Asian Studies, Regional Strategic Studies Programme, 1989.

Mills, Lennox A. *Malaya: A Political and Economic Appraisal.* Westport: Greenwood Press, 1958.

Milne, Robert Stephen. *Government and Politics in Malaysia.* Boston: Houghton Mifflin, 1967.

_____, and Diane K. Mauzy. *Singapore: The Legacy of Lee Kuan Yew.* Boulder, Colo.: Westview Press, 1990.

Quah, Jon S. T. "Meeting the Twin Threats of Communism and Communalism: The Singapore Response." In *Governments and Rebellions in Southeast Asia,* edited by Chandran Jeshurun, pp. 186-217. Singapore: Institute of Southeast Asian Studies, Regional Strategic Studies Programme, 1985.

_____, Chan Heng Chee, and Seah Chee Meow, eds. *Government and Politics of Singapore.* Rev. ed. Singapore: Oxford University Press, 1987.

Seah Chee Meow. *Community Centres in Singapore: Their Political Involvement.* Singapore: Singapore University Press, 1973.

Selvan, T. S. *Singapore, the Ultimate Island (Lee Kuan Yew's Untold Story).* Clifton Hill, Victoria, Australia: Freeway Books, 1990.

Silencing All Critics: Human Rights Violations in Singapore. New York: Asia Watch, 1990.

Tan, Wah Piow. *Let the People Judge: Confessions of the Most Wanted Person in Singapore.* Kuala Lumpur: Institut Analisa Sosial, 1987.

Vasil, Raj. K. *Governing Singapore.* Singapore: Eastern Universities Press, 1984.

Yeo Kim Wah. *Political Development in Singapore, 1945-55.* Singapore: Singapore University Press, 1973.

Constitution and Law

Ahmad Ibrahim. *Towards a History of Law in Malaysia and Singapore.* Singapore: Stamford College Press, 1970.

Allen, James de V., A. J. Stockwell, and L. R. Wright, eds. *A Collection of Treaties and Other Documents Affecting the States of Malaysia, 1761-1963.* Dobbs Ferry, N.Y.: Oceana Publications, 1981.

Harding, A. J. *Common Law in Singapore and Malaysia: A Volume of Essays Marking the 25th Anniversary of the Malaya Law Review.* Singapore: Butterworths, 1985.

Phang Boon Leong, Andrew. *The Development of Singapore Law: Historical and Socio-Legal Perspective.* Singapore: Butterworths, 1990.

Reprint of the Constitution of the Republic of Singapore: incorporating all amendments to the Constitution of Singapore (S.I. 1963 No. 1493) up to 31st March, 1980, and the Provisions of the Constitution of Malaysia Applicable to Singapore on that Date. Singapore: National Printers, 1980.

Sheridan, Lionel Astor. *Malaysia and Singapore, the Borneo Territories: The Development of Their Laws and Constitutions.* London: Stevens, 1961.

Political Parties

Barnett, A. Doak. *Reports on the Chinese in Singapore and Malaya.* AUFS Report. New York: American Universities Field Staff, 1955.

Brimmell, J. H. *A Short History of the Malayan Communist Party.* Singapore: D. Moore, 1956.

Chan Heng Chee. *The Dynamics of One Party Dominance: The PAP at the Grass Roots.* Singapore: Singapore University Press, 1976.

_____. *In the Middle Passage: The PAP Faces the Eighties.* University of Singapore, Department of Political Science Occasional Paper, No. 36. Singapore: Chopmen Enterprises, 1979.

Chong Peng Khaun, comp. *Problems in Political Development: Singapore.* Berkeley: McCutchan Pub. Corp., 1968.

Choo, Carolyn. *Singapore: the PAP & the Problem of Political Succession.* Petaling Jaya: Pelanduk Publications, 1985.

Lee Ting Hui. "The Communist Open United Front in Singapore, 1954-66." In *Armed Communists Movements in Southeast Asia,* edited by Lim Joo Jock and S. Vani, pp. 109-29. London: Gower, 1984.

Pang Cheng Lian. *Singapore's People's Action Party: Its History, Organization, and Leadership.* Oxford in Asia Current Affairs. Singapore: Oxford University Press, 1971.

Van der Kroef, Justus M. *Communism in Malaysia and Singapore.* The Hague: Martinus Nijhoff, 1967.

Armed Forces

Bilveer Singh, and Kwa Chong Guan. "The Singapore Defence Industries: Motivations, Organisation, and Impact." In *Arms and Defence in Southeast Asia,* edited by Chandran Jeshurun, pp. 96-124. Singapore: Institute of Southeast Asian Studies, Regional Strategic Studies Programme, 1989.

Chan Heng Chee. "Singapore." In *Military-Civilian Relations in South-East Asia*, edited by Zakaria Haji Ahmad and Harold Crouch, pp. 136-156. New York: Oxford University Press, 1985.

Chiang, Mickey. *Fighting Fit: The Singapore Armed Forces*. Petaling Jaya, Malaysia: Times Eds., 1990.

Chin Kin Wah. *The Defence of Malaysia and Singapore: The Transformation of a Security System, 1957-1971*. Cambridge, Eng.: Cambridge University Press, 1983.

_____. "Singapore: Threat Perception and Defence Spending in a City-State." In *Defence Spending in Southeast Asia*, edited by Chin Kin Wah, pp. 194-223. Singapore: Institute of Southeast Asian Studies, 1987.

Obaid ul Haq. "National Security in the Pacific Basin: A View from Singapore." In *National Security Interests in the Pacific Basin*, edited by Claude A. Buss, pp. 207-213. Hoover Publication, No. 319. Stanford: Hoover Institution Press, 1985.

Shorrick, N. *Lion in the Sky: The Story of Seletar and the Royal Air Force in Singapore*. Kuala Lumpur: Federal Publications, 1968.

The Singapore Artillery: 100th Year Commemorative Book. Singapore: Ministry of Defence, 1988.

Winsley, T. M. *A History of the Singapore Volunteer Corps*. Singapore: Govt. Printer, 1937.

Yong Mun Cheong. "The Military and Development in Singapore." In *Soldiers and Stability in Southeast Asia*, edited by J. Soedjati Djiwandono and Yong Mun Cheong, pp. 279-290. Singapore: Institute of Southeast Asian Studies, Strategic Studies Programme, 1988.

International Politics

Boyce, P. *Malaysia and Singapore in International Diplomacy: Documents and Commentaries*. Sydney: Sydney University Press, 1968.

Jackson, Karl, ed. *ASEAN in the Regional and Global Context.* Berkeley: University of California Press, 1986.

Lau Teik Soon. "National Threat Perceptions of Singapore." In *Threats to Security in East Asia-Pacific: National and Regional Perspectives,* edited by Charles E. Morrison, pp. 113-124. Lexington, Mass.: D. C. Heath, 1983.

_____, ed. *New Directions in the International Relations of Southeast Asia: The Great Powers and Southeast Asia.* Singapore: Singapore University Press, 1973.

Lee Lai To. *China's Changing Attitude Towards Singapore, 1965-1975.* Singapore: University of Singapore, Dept. of Political Science, 1975.

Lim, Linda Y. C. "The Foreign Policy of Singapore." In *The Political Economy of Foreign Policy in Southeast Asia,* edited by David Wurfel and Bruce Burton, pp. 125-145. New York: St. Martin's Press, 1990.

Morrison, Charles E., and Astri Suhrke. *Strategies of Survival: The Foreign Policy Dilemmas of Smaller Asian States.* St. Lucia, Australia: University of Queensland, 1978.

Seah Chee Meow. *Singapore's Position in ASEAN Cooperation.* Occasional Paper, No. 38. Singapore: Chopmen Enterprises, 1979.

Tilman, Robert O. *Southeast Asia and the Enemy Beyond: ASEAN Perception of External Threats.* Boulder: Westview Press, 1987.

Wilairat, Kawin. *Singapore's Foreign Policy: The First Decade.* Field Report Series, No. 10. Singapore: Institute of Southeast Asian Studies, 1975.

Wu Yuan Li. *Strategic Significance of Singapore: A Study in Balance of Power.* Washington: American Enterprise Institute for Public Policy Research, 1972.

Economy

General

Chen, Peter S. J. *Singapore: Development Policies and Trends*. Singapore: Oxford University Press, 1983.

Choe Kit Boey, Chew Moh Leen, and Elizabeth Su. *One Partnership in Development: UNDP and Singapore*. Singapore: United Nations Association of Singapore, 1989.

Clad, James. *Behind the Myth: Business, Money and Power in Southeast Asia*. London: Unwin Hyman, 1989.

Economic Survey of Singapore, 1990. Singapore: Ministry of Trade and Industry. Annual.

Goh Keng Swee. *The Practice of Economic Growth*. Singapore: Federal Publications, 1977.

Jayakumar, S. *Our Heritage and Beyond: A Collection of Essays on Singapore, Its Past, Present, and Future*. Singapore: Singapore National Trades Union Congress, 1982.

Krause, Lawrence B., Koh Ai Tee, and Lee Yuan. *The Singapore Economy Reconsidered*. Singapore: Institute of Southeast Asian Studies, 1987.

Lee Hsien Loong, ed. *The Singapore Economy: New Directions; Report of the Economic Committee*. Singapore: Ministry of Trade and Industry, 1986.

Lee Soo Ann. *Papers on Economic Planning and Development in Singapore*. Singapore: Federal Publications, 1971.

Lim Chong Yah, ed. *Policy Options for the Singapore Economy*. Singapore: McGraw-Hill, 1988.

_____, and Peter J. Lloyd, eds. *Singapore: Resources and Growth*. New York: Oxford University Press, 1986.

Lim Tay Boh. *The Development of Singapore's Economy*. Singapore: Donald Moore for Eastern Universities Press, 1960.

Ma, R., and You Poh Seng. *The Economy of Malaysia and Singapore.* Singapore: MPH Publications, 1966.

Sandhu, Kernial Singh, and Paul Wheatly, eds. *Management of Success: The Moulding of Modern Singapore.* Singapore: Institute of Southeast Asian Studies, 1989.

Saw Swee Hock, and R. S. Bhatal, eds. *Singapore in the Year 2000.* Singapore: Singapore University Press for the Association for the Advancement of Science, 1981.

Seah Chee Meow, ed. *Trends in Singapore.* Singapore: Singapore University Press; Institute of Southeast Asian Studies, 1975.

Silcock, Thomas Henry, ed. *Readings in Malayan Economics.* 4th ed. Singapore: D. Moore for Eastern Universities Press, 1961.

Towards Tomorrow: Essays on Development and Social Transformation in Singapore. Singapore: National Trades Union Congress, 1973.

Tregonning, Kennedy G. *Singapore, Its Successes & Future.* Singapore: J. M. Sassoon, 1980.

Wong, John. *ASEAN Economies in Perspective: A Comparative Study of Indonesia, Malaysia, the Philippines, Singapore and Thailand.* Philadelphia: Institute for the Study of Human Issues, 1979.

Woronoff, Jon. *Asia's "Miracle" Economies.* New York: M. E. Sharpe, 1991.

You Poh Seng, and Lim Chong Yah, eds. *The Singapore Economy.* Singapore: Eastern Universities Press, 1971.

_____, eds. *Singapore: Twenty-Five Years of Development.* Singapore: Nan Yang Xing Zhou Lilanhe Zaobao, 1984.

Finance

Asher, Mukul G., and Susan Osborne. *Issues in Public Finance in Singapore.* Singapore: Singapore University Press, 1980.

Drake, P. J. *Financial Development in Malaya and Singapore*. Canberra: Australian National University Press, 1969.

———, ed. *Money and Banking in Malaya and Singapore*. Singapore: MPH Publications, 1966.

Edwards, C. T. *Public Finances in Malaya and Singapore*. Canberra: Australian National University Press, 1970.

The Financial Structure of Singapore. 3d rev. ed. Singapore: Monetary Authority of Singapore, 1989.

Lee Sheng Yi. *The Monetary and Banking Development of Singapore and Malaysia*. 2d rev. ed. Singapore: Singapore University Press, 1986.

Papers on Monetary Economics. Singapore: Monetary Authority of Singapore, 1981.

Pridmore, F. *Coins and Coinages of the Straits Settlements and British Malaya 1786 to 1915*. Singapore: National Museum, 1975.

Singh, Saran. *The Encyclopaedia of the Coins of Malaysia, Singapore and Brunei, 1400-1986*. Kuala Lumpur: Malaysia Numismatic Society, 1986.

Skully, Michael T., ed. *Financial Institutions and Markets in Southeast Asia: A Study of Brunei, Malaysia, Philippines, Singapore, and Thailand*. New York: St. Martin's Press, 1984.

Soh, Doreen. *From Cowries to Credit Cards: Stories of Singapore's Money*. Singapore: Federal Publications, 1990.

Tan Chwee Huat. *Financial Markets and Institutions in Singapore*. 5th ed. Singapore: Singapore University Press, 1987.

Trade and Industry

Bauer, P. T. *The Rubber Industry: A Study in Competition and Monopoly*. Cambridge: Harvard University Press, 1948.

Chng Meng Kng, Linda Low, and Toh Mung Heng. *Industrial Restructuring in Singapore: for ASEAN-Japan Investment and Trade Expansion*. Asia Pacific Monograph, No. 3. Singapore: Chopmen Publishers, 1988.

_____, Linda Low, Tay Boon Nga, and Amina Tyabji. *Technology and Skills in Singapore*. Singapore: Institute of Southeast Asian Studies, 1986.

Chong Li Choy, Tan Chwee Huat, Wong Kwei Cheong, and Caroline Yeoh, eds. *Business, Society and Development in Singapore*. Singapore: Times Academic Press, 1990.

Coats, Austin. *The Commerce in Rubber: The First 250 Years*. Singapore: Oxford University Press, 1987.

Daniel, R. O. *Cooperative Societies in Singapore, 1925-1985*. Singapore: Singapore National Co-Operative Federation, 1987.

Doshi, Tilak. *Houston of Asia: The Singapore Petroleum Industry*. Honolulu: Resource Systems Institute, East-West Center, 1989.

Hughes, H., and You Poh Seng, eds. *Foreign Investment and Industrialization in Singapore*. Madison: University of Wisconsin Press, 1969.

Investor's Guide to the Climate of Singapore, 1991 (Revised up to October 1990). Singapore: Singapore International Chamber of Commerce. Annual.

Lee Soo Ann. *Industrialization in Singapore*. Victoria, Australia: Longman, 1973.

_____. *Singapore Goes Transnational: A Study of the Economic Impact of Investment by Multinational Corporations in Singapore*. Singapore: Eastern Universities Press, 1977.

Lim, Linda Y. C., and Pang Eng Fong. *Technology Choice and Employment Creation: A Case Study of Three Multinational Enterprises in Singapore*. Singapore: Chopmen Enterprises, 1982.

_____. *Trade, Employment and Industrialisation in Singapore*. Geneva: International Labour Organisation, 1986.

Mirza, Hafiz. *Multinationals and the Growth of the Singapore Economy*. New York: St. Martin's, 1986.

Productivity 2000. Singapore: National Productivity Board, 1990.

Puthucheary, J. *Ownership and Control in the Malayan Economy: A Study of the Structure of Ownership and Control, and Its Effects on the Development of Secondary Industries and Economic Growth in Malaya and Singapore*. Kuala Lumpur: University of Malaya Co-operative Bookshop, 1979.

Rodan, Garry. *The Political Economy of Singapore's Industrialization: National State and International Capital*. London: Macmillan, 1989.

Saw Swee Hock. *Investment Management in Singapore*. Singapore: Longman Singapore and Stock Exchange of Singapore, 1989.

Sharma, Shankar. *Role of the Petroleum Industry in Singapore's Economy*. Singapore: Institute of Southeast Asian Studies, ASEAN Economic Research Unit, 1989.

Soon Lee Ying. *Foreign Direct Investment in ASEAN*. Kuala Lumpur: Malaysian Economic Association, 1990.

Tan, Loong-Hoe, and Chia Siow Yue. *Trade, Protectionism, and Industrial Adjustment in Consumer Electronics: Asian Responses to North America*. Field Report Series, No. 22. Singapore: Institute of Southeast Asian Studies, 1989.

Wong Kum Poh, and M. Tan, eds. *Singapore in the International Economy*. Singapore: Singapore University Press for the Economic Society of Singapore, 1972.

Yoshihara, Kunio. *Foreign Investment and Domestic Response: A Study of Singapore's Industrialization*. Singapore: Eastern Universities Press, 1976.

Labor

Balakrishna, V. R. *A Brief History of the Singapore Trade Union Movement*. Singapore: National Trades Union Congress, 1980.

Gamba, C. *The Origins of Trade Unionism in Malaya: A Study of Colonial Labour Unrest*. Singapore: D. Moore for Eastern Universities Press, 1962.

Pang Eng Fong. *Education, Manpower and Development in Singapore*. Singapore: Singapore University Press, 1982.

Saw Swee Hock. *The Labour Force of Singapore*. Singapore: Department of Statistics, 1984.

_____. *New Population and Labour Force Projections and Policy Implications for Singapore*. Singapore: Institute of Southeast Asian Studies, 1987.

Thompson, Virginia. *Labour Problems in Southeast Asia*. New Haven: Yale University Press, 1947.

Company Histories

Cunyngham-Brown, Sjovald. *The Traders; A Story of Britain's South-East Asian Commercial Adventure*. London: Newman Neame, 1971.

A French Bank in Perspective: 1905-1985 Banque Indosuez in Singapore. Singapore: Banque Indosuez, 1986.

Helfferich, Emil. *Behn Meyer & Co. and Arnold Otto Meyer*. Hamburg: 1981.

Hongkong and Shanghai Banking Corporation. *A Century in Singapore*. Hong Kong: Hongkong and Shanghai Banking Corporation, 1978.

Hutton, Peter. *Make What I Can Sell: The Story of Jack Chia-MPH*. Singapore: Jack Chia-MPH, 1978.

Jennings, Eric. *Cargoes: A Centenary Story of the Far Eastern Freight Conference*. Singapore: Meridian Communications (South-East Asia), 1980.

_____. *Mansfields: Transport and Distribution in Southeast Asia*. Singapore: 1973.

_____. *Wheels of Progress: 75 Years of Cycle and Carriage*. Singapore: Meridian, 1975.

Tregonning, Kennedy G. *Home Port Singapore; A History of Straits Steamship Company Limited, 1890-1965*. London: Oxford University Press for Straits Steamship Co., Ltd., 1967.

_____. *Straits Tin: A Brief Account of the First Seventy Five Years of the Straits Trading Company Limited, 1887-1962*. Singapore: Straits Times Press, 1962.

Geography

Atlases and Gazetteers

The ASEAN Climatic Atlas. Scale 1:10,000,000. Jakarta: ASEAN Subcommittee on Climatology, ASEAN Committee on Science and Technology, ASEAN Secretariat, 1982.

The ASEAN Compendium of Climatic Statistics. Jakarta: ASEAN Sub-committee on Climatology, ASEAN Committee on Science and Technology, ASEAN Secretariat, 1982.

Atlas for Singapore. Editorial advisor: Ooi Jin Bee. Research Associate: J. W. Humphries. Singapore: Collins-Longman, 1979.

Atlas of Southeast Asia. With an introd. by D. G. E. Hall. London: Macmillan, 1964.

Malaysia, Singapore, and Brunei; Official Standard Names Approved by the United States Board on Geographic Names. 2d ed. Gazetteer, no. 10. Washington: Geographic Names Division, 1971.

Fell, R. T. *Early Maps of South-East Asia*. Singapore: Oxford University Press, 1988.

General

Chia Lin Sien, Ausafur Rahman, and Dorothy Tay B. H., eds. *The Biophysical Environment of Singapore*. Singapore: Singapore University Press for the Geography Teachers Association of Singapore, 1991.

Chia Lin Sien and Colin MacAndrews, eds. *Southeast Asian Seas: Frontiers for Development*. Singapore: McGraw-Hill, 1981.

Dobby, Ernest H. G. *Southeast Asia*. 11th ed. London: University of London Press, 1973.

Dutton, Geoffrey. *Impressions of Singapore*. Photographs by Harri Peccinotti. Singapore: Times Books International, 1981.

Jackson, R. N. *Immigrant Labour and the Development of Malaya, 1786-1920*. Kuala Lumpur: Government Press, 1961.

Ooi Jin Bee. *Land, People and Economy in Malaya*. London: Longmans, 1963.

_____, and Chia Lin Sien. *The Climate of West Malaysia and Singapore*. Singapore: Oxford University Press, 1974.

Robequain, Charles. *Malaya, Indonesia, Borneo and the Philippines: A Geographical, Economic and Political Description*. Translated by E. D. Laborde. New York: John Wiley, 1954.

Demography

Chang Chen Tung, Ong Jin Hui, and Peter S.J. Chen. *Culture and Fertility: The Case of Singapore*. Research Notes and Discussions Paper, No. 21. Singapore: Institute of Southeast Asian Studies, 1980.

Chen, Peter S. J., and James T. Fawcett, eds. *Public Policy and Population Change in Singapore*. New York: Population Council, 1979.

Cheng Siok Hwa. *Population Structure and Trends in Singapore: A Historical Survey*. Occasional Paper Series, no. 107. Singapore: Nanyang University, Institute of Humanities and Social Sciences, 1979.

Kuo, Eddie C. Y., and Chiew Seen Kong. *Ethnicity and Fertility in Singapore*. Research Notes and Discussions Paper, No. 48. Singapore: Institute of Southeast Asian Studies, 1984.

Saw Swee Hock. *Changes in the Fertility Policy of Singapore.* IPS Occasional Paper, No. 2. Singapore: Institute of Policy Studies, Times Academic Press, 1990.

_____. *Population Control for Zero Growth in Singapore.* Singapore: Oxford University Press, 1980.

_____. *Singapore Population in Transition.* Philadelphia: University of Pennsylvania Press, 1970.

Urbanization

Chew Soo Beng. *Fishermen in Flats.* Monash Papers on Southeast Asia, No. 9. Melbourne: Monash University Centre of Southeast Asian Studies, 1982.

Chia Lin Sien. "Ethical Dilemmas Arising from Urban Development and Environmental Change." In *Ethical Dilemmas of Development in Asia,* edited by Godfrey Gunatilleke, Neelan Tiruchelvam, and Radhika Coomaraswamy, pp. 223-241. Lexington, Mass.: Lexington Books, 1983.

Gamer, Robert E. *The Politics of Urban Development in Singapore.* Ithaca, N.Y.: Cornell University Press, 1972.

Lee Boon Hiok. "Decentralization for Urban Development: The Residents' Committees in Singapore." In *Building from Below: Local Initiatives for Decentralized Development in Asia and Pacific,* edited by Anil Bhatt, Ledivina V. Carino, Khalid Shams, Heinrich Siedentoff, and Gaudioso Sosmena, Jr., Vol. 2, pp. 317-340. Kuala Lumpur: Konrad Adenauer Stiftung and Asian and Pacific Development Centre, 1987.

Riaz Hassan. *Families in Flats: A Study of Low Income Families in Public Housing.* Singapore: Singapore University Press, 1977.

Wong, Aline K., and Stephen H. K. Yeh, eds. *Housing a Nation: 25 Years of Public Housing in Singapore.* Singapore: Housing and Development Board, 1985.

Yeung Yue Man. *Cities that Work: Hong Kong and Singapore*. Occasional Paper, no. 72. Hong Kong: Chinese University of Hong Kong, Geography Department, 1985.

_____. *National Development Policy and Urban Transformation in Singapore: A Study of Public Housing and the Marketing System*. Chicago: University of Chicago, Dept. of Geography, 1973.

Transportation and Communication

Heidt, Erhard U. *Television in Singapore: An Analysis of a Week's Viewing*. Research Notes and Discussions Paper, No. 44. Singapore: Institute of Southeast Asian Studies, 1984.

Kuo, Eddie C. Y., and Peter S. J. Chen. *Communication Policy and Planning in Singapore*. Honolulu: East-West Communication Institute, 1983.

The Land Transport of Singapore: From Early Times to the Present. Singapore: Archives and Oral History Department, 1981.

Tan Teng Lang. *The Singapore Press: Freedom, Responsibility, and Credibility*. Singapore: Times Academic Press, 1990.

Watson, Peter L., and Edward P. Holland. *Relieving Traffic Congestion: The Singapore Area License Scheme*. Washington, D.C.: World Bank, 1987.

Wong Soon Chong, and Lian Fook Shin. "Singapore." In *Broadcasting in Asia and the Pacific: A Continental Survey of Radio and Television*, edited by John A. Lent, pp. 155-162. Philadelphia: Temple University Press, 1978.

Neighborhoods and Pictorial Works

Berry, Linda. *Singapore's River, A Living Legacy*. Singapore: Eastern Universities Press, 1982.

Chinatown : An Album of A Singapore Community. Singapore: Times Books International: Archives and Oral History Dept., 1983.

The Development of Nee Soon Community. Singapore: Grassroots Organisations of Nee Soon Constituency: National Archives, Oral History Dept., 1987.

Dioramas, a Visual History of Singapore. Singapore: National Museum, 1985.

Geylang Serai, Down Memory Lane. Singapore: Heinemann Asia: National Archives, 1986.

Lee Kip Lin. *Emerald Hill: The Story of a Street in Words and Pictures.* Singapore: National Museum, 1984.

_____. *Telok Ayer Market: A Historical Account of the Market from the Founding of the Settlement of Singapore to the Present Time.* Singapore: Archives & Oral History Dept., 1983.

A Pictorial History of Nee Soon Community. Singapore: Grassroots Organisations of Nee Soon Constituency: National Archives, Oral History Dept., 1987.

Siddique, Sharon, and Nirmala Shotam-Gore. *Serangoon Road: A Pictorial History.* Singapore: Educational Publications Bureau, 1983.

Singapore Rediscovered: A Visual Documentation of Early Singapore. Singapore: National Museum, 1983.

Tan, Sumiko. *Streets of Old Chinatown Singapore.* Photographs by Michael Liew. Singapore: Page Media, 1990.

Tanjong Pagar: A Pictorial Journey, 1819-1989. Singapore: Tanjong Pagar Constituency, 1989.

Tanjong Pagar: Singapore's Cradle of Development. Singapore: Tanjong Pagar Constituency, 1989.

Tanzer, Marlene, ed. *Singapore Lifeline: The River and Its People.* Singapore: Times Books International: Oral History Department, 1986.

Society

Anthropology

Cole, Fay Cooper. *The Peoples of Malaysia*. New York: D. van Nostrand, 1945.

Neoh Thean Chye. *Cultural Background of the Peoples of Malaya*. Ipoh: Perak Publishing House, 1960.

Ryan, N. J. *The Cultural Heritage of Malaya*. 2d ed. Kuala Lumpur: Longman Malaysia, 1971; first published in 1962.

Sopher, David E. *The Sea Nomads: A Study of the Maritime Boat People of Southeast Asia*. Singapore: National Museum, 1977.

Wu Teh Yao. *The Singapore Traditional Culture: Changes in Response to the Impact of Western Culture*. Occasional Paper Series, No. 15. Singapore: University of Singapore, Dept. of Political Science, 1975.

Chinese

Blythe, W. L. *The Impact of the Chinese Secret Societies in Malaya*. London: Issued under the auspices of the Royal Institute of International Affairs by Oxford University Press, 1969.

Carstens, Sharon A. *Chinese Associations in Singapore Society: An Examination of Function and Meaning*. Occasional paper, no. 37. Singapore: Institute of Southeast Asian Studies, 1975.

Cheng Lim-Keak. *Social Change and the Chinese in Singapore: A Socio-Economic Geography with Special Reference to Bang Structure*. Singapore: Singapore University Press, 1985.

Chia, Felix. *Ala Sayang: A Social History of the Babas and Nonyas*. Singapore: Eastern Universities Press, 1983.

_____. *The Babas*. Singapore: Times Books International, 1980.

Clammer, John. *Straits Chinese Society: Studies in the Sociology of the Baba Communities of Malaysia and Singapore*. Singapore: Singapore University Press, 1980.

Comber, L. *Chinese Secret Societies in Malaya: A Survey of the Triad Society from 1800 to 1900*. Locust Valley, N. Y.: J. J. Augustin for the Association for Asian Studies, 1959.

Cushman, Jennifer W., and Wang Gungwu, eds. *Changing Identities of the Southeast Asian Chinese Since World War II*. Hong Kong: Hong Kong University Press, 1988.

Fitzgerald, C. P. *The Southern Expansion of the Chinese People*. New York: Praeger, 1972.

Freedman, M. *Chinese Family and Marriage in Singapore*. London: H.M. Stationery Off., 1957.

_____. *The Study of Chinese Society: Essays by Maurice Freedman*. Selected and Introduced by G. William Skinner. Stanford: Stanford University Press, 1979.

Gaw, Kenneth. *Superior Servants: The Legendary Cantonese Amahs of the Far East*. New York: Oxford University Press, 1988.

Jones, Russell. *Chinese Names: Notes on the Use of Surnames and Personal Names by the Chinese in Malaysia and Singapore*. Petaling Jaya: Pelanduk Publications, 1984.

Lee Lai To, ed. *Early Chinese Immigrant Societies: Case Studies from North America and British Southeast Asia*. Singapore: Heinemann, 1988.

Lim How Seng, Lim Guan Hock, and Kua Bak Lim, eds. *History of the Chinese Clan Associations in Singapore*. Singapore: National Archives, 1986.

Lim, Linda Y. C., and L. A. Peter Gosling, eds. *The Chinese in Southeast Asia*. Singapore: Maruzen, 1983.

Mak Lau Fong. *The Sociology of Secret Societies: A Study of Chinese Secret Societies in Singapore and Peninsular Malaysia*. Kuala Lumpur: Oxford University Press, 1981.

Pan, Lynn. *Sons of the Yellow Emperor: A History of the Chinese Diaspora*. Boston: Little, Brown and Co., 1990.

Peranakan Heritage: National Museum of Singapore. Singapore: Friends of the National Museum, 1988.

Suryadinata, Leo, ed. *The Ethnic Chinese in the ASEAN States: Bibliographical Essays*. Singapore: Institute of Southeast Asian Studies, 1989.

Tan Tsu Wee, Thomas. *Chinese Dialect Groups: Traits and Trades*. Singapore: Opinion Books, 1990.

_____. *Your Chinese Roots: The Overseas Chinese Story*. Singapore: Times Books International, 1986.

Vaughan, J. D. *The Manners and Customs of the Chinese of the Straits Settlements*. With an introd. by Wilfred Blythe. Kuala Lumpur: Oxford University Press, 1971.

Wang Gungwu. *China and the Chinese Overseas*. Singapore: Times Academic Press, 1991.

_____. *Community and Nation: Essays on Southeast Asia and the Chinese*. Singapore: Singapore University Press, 1981.

Wynne, Mervyn Llewelyn. *Triad and Tabut: A Survey of the Origin and Diffusion of Chinese and Mohamedan Secret Societies in the Malay Peninsula, A.D. 1800-1935*. Singapore: Government Printer, 1941.

Malays

Djamour, Judith. *Malay Kinship and Marriage in Singapore*. London: Athlone Press, 1965.

_____. *The Muslim Matrimonial Court in Singapore*. London: Athlone Press, 1966.

Hussin Zoohri, Wan. *The Singapore Malays: The Dilemma of Development*. Singapore: Ke-Satuan Guru-guru Melayu Singapura (Singapore Malay Teachers' Union), 1990.

Li, Tania. *Malays in Singapore: Culture, Economy and Ideology*. East Asian Social Science Monographs. Singapore: Oxford University Press, 1989.

Sharom Ahmat and James Wong, eds. *Malay Participation in the National Development of Singapore*. Singapore: Eurasia Press, 1971.

Vredenbregt, J. "Bawean Migration: Some Preliminary Notes." *Bijdragen tot de Taal-, Land- en Volkenkunde*, Vol. 120 (1964), pp. 109-137.

Indians and Other Ethnic Groups

Ampalavanar, Rajeswary. *The Indian Minority and Political Change in Malaya, 1945-1957*. East Asian Historical Monographs. Kuala Lumpur: Oxford University Press, 1981.

Arasaratnam, Sinnapah. *Indians in Malaysia and Singapore*. Rev. ed. Kuala Lumpur: Oxford University Press, 1979.

Crabb, Charles Henry. *Malaya's Eurasians: An Opinion*. Singapore: D. Moore for Eastern Universities Press, 1960.

Daus, Ronald. *Portuguese Eurasian Communities in Southeast Asia*. Singapore: Institute of Southeast Asian Studies, 1989.

Nathan, Eze. *The History of Jews in Singapore 1830-1945*. Singapore: Herbilu Editorial & Marketing Services, 1986.

Netto, George. *Indians in Malaya: Historical Facts and Figures*. Singapore: The Author, 1961.

Rabinowitz, Louis Isaac. *Far East Mission*. Johannesburg: Eagle Press, 1952.

Raja Singam, S. Durai. *A Hundred Years of Ceylonese in Malaya and Singapore, 1867-1967*. Kuala Lumpur: N. Thamotharam Pillay, 1967.

Sandhu, Kernial Singh. *Indians in Malaya*. London: Cambridge University Press, 1969.

Siddique, Sharon, and Nirmala Puru Shotam. *Singapore's Little India: Past, Present and Future*. Singapore: Institute of Southeast Asian Studies, 1982.

Education

Chang Min Phang, Paul. *Educational Development in a Plural Society*. Singapore: Academia Publications, 1973.

Gopinathan, Saravanan. *Towards a National System of Education in Singapore, 1945-1973*. Singapore: Oxford University Press, 1974.

Hu Shi Ming. *Education in a Multi-Racial Society: The Republic of Singapore*. Stony Brook: State University of New York, American Historical Association Education Project, 1974.

Lee Boon Hiok. *Planning and Management of the University of Singapore and Nanyang University Prior to Merger*. Singapore: Regional Institute of Higher Education and Development, 1983.

Lim Chong Yah. *Education and National Development*. Singapore: Federal Publications, 1983.

Lind, Andrew W. *Nanyang Perspective: Chinese Students in Multiracial Singapore*. Asian Studies at Hawaii, no. 13. Honolulu: University Press of Hawaii, 1974.

Loh Fook Seng, Philip. *Seeds of Separatism: Educational Policy in Malaya 1874-1940*. Kuala Lumpur: Oxford University Press, 1975.

Seah Chee Meow, and Suratno Partoatmodjo. *Higher Education in the Changing Environment: Case Studies, Singapore and Indonesia*. Singapore: Regional Institute of Higher Education and Development, 1979.

Siddique, Sharon, and Yang Razali Kassim, eds. *Muslim Society, Higher Education and Development in Southeast Asia.* Singapore: Institute of Southeast Asian Studies, 1987.

Skolnik, Richard L. *An Introduction to the Nation-Wide Learning System of Singapore.* Occasional Paper, no. 42. Singapore: Institute of Southeast Asian Studies, 1976.

Tham Seong Chee. *Schools and Value Development in Singapore.* Singapore: Regional Institute of Higher Education and Development, 1983.

Wijeysingha, E. *The Eagle Breeds a Gryphon: The Story of the Raffles Institution, 1823-1985.* Singapore: Pioneer Book Centre, 1989.

Wilson, Harold E. *Educational Policy and Performance in Singapore, 1942-1945.* Occasional Paper, No. 16. Singapore: Institute of Southeast Asian Studies, 1973.

_____. *Social Engineering in Singapore: Educational Policies and Social Change, 1819-1972.* Singapore: Singapore University Press, 1978.

Wong Hoy Kee, Francis, and Gwee Yee Hean. *Perspectives: The Development of Education in Malaysia and Singapore.* Singapore: Heinemann Educational Books, 1972.

Yip Soon Kwong, John, and Sim Wong Kooi, eds. *Evolution of Educational Excellence: 25 Years of Education in the Republic of Singapore.* Singapore: Longman Singapore Pub. Ltd., 1990.

Philosophy and Religion

Ahmad Ibrahim. *Islamic Law in Malaya.* Ed. by Shirle Gordon. Singapore: Malaysian Sociological Research Institute, 1965.

Babb, L. A. *Thaipusam in Singapore: Religious Individualism in a Hierarchical Culture.* Singapore: Chopmen Enterprise, 1976.

Chatfield, G. A. *The Religions and Festivals of Singapore.* Singapore: Eastern Universities Press, 1962.

Clammer, John. *Studies in Chinese Folk Religion in Singapore and Malaysia*. Contributions to Southeast Asian Ethnography, No. 2. Singapore: Institute of Southeast Asian Studies, 1983.

Comber, L. *Chinese Temples in Singapore*. Singapore: Eastern Universities Press, 1958.

Doraisamy, Theodore R., ed. *Forever Beginning II: One Hundred Years of Methodism in Singapore*. Singapore: The Methodist Church in Singapore, 1986.

Elliott, A. J. A. *Chinese Spirit and Medium Cults in Singapore*. Singapore: D. Moore, 1964.

Hinton, Keith. *Growing Churches Singapore Style: Ministry in an Urban Context*. Singapore: Overseas Missionary Fellowship, 1985.

Ho Wing Meng. *Asian Values and Modernisation: A Critical Interpretation*. Occasional Paper, No. 1. Singapore: University of Singapore, Dept. of Philosophy, 1976.

Kuo, Eddie C. Y. *Confucianism and the Chinese Family in Singapore: Continuities and Changes*. Singapore: National University of Singapore, Dept. of Sociology, 1987.

Lee, Felix George. *The Catholic Church in Malaya*. Singapore: D. Moore for Eastern University Press, 1963.

Mialaret, Jean Pierre. *Hinduism in Singapore: A Guide to the Hindu Temples of Singapore*. Singapore: Donald Moore for Asia Pacific Press, 1969.

Muslims in Singapore: A Photographic Portrait. Singapore: MPH Magazine for Muslim Religious Council of Singapore, 1984.

Quah, Jon S. T. *In Search of Singapore's National Values*. Singapore: Times Academic Press, 1991.

Seah Chee Meow. *Asian Values and Modernization*. Singapore: Singapore University Press, 1977.

Semple, Edgar George. *Singapore Religions*. Singapore: Methodist Publishing House, 1927.

Siddique, Sharon. "The Administration of Islam in Singapore." In *Islam and Society in Southeast Asia*, edited by Taufik Abdullah and Sharon Siddique, pp. 315-331. Singapore: Institute of Southeast Asian Studies, 1986.

Tamney, Joseph B., and Riaz Hassan. *Religious Switching in Singapore: A Study of Religious Mobility*. Singapore: Select Books, 1987.

Tan Chee Beng. *The Development and Distribution of Dejiao Associations in Malaysia and Singapore: A Study on a Chinese Religious Organization*. Occasional Paper, no. 79. Singapore: Institute of Southeast Asian Studies, 1985.

Teoh Eng Soon. *Malayan Buddhism: A Critical Examination*. Singapore: Eastern University Press, 1963.

Tham Seong Chee. *Religion and Modernization: A Study of Changing Rituals among Singapore's Chinese, Malays and Indians*. Singapore: Graham Brash, 1985.

Tu Wei Ming. *The Way, Learning and Politics in Classical Confucian Humanism*. Occasional Paper and Monograph Series, No. 2. Singapore: Institute of East Asian Philosophies, 1985.

Weyland, Petra. "International Muslim Networks and Islam in Singapore." *Sojourn*, Vol. 5, No. 2 (August 1990), pp. 219-254.

Sociology and Social Conditions

Chee Heng Leng. "Babies to Order: Recent Population Policies in Malaysia and Singapore." In *Structures of Patriarchy: The State, the Community, and the Household*, edited by Bina Agarwal, pp. 164-174. London: Zed Books, 1988.

Chen Ai Ju, and Gavin Jones. *Ageing in ASEAN: Its Socio-Economic Consequences*. In collaboration with Lita Domingo *et al*. Singapore: Institute of Southeast Asian Studies, 1989.

Chen, Peter S. J., and Hans Dieter Evers, eds. *Studies in ASEAN Sociology: Urban Society and Social Change*. Singapore: Chopmen Enterprises, 1978.

_____, Eddie Kuo C. Y., and Betty J. Chung. *The Dilemma of Parenthood: A Study of the Value of Children in Singapore*. Singapore: Maruzen Asia, 1982.

_____, and Tai Ching Ling. *Social Ecology of Singapore*. Singapore: Federal Publications, 1977.

Chew Sock Foon, and John A. MacDougall. *Forever Plural: The Perception and Practice of Inter-Communal Marriages in Singapore*. Papers in International Studies: Southeast Asia Series, No. 45. Athens, Ohio: Ohio University, Center for International Studies, 1977.

Chung, Betty J., Peter S. J. Chen, Eddie C. Y. Kuo, and Nirmala Srirekam Purushotam. *The Dynamics of Child-Rearing Decisions: The Singapore Experience*. Singapore: Maruzen Asia, 1981.

Clammer, John. *Singapore: Ideology, Society, Culture*. Singapore: Chopmen Enterprises, 1985.

Drysdale, J. G. S. *In the Service of the Nation*. Singapore: Federal Publications, 1985.

Hodge, Peter, ed. *Community Problems and Social Work in Southeast Asia; The Hong Kong and Singapore Experience*. Hong Kong: Hong Kong University Press, 1980.

Iskander Mydin. *Pioneers of the Streets*. Singapore: Art, Antiques, and Antiquities, 1989.

Kaye, Barrington. *Upper Nankin Street, Singapore: A Sociological Study of Chinese Households Living in a Densely Populated Area*. Singapore: University of Malaya Press, 1960.

Kua Ee Heok, and Tsoi, Wing Foo. *Drug Dependence and Drug Abuse in Singapore*. Singapore: Heinemann Asia, 1986.

Kuo, Eddie C. Y. , and Aline K. Wong, eds. *The Contemporary Family in Singapore: Structure and Change*. Singapore: Singapore University Press, 1979.

Lau Teik Soon. *Majority-Minority Situation in Singapore*. Occasional Paper Series, No. 7. Singapore: Dept. of Political Science, University of Singapore, 1974.

Lee Yong Kiat. *The Medical History of Early Singapore*. SEAMIC Publication, No. 14. Tokyo: Southeast Asian Medical Information Center, 1978.

Neville, Mollie, and Warwick Neville. *Singapore: A Disciplined Society*. Singapore: Heinemann, 1980.

Ong Teck Hong (Wang Te Feng). *Drug Abuse in Singapore: A Psychosocial Perspective*. Singapore: Hillview Publications, 1989.

The People's Association, 1960-1990: 30 Years with the People. Singapore: The Association, 1990.

Quah, Stella R. *Balancing Autonomy and Control: The Case of Professionals in Singapore*. Cambridge, MA: Massachusetts Institute of Technology, Center for International Studies, 1984.

_____, ed. *The Family as an Asset: A International Perspective on Marriage, Parenthood and Social Policy*. Singapore: Times Academic Press, 1990.

_____, and Jon S. T. Quah. *Friends in Blue: The Police and the Public in Singapore*. Singapore: Oxford University Press, 1987.

_____, ed. *The Triumph of Practicality: Tradition and Modernity in Health Care Utilization in Selected Asian Countries*. Social Issues in Southeast Asia. Singapore: Institute of Southeast Asian Studies, 1989.

Riaz Hassan. *Ethnicity, Culture and Fertility: An Exploratory Study of Fertility Behaviour and Sexual Beliefs*. Singapore: Chopmen, 1980.

_____. *Interethnic Marriage in Singapore: A Study in Interethnic Relations*. Occasional Paper, No. 21. Singapore: Institute of Southeast Asian Studies, 1976.

_____, ed. *Singapore: Society in Transition*. Kuala Lumpur: Oxford University Press, 1976.

_____. *A Way of Dying: Suicide in Singapore*. Kuala Lumpur: Oxford University Press, 1983.

Saw Swee Hock, and Aline K. Wong. *Youths in Singapore: Sexuality, Courtship, and Family Values*. Singapore: Singapore University Press for Family Association of Singapore, 1981.

Shaw, K. E., Peter S. J. Chen, Lee Sheng Yi, and George G. Thomson. *Elites and National Development in Singapore*. Tokyo: Institute of Developing Economies, 1977.

Vente, R. E., R. S. Bhathal, and R. M. Nakhooda, eds. Cultural *Heritage vs. Technological Development*. Singapore: Maruzen Asia, 1981.

Warren, James F. "Prostitution in Singapore Society and the Karayuki-san." in *The Underside of Malaysian History: Pullers, Prostitutes, Plantation Workers*, edited by Peter J. Rimmer and Lisa M. Allen, pp. 161-178. Singapore: Singapore University Press for the Malaysia Society of the Asian Studies Association of Australia, 1990.

Wu Teh Yao, ed. *Political and Social Change in Singapore*. Southeast Asian Perspectives, No. 3. Singapore: Institute of Southeast Asian Studies, 1975.

Yeh, Stephen H. K. *Marriage and Family in a Developing Society*. Singapore: Donald Moore for Eastern Universities Press, 1968.

Women

Ahmad Ibrahim. *The Legal Status of Muslim Women in Family Law in Malaysia, Singapore and Brunei*. Singapore: Malayan Law Journal, 1965.

Cheng Siok Hwa. *Women in Singapore: Legal, Educational and Economic Aspects*. Occasional Paper, No. 92. Singapore: Institute of Humanities and Social Sciences, College of Graduate Studies, Nanyang University, 1976.

Fong, Monica Skantze. *Female Labor Force Participation in a Modernizing Society: Malaya and Singapore, 1921-1957*. Honolulu: East-West Population Institute, 1975.

Heng, Geraldine, ed. *The Sun in Her Eyes: Stories by Singapore Women*. Singapore: Woodrose Publications, 1976.

Labour Pains: Coming to Grips with Sexual Inequality. Singapore: Asiapac, 1984.

Lebra, Joyce, and Joy Paulson. *Chinese Women in Southeast Asia*. Singapore: Times Books International, 1980.

Lim, Linda Y. C. *Women in the Singapore Economy*. ERC Occasional Paper, No. 5. Singapore: Chopmen, 1982.

_____. *Women Workers in Multinational Corporations: The Case of Electronics Industry in Malaysia and Singapore*. Michigan Occasional Papers in Women's Studies, No. 9. Ann Arbor: University of Michigan, Women's Studies Program, 1978.

Manderson, Lenore. *Women's Work and Women's Roles: Economics and Everyday Life in Indonesia, Malaysia, and Singapore*. Canberra: Australian National University Press, 1983.

Quah, Stella R. *Between Two Worlds: Modern Wives in a Traditional Setting*. Singapore: Institute of Southeast Asian Studies, 1988.

Wong, Aline K. *Economic Development and Women's Place: Women in Singapore*. Change International Reports, No. 1. London: Change, 1980.

_____. *Women in Modern Singapore*. With the assistance of Chew Oon Ai and others. Singapore: University Education Press, 1975.

_____, and Ko Yiu Chung. *Women's Work and Family Life: The Case of Electronics Workers in Singapore*. Women in International

Development Working Paper Series, No. 64. East Lansing: Michigan State University, 1984.

Culture

Architecture

Augustin, Andreas. *The Raffles Treasury: Secrets of a Grand Old Lady*. 5th ed. Singapore: s.n., 1989.

Beamish, Jane, and Jane Ferguson. *A History of Singapore Architecture: The Making of a City*. Singapore: G. Brash, 1985.

Doggett, Marjorie. *Characters of Light*. Singapore: Times Books International, 1985.

Edwards, Norman. *The Singapore House and Residential Life, 1819-1939*. New York: Oxford University Press, 1990.

Gretchen, M. *Pastel Portraits: Singapore's Architectural Heritage*. Photographs by R. Ian Lloyd and Ian C. Stewart. Singapore: Singapore Coordinating Committee, distributed by Select Books, 1984.

Hancock, T. H. H., and C. A. Gibson Hill. *Architecture in Singapore*. Singapore: 1954.

Hooi, Christopher. *National Monuments of Singapore*. Singapore: National Museum, 1982.

Kohl, David G. *Chinese Architecture in the Straits Settlements and Western Malaya: Temples, Kongsis and Houses*. Kuala Lumpur: Heinemann Asia, 1984.

Lee, Edwin. *Historic Buildings of Singapore*. Singapore: Preservation of Monuments Board, 1990.

Lee Kip Lin. *The Singapore House, 1819-1942*. Singapore: Times Editions, Preservation of Monuments Board, 1988.

Lip, Evelyn. *Chinese Temple Architecture in Singapore*. Singapore: University of Singapore Press, 1983.

National Monuments. Singapore: Preservation of Monuments Board, 1985.

Powell, Robert. *Innovative Architecture of Singapore*. Singapore: Select Books, 1989.

Ramachandra, S. *Singapore Landmarks: Past and Present*. Singapore: D. Moore for Eastern Universities Press, 1961.

Singapore Historical Postcards from the National Archives Collection. Singapore: Times Editions, 1986.

Customs

Alwi bin Sheikh Alhady. *Malay Customs and Traditions*. Singapore: Donald Moore, 1962.

Arasaratnam, Sinnapah. *Indian Festivals in Malaya*. Kuala Lumpur: University of Malaya, Dept. of Indian Studies, 1966.

Cheo Kim Ban. *Baba Folk Beliefs and Superstitions*. Singapore: Landmark Books, 1988.

Comber, L. *Chinese Magic and Superstition in Malaya*. Singapore: Donald Moore, 1955.

_____. *Chinese Ancestor Worship in Singapore*. Singapore: Eastern Universities Press, 1958.

Craig, JoAnn. *Culture Shock!: Singapore [and] Malaysia*. Rev. ed. Singapore: Times Books International, 1986.

Lip Mong Har. *Chinese Geomancy*. Singapore: Times Books International, 1979.

Lo, Dorothy, and L. Comber. *Chinese Festivals in Malaya*. Singapore: Eastern Universities Press, 1958.

Art and Music

Falconer, John. *A Vision of the Past: A History of the Early Photography of Singapore and Malaya: The Photographs of G. R. Lambert & Co., 1880-1910*. Singapore: Times Editions, 1987.

Ho Wing Meng. *Straits Chinese Porcelain: A Collector's Guide*. Singapore: Times Books International, 1983.

_____. *Straits Chinese Silver: A Collector's Guide*. Singapore: Times Books International, 1984.

Singapore Artists. Singapore: Singapore Cultural Foundation and Federal Publications, 1982.

Yeo, R. "The Arts in Singapore: The Last Ten Decades and Beyond." In *Singapore--A Decade of Independence*, edited by Charles Ng and T. P. B. Menon, pp. 45-67. Singapore: Alumni International Singapore, 1975.

Zubir Said: His Songs. Singapore: Times Books International for Singapore Cultural Foundation, 1990.

Printing and Publishing

Byrd, Cecil K. *Books in Singapore: A Survey of Publishing, Printing, Bookselling and Library Activity in the Republic of Singapore*. Singapore: Chopmen Enterprises, 1970.

Byrd, Cecil K. *Early Printing in the Straits Settlements 1806-1858: A Preliminary Inquiry*. Singapore: National Library, 1970.

Chen Mong Hock. *The Early Chinese Newspapers of Singapore, 1881-1912*. Singapore: University of Malaya Press, 1967.

Pages from Yesteryear: A Look at the Printed Works of Singapore, 1819-1959. Singapore: Singapore Heritage Society in association with the Heritage Departments of Singapore, 1989.

Language and Literature

Afendras, Evangelos A., and Eddie C. Y. Kuo. *Language and Society in Singapore*. Singapore: Singapore University Press, 1980.

Anbalagan, K., ed. *Proceedings of the Conference on Tamil Language and Literature in Singapore*. Singapore: Tamil Language Society, 1981.

Bennett, Bruce, Ee Tiang Hong, and Ron Shepherd, eds. *The Writer's Sense of the Contemporary: Papers in Southeast Asian and Australian Literature*. Nedlands, W.A.: University of Western Australia, Centre for Studies in Australian Literature, 1982.

Coulmas, Florian, ed. *With Forked Tongues: What Are National Languages Good For?* Ann Arbor, Mich.: Karoma Publishers, 1988.

Crewe, William. *The English Language in Singapore*. Singapore: Eastern Universities Press, 1977.

Focus on Malaysia and Singapore: Stories, Poems, Articles. Nedlands, W. A.: University of Western Australia Press, 1971.

Kuo, Eddie C. Y. *Language Management in a Multilingual State: The Case of Planning in Singapore*. Singapore: National University of Singapore, Dept. of Sociology, 1988.

Llamzon, Teodoro A. *Papers on Southeast Asian Languages: An Introduction to the Languages of Indonesia, Malaysia, the Philippines, Singapore, and Thailand*. Singapore: Singapore University Press for SEAMEO Regional Language Center, 1979.

Nair, Chandran, ed. *Singapore Writing*. Singapore: Woodrose Publications for the Society of Singapore Writers, 1977.

Noss, Richard B., ed. *An Overview of Language Issues in South East Asia, 1950-1980*. Singapore: Singapore University Press, 1984.

Singh, Kirpal, ed. *The Writer's Sense of the Past: Essays on Southeast Asian and Australasian Literature*. Singapore: Singapore University Press, 1987.

Tay Wan Joo, Mary. *Trends in Language, Literacy and Education in Singapore*. Census Monograph, No. 2. Singapore: Department of Statistics, 1983.

Tham Seong Chee, ed. *Essays on Literature and Society in Southeast Asia: Political and Sociological Perspectives*. Singapore: Singapore University Press, 1981.

Thumboo, Edwin, and others, eds. *The Poetry of Singapore: Anthology of ASEAN Literature*. Anthology of ASEAN Literatures, vol. 1. Singapore: ASEAN Committee on Culture and Information, 1985.

Thumboo, Edwin, general ed., and others. *The Fiction of Singapore*. 3 vols.: Anthology of ASEAN Literature, vols. 2, 2A, & 3. Singapore: ASEAN Committee on Culture and Information, 1990.

Tongue, R. K. *The English Language of Singapore and Malaysia*. Singapore: Eastern Universities Press, 1979.

Wignesan, T., ed. *Bunga Emas: An Anthology of Contemporary Malaysian Literature, 1930-1963*. London: A. Blond, 1964.

Wong Meng Voon, and Wong Yoon Wah, eds. *An Anthology of Singapore Chinese Literature*. Singapore: Singapore Association of Writers, 1983.

Yap, Arthur. *A Brief Critical Survey of Prose Writing in Singapore and Malaysia*. Singapore: Educational Publication Bureau, 1972.

Fiction

Barber, Noel. *Tanamera: A Novel of Singapore*. New York: Macmillan, 1981.

Chin Kee Onn. *Ma-rai-ee*. London: Harrap, 1952.

Clavell, James. *King Rat*. London: Michael Joseph, 1963.

Farrell, J. G. *The Singapore Grip*. London: Weidenfeld and Nicolson, 1978.

Finlay, M. H. *The Lim Family of Singapore*. London: Pickering & Inglis, 1965.

Fraser, George MacDonald. *Flashman's Lady*. New York: Knopf, distributed by Random House, 1978.

George, Sydney Charles. *Bright Moon in the Forest*. London: Jarrolds, 1946.

Glaskin, G. M. *Lion in the Sun*. London: Barrie & Rockliff, 1960.

Han Suyin. *Cast but One Shadow*. London: Cape, 1959.

Lim, Catherine. *Little Ironies: Stories of Singapore*. Singapore: Heinemann Educational Books, 1978.

_____. *O Singapore!: Stories in Celebration*. Singapore: Times Books International, 1989.

Lim Thean Soo. *Southward Lies the Fortress: The Siege of Singapore*. Singapore: 1971.

Lin Yutang. *Juniper Loa*. London: Heinemann, 1964.

Theroux, Paul. *Saint Jack*. Harmondsworth, Middlesex: Penguin Books, 1976.

The Lighter Side
Chia, Corinne, K. K. Seet, and Pat M. Wong. *Made in Singapore*. Cartoons by Collette. Singapore: Times Books International, 1985.

Chiang, Michael. *Army Daze: The Assorted Misadventures of a National Serviceman*. Singapore: Times Books International, 1985.

Kitchi Boy. *Oh No, It's the Kitchi Boy Gang!* Singapore: Times Books International, 1985.

Macaw. *A Bird's Eye View of Singapore*. Cartoons rendered by Patrick Chia. Singapore: Times Books International, 1985.

Padulo, Michael Anthony. *Kampong Capers*. Singapore: Longman, 1987.

Toh Paik Choo, Sylvia. *Eh, Goondu!* Singapore: Eastern Universities Press, 1982.

_____. *Friendship, Courtship, Hatred, Love....* Singapore: Times Books International, 1983.

_____. *Lagi Goondu!* Singapore: Times Books International, 1986.

_____. *On the Buses.* Singapore: Landmark Books, 1987.

_____. *The Pick of Paik Choo.* Singapore: Times Books International, 1982.

Wu, B. J. *Singapore Accent.* Singapore: C. Nair for Times Distributors, 1981.

Reference Works

Encyclopaedias

Embree, Ainslie T., ed. *Encyclopedia of Asian History.* New York: Charles Scribner's Sons, 1988.

Louis-Frédéric. *Encyclopaedia of Asian Civilizations.* Villecresnes: L. Frederic Pub., 1977.

Yearbooks and Handbooks

Asia Yearbook. Hongkong: Far Eastern Economic Review, 1962- Annual.

Foo Kok Pheo, ed. *Common Abbreviations and Acronyms in Singapore.* Singapore: Hillview Publications, 1990.

Singapore. 1964-   . Singapore: Govt. Print. Off.   Annual.

Southeast Asian Affairs. 1974-   . Singapore: Institute of Southeast Asian Studies. Annual.

Straits Times Annual. Singapore: Straits Times. Annual.

Vreeland, Nena. *Area Handbook for Singapore*. Washington, D.C.: U.S. Govt. Print. Off., 1977.

Yearbook of Statistics: Singapore. 1967-   . Singapore: Dept. of Statistics. Annual.

Directories and Biographical Dictionaries

The Diplomatic Press Directory of the State of Singapore 1960-61, including Trade Index and Biographical Section. London, The Diplomatic Press and Pub. Co., 1961.

Straits Times Directory of Singapore. 1974-   Singapore: Straits Times, Annual.

Weinstock, Joseph A., comp. *Malaysia, Singapore, & Brunei Studies: Personnel/Programs/Resources: Directory*. Ann Arbor: Malaysia, Singapore & Brunei Studies Group, Southeast Asia Regional Council, Association for Asian Studies, 1978.

Who's Who in Malaysia and Singapore. 1955-   Kuala Lumpur: Who's Who Pub.

Who's Who in Malaysia and Singapore Business Community and Directory. Kuala Lumpur: Continental Enterprise, 1989.

Who's Who in Singapore. 1981/82-   . Singapore: City Who's Who Pte. Ltd. Irregular.

Indexes

Berita. Vol. 1 (1975)-   . Ann Arbor: Association for Asian Studies, Malaysia/Singapore/Brunei Group. Quarterly.

Index to Periodical Articles Relating to Singapore, Malaysia, Brunei, ASEAN. 1980/82-   Singapore: National University of Singapore Library.

Lim Huck Tee, and D. E. K. Wijasuriya. *Index Malaysiana: An Index to the Journal of the Straits Branch of the Royal Asiatic Society and the Journal of the Malayan Branch Royal Asiatic Society,*

1878-1963. Kuala Lumpur: Malaysian Branch, Royal Asiatic Society, 1970. *Supplement 1-2*, 1964/75-

Singapore Periodicals Index. 1969/70-   . Singapore: National Library.

Willer, Thomas F., comp. *Southeast Asia References in the British Parliamentary Papers, 1801-1972/73: An Index*. Papers in International Studies, Southeast Asia Series, no. 8. Athens, Ohio: Ohio University, Center for International Studies, 1978.

Major English Language Journals and Newspapers

Commentary, Vol. 1 (1968)-   . University of Singapore Society. Irregular.

Contemporary Southeast Asia. Vol. 1 (1979)-   . Institute of Southeast Asian Studies. Quarterly.

Economic Bulletin. Singapore International Chamber of Commerce. Monthly.

Heritage. No. 1 (1977)- . Singapore National Museum. Semiannual.

Journal of Southeast Asian Studies. 1970-   . Superseded the *Journal of Southeast Asian History*. McGraw-Hill Far Eastern Publishers. Semiannual.

Journal of the History Society. 1976/77-   . National University of Singapore History Society.

Journal of the Indian Archipelago and Eastern Asia. Vol. 1-9 (1847-1855); New Series, Vol. 1-4 (1956-1963). Reprinted by Kraus Reprint, 1970.

Journal of the Malaysian Branch of the Royal Asiatic Society. Vol. 1 (1923)-   . Semiannual.

Journal of the Straits Branch of the Royal Asiatic Society. Nos. 1-86 (1878-1922). Reprinted by Kraus Reprint, 1965.

The Mirror. 1965-   . Singapore Ministry of Culture. Biweekly.

Performing Arts. Vol. 1 (1984)- . Singapore National Theatre Dance Circle. Annual.

Singa: Literature and the Arts in Singapore. No. 1 (1980)- . Singapore Ministry of Culture. Semiannual.

Singapore Bulletin. 1972- . Singapore Ministry of Culture. Monthly.

Singapore Economic Review. Vol. 28 (1983)- . Superseded the *Malayan Economic Review*. Vol. 1-27. Economic Society of Singapore and the National University of Singapore. Semiannual.

Singapore Heritage. No. 1 (1983)- . Singapore Ministry of Culture. Quarterly.

Singapore Journal of Education. Vol. 1 (1978)- . Singapore Institute of Education.

Singapore Journal of Tropical Geography. 1980- . National University of Singapore, Dept. of Geography. Semiannual.

Sojourn. Vol. 1 (1986)- . Institute of Southeast Asian Studies. Semiannual.

Straits Times. Straits Times Press. Daily newspaper and weekly overseas edition.

Map Credits

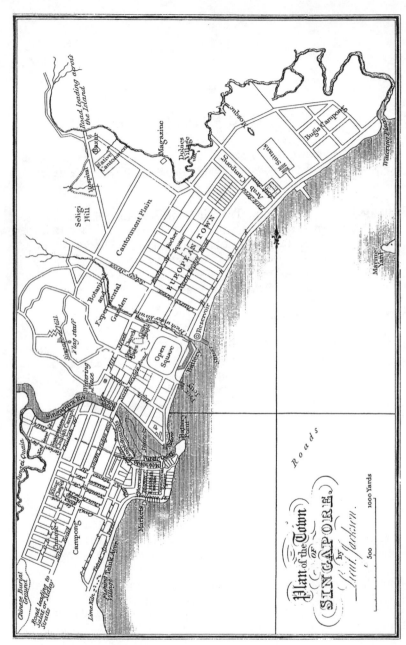

Oldest Town Plan of Singapore, 1828

INDEX TO DICTIONARY

241

248

Opium farm 27, 59, 111, 130, 149
Orang Laut 34, 38, 112, 120
Orang Selat. See Orang Laut
Ord, Colonel Sir Harry St. George 43, 112, 119
Overseas Chinese Association 90, 96, 112, 113, 146
Overseas Chinese Banking Corporation (OCBC) 85, 146, 162
Pan-Malayan Council of Joint Action (PMCJA) 26, 49, 113, 146
Pan-Malayan Federation of Trade Unions (PMFTU) 26, 97, 114, 137
Parliament 31, 35, 38, 39, 43, 44, 68, 75, 88, 90, 105, 108, 109, 110, 114, 121, 122, 132-134, 136, 139, 150, 152, 161, 163
Parti Rakyat Brunei 31
Penang 30, 32, 37, 48, 56, 65, 70, 89, 92, 94, 95, 114, 115, 119, 121, 123, 124, 134, 135, 142-144, 151, 155
Peninsular Malaysia 23, 115, 117
People's Action Party (PAP) 23, 24, 26, 30, 31, 36, 39, 43, 51, 52, 54, 56, 57, 61, 62, 66, 67, 73, 85-87, 91, 92, 100, 103-105, 107, 109, 110, 115, 117, 124, 126, 127, 132-136, 138, 141, 152, 154, 157, 160, 161
People's Association(s) 117
People's Republic of China 40, 41, 47, 61, 84, 119
Pepper 50, 58, 78, 130, 150
Perak 95, 99, 101, 130, 144, 161
Peranakan 24, 30, 118, 142
Peranakan Keling 24, 118

Peranakan Kling. See Peranakan Keling
Perankkan. See Peranakan; Baba
Percival, Lieutenant-General Arthur 33, 118
Philippines 29, 66, 74, 118, 156, 162
Pickering, William 42, 119, 140
Pillai, Narayana 119
Pinyin 35, 39, 41, 47, 64, 66, 68, 78, 82, 84, 119, 131, 146
Piracy 120
Pirate 112
Plen, The. See Fang Chuang Pi
Post Office Riots 120
Pownall, General Sir Henry 33
President 46, 48, 71, 80, 86, 90, 92, 102, 104, 105, 113, 114, 121, 122, 127, 128, 132-136, 143, 145-149, 151, 158, 163
Presidential Council 122, 145, 151
Prime Minister 23, 24, 35, 46, 51, 60-62, 65, 85, 87, 93, 98, 110, 114, 118, 121, 127, 141, 152, 157, 163
Privatization 122, 141
Progressive Party 26, 84, 86, 89, 92, 102, 122, 136, 142, 145, 146
Pulau Senang 123, 132
Puthucheary, Dominic 135
Puthucheary, James 51, 123, 135, 156, 160
Raffles, Sir Thomas Stamford 23, 24, 31, 44, 45, 48, 51, 56, 57, 59, 69, 77, 115, 119, 120, 124, 126, 139, 144
Raffles College 61, 85, 98, 125, 152, 156
Raffles Hotel 126